The New Mazda RX-7 and Mazda Rotary Engine Sports Cars

RX-7

The New Mazda RX-7 and Mazda Rotary Engine Sports Cars

By Jack K. Yamaguchi

Edited by Ron Wakefield

Driving impressions by Paul Frère

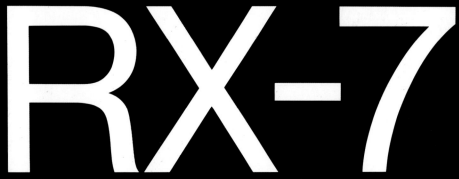

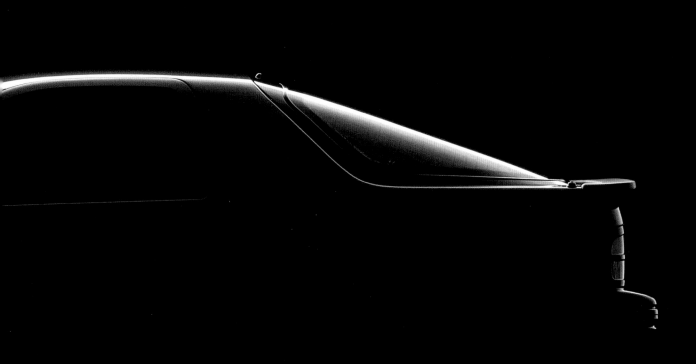

St. Martin's Press
New York

THE NEW MAZDA RX-7 AND MAZDA ROTARY ENGINE SPORTS CARS BY JACK K. YAMAGUCHI. ©1985 by Dai Nippon Printing Co., Ltd.
Library of Congress Catalog Card Number 85-62339
ISBN 0-312-69456-3
First U. S. Edition
10 9 8 7 6 5 4 3 2 1

4
THE ROTARY PEOPLE

5
THE ROTARY ON THE TRACK

MAZDA ROTARY ENGINES

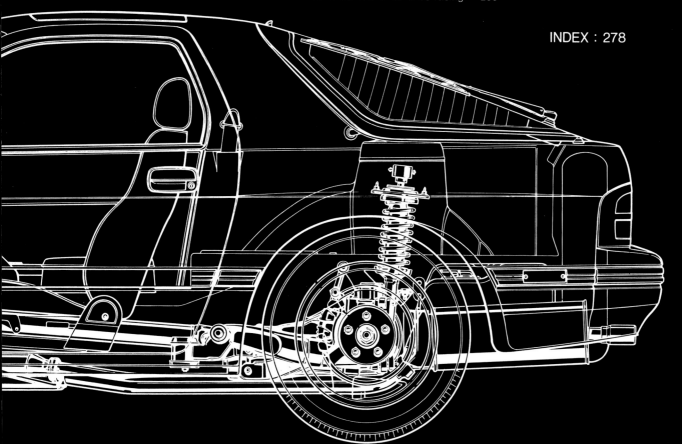

FOREWORD

WE COMPLETED OUR first prototype rotary engine almost a quarter of a century ago. The Wankel rotary engine captivated the world's mechanical engineers and followers of automotive engineering, and was at the time heralded as a "dream engine." The engine produced high power through the classical Otto four-stroke cycle in almost pure rotary motion—indeed, a revolution sought by many a designer and engineer for more than a century of the internal-combustion engine's history.

There were difficulties and hardships, associated with the development of any revolutionary invention. We have had more than a fair share of them; however, we at Mazda were determined that the rotary could be perfected—through innovative engineering efforts and continuous development. We have placed the engine in the most demanding and rigorous tests—on roads and tracks of the world. The new RX-7 is powered by an engine that is well tried and proven, yet incorporating innovative new features we have developed.

However powerful and efficient an engine may be, it does not make a good sports car by itself. Our new car must be as innovative as the engine. The new RX-7, the subject of Jack Yamaguchi's book, is such a car—a new-generation sports car that establishes an unparalled value in performance and owner satisfaction. I am confident that the car will become a harbinger of modern sports cars.

Jack Yamaguchi must have had unwavering faith in the rotary engine, just as we at Mazda have, for I remember seeing him and talking with him on the future of this great invention on numerous occasions, including those darker days. I am pleased that he has undertaken to write this informative account of the quarter-century history of the Mazda rotary engine and sports cars powered by it. I should like to join readers of this book in expressing gratitude to him for his efforts.

Kenichi Yamamoto
President, Mazda Motor Corporation

PREFACE

UPON LEARNING THAT a new Mazda sports car was being developed, I approached the Hiroshima company with the idea of documenting the new car's conception and developement with a commemorative book. Mazda quickly agreed, and gave me full access to the people, places and processes behind the new P747 RX-7, as well as the company's historical documentation of its predecessor and the long road to perfecting the rotary engine. The RX-7 story is an account of how a car maker conceives, designs and engineers a new car in our time — a new car that has a tough act to follow, an innovative tradition to continue, unique success to repeat.

One could hardly be content just to tell the *new* RX-7 story. No account of this important new sports car would be complete without the story of its pioneering predecessor, nor a chronicle of Mazda's dogged determination to make the rotary engine work when the world was saying it wouldn't. Behind these pieces of hardware are real, live, warm-blooded human beings—the Rotary People who believed in a unique engine concept, in their company, in the inseparability that had evolved between Mazda's reputation and the extraordinary engine.

It needs saying that after the difficulties of the Seventies, most large corporations would have simply abandoned Felix Wankel's engine; indeed, the world's largest car maker did. But Mazda's decision was based neither on cold business nor a short-term viewpoint. Certain people there had a vision, and it was to be fulfilled.

The decision to build the first RX-7, made in that time of crisis, rested upon this belief that the Wankel rotary engine could be perfected; on the knowledge that it was especially suited to a sports car; and on a surprising understanding of America's romance with sports cars.

I have been fortunate in having tutors on the state-of-art development of the Mazda rotary engine in President Yamamoto, Managing Director Takashi Kuroda and lately Department Manager Hiroshi Ohzeki.

Two people have been especially helpful in tracing Mazda sports cars, born and aborted: Managing Director Masataka Matsui and his remarkable small notebook full of data and fascinating episodes, and P747 project manager Akio Uchiyama, who has seen most of Mazda's sports cars being planned, designed, developed and more frequently abandoned. I am glad his determination and untiring efforts have been handsomely rewarded by two generations of the RX-7.

I should like to thank Mazda's design chief Matasaburo Maeda who went to the trouble of saving a box–full of old prototype photographs destined for shredding; they included those of the Corvette beater X020G, the R16A roadster and the RX500 midship car. Maeda caught a bad cold while searching for them in a dusty storage room.

I am indebted to many other people in the company, whose names may have escaped this book. And I am grateful to Editors John Dinkel of *Road & Track* and Shotaro Kobayashi of *Car Graphic*, as well as Publisher Osami Suzuki of *Moter Fan* for permission to quote and reprint parts of their excellent publications.

And my hearty thanks to my collaborators in this endeavor; my friend Paul Frère for taking time to test–drive and write impressions on the new RX-7—in pouring rain for two consecutive days! To Editor Ron Wakefield for cleaning up and sorting my heavily Japanese-accented text. And to talented photographer Haru Tajima, whom I asked to capture the new RX-7 in his lens, "make it breathe and speak to the readers." He did just that.

Jack K. Yamaguchi

Driving the P747 RX-7

by Paul Frère

THE FIRST VERSION of the RX-7 was a very pleasant, well mannered sports car for its price. It had a fairly good performance and was space-efficient, reasonably silent and beautifully smooth. A good friend of mine who is a top executive at Rolls-Royce Motors and judges cars by Rolls-Royce standards already runs his second RX-7 as his personal car and he loves it: that must mean something! But it must be admitted that a rigid rear axle, however well located it may be, is a compromise hardly acceptable in a sports car whose production is to continue well into the Nineties,

especially if it is to compete with the best in terms of performance and power. Mazda Motor Corporation realized this, and as early as the fall of 1983, I was invited to Japan to try and comment on an early prototype of the new model, which was extremely promising. After a year of further development, the car was nearly finalized and I was again invited to drive it, this time on the most exciting test course imaginable: the old Nürburgring in Germany, a single lap which measures no less than 21 kilometers (13 miles). It used to be 22.8 km, but since the new Grand Prix course was built, a bypass was constructed, eliminating the pit area so that the old course could be used for testing without interfering with the activities of the new circuit. No other test course shows up the merits and the defects of a car better than the old Nürburgring. For me it is a wonderful base of comparison, since I have driven there for more than 30 years, completing nearly 2000 laps racing and testing cars ranging from Formula 1 to family models.

Tadayuki Masuda, Division Manager, Testing and Development, and the author listen to Paul Frère

Here the handling of the P747 RX-7 was a revelation—so precise, so crisp and responsive that it felt nearly like a racing car—and this was not achieved at the expense of comfort, which remained quite reasonable by sports-car standards. Sports cars of other famous makes were on hand for comparison, but as far as handling was concerned, none of them reached the standards set by the new RX-7. It was also some 12 to 13 seconds faster over the complete lap than the now "old" model, both using naturally aspirated engines to European specifications.
But even though the new car had more power than the previous model, the chassis was just crying for more. That is just what is provided by the two turbocharged cars I drove on two different test tracks in Japan, just before series production of the new RX-7 began. One of these courses was Mazda's own, completely new 3.4-km (2.1-mi.) Global Course, which is not only a very complete and varied handling course, but which also reproduces a variety of road surfaces, some of which are far less than smooth. The other was the Nishi Nippon circuit, a small but excellent race course in the extreme western part of Honshu, Japan's main island.

Performance, however, is not the whole story. Get into the car and you will find that ingress is easy through the large, wide-opening doors. Once in your seat, you are faced by a beautifully styled, leather-covered steering wheel, adjustable for height, of just the right size and providing plenty of grip. The horn is operated by a large pad in its center, the only place where it can be found immediately, whatever the position of the steering wheel. In the manual-transmission version, the brake and accelerator pedals are ideally placed for "heel-and-toeing"; for me this is of vital importance. There is even a well placed footrest to the left of the clutch pedal—proof that the development and testing engineers are experienced drivers. In front of you are all the vital instruments: large, no-nonsense, mostly circular dials with proper needles. I only wished the figures and lettering were white rather than red on black, so that they could be read even better.

Once on the move, the P747 RX-7 is a real delight. The smoothness of the rotary engine is something that must be experienced. In the lower speed ranges it is more silent than a good reciprocating engine, but it is quite remarkable how little its noise increases as the revolutions rise. Add that it also revs with exceptional willingness, and you will soon be convinced that the buzzer reminding you that 7000—not the sky—is the limit, is by no means a futile gadget.

Naturally, my preference goes to the turbocharged version, which has enough power to do justice to the wonderful chassis—especially as the turbo is effective at quite low engine speeds and its response is not far short of immediate. Mid-range torque is good and it is typical of the engine's good flexibility that on the Nishi Nippon circuit in pouring rain, there were two rather sharp bends in which it was better to stay in third gear and pick up from 4000 rpm, rather than use second and pick up from 5800 rpm. Engine, clutch and gearbox make an admirable powertrain; the clutch is easy to operate with fairly short pedal travel in spite of the high torque to be transmitted, and the gearshift mechanism is very precise and positive, if perhaps a little "notchy."

An admirable feature is the car-speed and side-force-sensitive power steering, which is finger-light at parking and lower town speeds, but provides plenty of feel at high speeds, when the assistance becomes virtually zero. Just as important is the fact that under fast cornering conditions, without becoming heavy, it fully reflects the inputs. This is another feature of the new RX-7 and apparently results from both the quick steering ratio (15.2:1) and rear suspension geometry designed to accelerate the response in the transient stage without inducing understeer under steady cornering conditions. For a competent driver, this is an admirable feature, though the less expert may find the very quick response disconcerting if he/she is called upon to act in an emergency at speed. To sum up the situation, I would say that the P747 RX-7 is a car to be driven "with fingers," rather than with the fists or the forearms.

This being said, and even though straight-line stability at speed is very good, winding roads are certainly the RX-7's favorite element. Here its ability and cornering agility really come into their own, and fast driving is encouraged by the car's minimal parasitic movements, such as roll, dive and squat. And the well shaped seats help spirited driving by providing excellent lateral support. It is also encouraged by excellent four-wheel disc brakes which, in the versions I drove, feature racing-type four-piston aluminum calipers on the front wheels and internally vented discs all around. In really tight bends, the driver's-side front pillar tends to interfere with the line of vision, but the very wet conditions prevailing when I drove the two turbocharged cars on the Nishi Nippon circuit emphasized the excellent traction resulting from both the balanced weight distribution and the clever rear suspension design, even though no limited-slip differential was fitted.

Even with the automatic transmission, the Turbo proved to be a very good performer, though I think that for a sports car it would be more appropriate if fourth were a normal driving gear rather than an overdrive. But in itself, the combination of a torque-converter transmission and a turbocharged engine is a logical one: at low engine revolutions, when the turbo has little effect, the torque converter multiplies the torque reaching the driving wheels, and as the revolutions rise and the converter becomes ineffective, the boost pressure starts rising, providing the required

Mazda's new Global Course at Miyoshi Proving Ground

increased torque.

In practice, even under fast driving conditions, the automatic version does not lag far behind the five-speed manual. The proof is that, under very wet conditions, I lapped the Nishi Nippon circuit in 1 minute 37.0 seconds with the five-speed Turbo and in 1 min. 38.7 sec. with the automatic, a difference of only 1.18 percent. This was, of course, operating the selector lever manually to shift down before corners where necessary, and for this I would have preferred the selector to move freely between positions "2" and "D" to avoid moving the selector into first or neutral when operating it in a hurry.

In whatever form, the P747 RX-7 with its controversial, but fascinating rotary engine is an exciting car to drive, and its performance and handling do full justice to its advanced specifications.

i

A NEW RX-7 IS BORN

Agonizing over the name

THE DECISION TO develop a new Mazda sports car to replace the popular, lucrative but aging RX-7 was straightforward: nearly every car, no matter how good or successful, eventually has to be replaced by a new one.

Just what form the new car would take and what it would be called were more difficult questions. As the car took shape under the internal code P747, there was a long and heated debate at Mazda about its name. Progress was the keynote in its conception and development, and a faction of the planning-development group wanted a numerical progression as well. Indeed, that was already a tradition with Mazda's rotary-powered cars. After the simplifying leap from the R100 to the RX-2, only the "6" had been skipped (because *eks* and *six* don't roll too well on the Japanese tongue) on the way to the RX-7—although the RX-5 was called Cosmo in some markets. To some, it seemed supremely logical to move up the numerical scale; a daring copywriter even suggested jumping from 7 to 11.

A bit of anxiety about the number was justified, for Project P747 was to be a new car from the ground up. To be positioned a class above the incumbent series, it would compete squarely with the world elite of sports cars and GTs—including those from Stuttgart-Zuffenhausen. It would also serve as a new flagship, raising the Hiroshima-based company's technological image. In the end, however, the project group's mainstream, headed by Chief Project Engineer Akio Uchiyama, prevailed: the new car would inherit the RX-7 designation.

The rationale was that the RX-7 had become a household word, particularly in the all-important American market, that would continue to strike the right note with the world's enthusiasts. Further, reasoned the "7" proponents, if the car is good, the name should be good; if the breed improved, the established name would take on the intended connotation of newness and increased product value.

Parenthetically, the development code P747 has no particular meaning; it was chosen by Uchiyama so as not to give any hint about the vehicle's type, year, configuration or engine type. Mazda had been using numerals (on a series of long-distance racing cars built by its competition subsidiary) that would have ultimately led to 747; the 1983 Le Mans car was Type 717C and the 1984 version progressed to 727C. The stretched 1985 model was 737C (the suffix is for Group C-2) and the new IMSA GTO racer, based on the P747 and designed parallel to the production model, bears a clear and intentional resemblance to those Le Mans-type mid-engine racers.

Whatever the logic—will the name be seen as an honorable succession in Mazda's sports car lineage or merely a misnomer for a car that is a quantum leap over its predecessor?—Project P747 has become the second-generation Mazda RX-7.

The toughest decision: choosing a concept

IT WAS in June 1981, three years after the original model (Project X605) had been launched, when the development proposal for an RX-7 successor was officially made at Mazda. Unusually long by Japanese industry standards, this period before starting on the successor was devoted to nurturing the original X605 concept, itself a modest and straightforward design that borrowed many components from Mazda's volume-production parts bins of the time. An upward swing in sports-car performance and equipment was now the trend, so this nurturing had taken the form of developing more powerful, better equipped versions of the RX-7. The Type P132 GSL-SE for the American market, powered by the revived 13B fuel-injected engine, and a Turbo version propelled by a turbocharged 12A engine for the Japanese performance segment, were such offerings.

The June 1981 proposal presented three alternative courses P747 could take.

Concept One was an evolutionary car, having the same wheelbase and outside dimensions of the X605; Uchiyama termed it the Realistic Sports Car. It would retain most of the basic X605's homely features: live rear axle, front disc/rear drum brakes and 13-inch wheels. About the only new major engineering feature would be rack-and-pinion steering; even that was a reluctant concession, granted by the planners halfway through its conception.

Concept Two, called the Technologically Advanced Sports Car, was at the opposite end of the scale. It would be a compact 2+2 on a wheelbase *shorter* than the X605's having such high-tech features as an active suspension system combining a novel independent rear end, electronically controlled variable springs, shock absorbers and anti-roll bars; rear transaxle à la Porsche, variable-assist power steering, four-wheel disc brakes and the inevitable electronic instrument display.

The third option was to be a Civilized Sports Car somewhere between the two extreme proposals. This too would be a 2+2, but on a slightly longer wheelbase: 2455 mm (96.7 in.) versus the X605's 2420 (95.3). It would have advanced independent rear suspension and four-wheel disc brakes like Concept Two, but no far-out chassis electronics, and include rack-and-pinion steering and 14-in. wheels, larger than the basic X605 wear, but like that of the upmarket GSL-SE version. Power options would range from a base 110 bhp to turbocharged 180 bhp, with which the new car should accelerate from zero to 60 mph in under 8 seconds.

In spring 1982, the three concepts were shown at a series of product clinics in the U.S. Estimated prices of $9,000–12,000, $13,000–15,000 and $11,000–13,000 for Concepts One, Two and Three were given to the sample audience; at the time, the production RX-7's median price fell just short of $10,000.

From the outset the Mazda planners were determined that Concept Three should be their entry in the late-Eighties sports car battle, which would be intensified by several updated and new models from the established makes as well as aspiring new entries from Japan. The status-quo Concept One would be hard-pressed by the relatively inexpensive, lightweight newcomers expected from Honda, Toyota and Nissan. On the other hand, because the new car would replace the current RX-7 rather than complement it, it could not be too far-fetched in technology or venture too far toward outright luxury price brackets. Concept Two was judged premature.

In fact, the two alternative concepts were shown rather perfunctorily, both initially to company management and later in the clinics, mainly to highlight the strong viability and soundness of Concept Three. They progressed no further than paper proposals; their contribution was mainly to pave the way for Concept Three.

The new RX-7: a civilized sports car

LIKE MANY Japanese-concocted descriptive phrases translated into English, "civilized sports car" could be misleading. It might, for instance, raise expectations of additional comfort, convenience and entertainment features. But those add weight, the perpetual enemy of performance. They would also take the RX-7 in the ZX direction, a tack Mazda people dislike almost to the point of abhorrence—although they concede the ZX's enviable commercial record. "Our new RX-7 will not become a high-performance luxury car. It is and will remain a sports car of superior quality," affirms project chief Uchiyama. Thus in the Mazda context, "civilized" translates into technological sophistication and engineering innovation. And the RX-7 is absolutely brimming with both.

In the course of design and development, the smaller-displacement 12A engine that has been under the hoods of all RX-7s but the GSL-SE was dropped altogether, for two reasons. A base carbureted engine would be hard-put to propel a larger and more sophisticated car that would, despite Uchiyama's vow, inevitably gain some weight. And a highly tweaked smaller engine might not have attained optimum fuel efficiency.

So the new RX-7's engine family is exclusively the larger 13B, previously reserved for the top U.S.-market model GSL-SE. It is initially offered in an updated fuel-injected version with charge dynamics and acoustic induction (DEI, Dynamic Effect Intake), rated at 146 bhp SAE or 11 bhp more than the previous GSL-SE engine. Later a turbocharged DEI 13B will be added. It features twin-scroll turbocharging, an ingeniously simple system that provides the effect of variable turbocharger geometry and thus combines low-end response and high-end power. The turbo 13B puts out 182 bhp, with a strong and even spread of torque across its usable speed range. In either form, the engine is now electronically managed by a central computer, for an optimum combination of performance, fuel efficiency and driveability. Transmission options include two five-speed manual gearboxes: an improved, reinforced version of the Type M box as used in the previous GSL-SE, and a heftier Type R for the Turbo. Optional with the naturally aspirated engine is a JATCO (Japan Automatic Transmission Co.) four-speed automatic with a torque-converter lockup clutch. The long-snout final drive unit is mounted on a subframe and drives the rear wheels through universal-jointed halfshafts; a multi-plate limited-slip differential is standard on the naturally aspirated GXL and may be optionally offerred on the Turbo. Front suspension is by the ubiquitous MacPherson-strut system, but the components are all new and include aluminum hubs and aircraft-quality forged aluminum lower A-arms. At the rear, the new RX-7 finally gets independent suspension; it is unique and must rank as one of the more significant recent developments, right up there with Porsche's Weissach system and Daimler-Benz's heralded multi-link arrangement. The new rear suspension is basically a semi-trailing-arm system, but has a triad-pivot hub that controls toe angle under various operating loads and a linkage that compensates for camber changes. These refinements are aimed at improving the compromise between high-speed stability and dynamic response, two virtues not always combined ideally in semi-trailing rear ends. The RX-7 Turbo has sportier calibrations than other versions, featuring firmer springs and shock absorbers. The upper GXL may be specified either with the Turbo's Sports package or AAS, an electronically controlled adjustable shock-absorber system that allows the driver to choose between Normal and firmer Sport damping settings.

Now by rack and pinion, the RX-7's steering is as sophisticated as its suspension. The standard manual steering rack is supported by a yoke-and-roller-bearing combination that exerts variable forces on the rack; quick and precise response to initial steering input, reasonable quickness and acceptably light efforts are claimed. Standard on the GXL and Turbo and optional on the base model, the power steering has an electronic "brain" that tailors power assist to driving conditions and road surfaces. Its computer gathers data on vehicle speed and steering angle for a calculation of the lateral acceleration or "g." It even takes the road's coefficient of friction into account and, via twin tandem hydraulic pumps, doles out just the right amount of assistance.

The brakes are vacuum-assisted discs, the front ones ventilated. Top-of-the-line naturally aspirated models with 15-in. cast aluminum wheels have ventilated discs all around, the front pair featuring aluminum calipers with quad-opposed pistons. For the Turbo, Mazda has provided not only this premium brake system but the 16-in. wheels as standard; to be offered later as an option is the Bosch-patented ABS (Anti-skid Braking System) with a further refinement by Mazda that eliminates the excessive pedal kickback sometimes associated with such systems.

Footwear for the new RX-7 ranges from the base set of 185/70HR-14 tires on 14 × 5.5JJ stamped steel wheels to the top models' 205/60VR-15 on cast aluminum 15 × 6JJ wheels. On the Turbo, 205/55VR-16 tires on 16 × 7JJ alloys are standard. As before, the P747 RX-7 comes in only one body style; riding on a wheelbase 2430 mm (95.7 inch) long, it is just over an inch shorter than its predecessor at 4290 cm/168.9 in.. And yet, remarkably, it will be available as a 2+2, with small folding rear seats much like those of the Porsche 944. Actually, the previous RX-7 had also been offered in Japan as a 2+2, but stringent U.S. rear-end crash standards had precluded offering it there. The P747 solves this problem belatedly by caging the rear compartment with sturdy side-frame extensions.

RX-7 mechanical layout: the engine is placed "front midships," aft of the front wheel centerline

At 1690 mm or 66.5 in., the new RX-7 is 0.8 in. wider than the old and as wide as Japanese designers would dare, being the customary 10 mm short of the maximum allowed for Japan's "small" passenger-car class. At anything over 1700 mm, the annual tax on a car doubles. (For this reason even the most powerful turbocharged Nissan ZX still has a body within the width limit, and inboard of the Toyota Supra's exaggerated add-on flares the body proper is rather narrow.) At 1450 mm front/1440 mm rear (57.1/56.7 in.) the P747's tracks utilize the available body width to the limit and add more than an inch at either end over the predecessor. The new car's height is almost identical to that of the old: 1265 mm (49.8 in.).

Weight, the enemy of performance, vehicle dynamics and fuel efficiency, threatened the P747's very birth halfway through the project. The engineering improvements and innovations could have resulted in a considerable weight penalty for the P747, quite aside from the various comfort and convenience features it needed to be worthy of its new performance and quality status. Project chief Uchiyama saw early on that to meet fuel-economy targets, the car with manual transmission would have to squeeze into the U.S. Environmental Protection Agency's 2875-lb weight class, and with automatic transmission into the EPA 3000-lb class.

A still more serious concern for Mazda was America's dreaded Gas Guzzler Tax, which the RX-7 buyer would have to pay if its combined city-highway mileage fell below the 1986 minimum of 22.5 miles per gallon. The 1985 RX-7 GSL-SE had barely cleared that year's 21.5-mpg hurdle; Mazda would do anything and everything to avoid the tax. (Uchiyama, recalling Mazda's bleak days in the wake of the 1973 oil crisis, vows: "Once was enough. Never again will we be called a guzzler.")

To reappraise the project's feasibility in the face of the looming weight barrier, Mazda management went so far as to order a freeze for a full month in May 1983, even though most of the design work on major components had been completed. Subsequently, Uchiyama's people put up a renewed and determined fight against their common enemy. As a result, the P747 has more light-alloy components than any Mazda since the very first (the diminutive R360 two-seater coupe at 380 kg/838 lb!), and for that matter probably more than any other current production Japanese car. They include front suspension arms, engine-mount bracket, front brake calipers, final drive rear casing-cum-mount member, spare wheel and—on certain weight-critical models—an aluminum hood. Uchiyama sent one of his people to a specialist manufacturer at Greifenstein-Allendorf near Frankfurt, Germany to procure an aluminum jack that would save 3 lb over a steel one; it is standard equipment on every new RX-7.

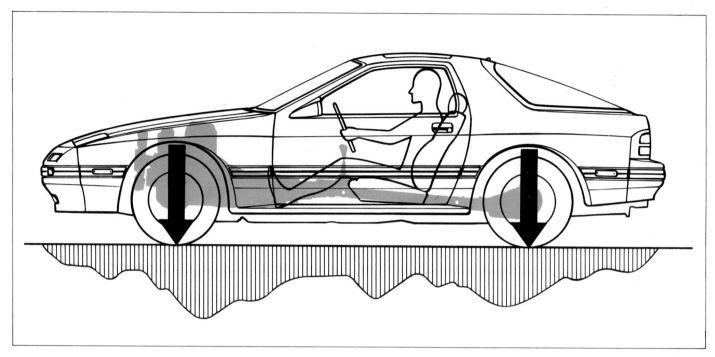

With two occupants and a full tank of fuel, weight distribution works out 50/50

In its comprehensively equipped two-seater GXL guise, the new RX-7 scales 1190.5 kg (2625 lb) curb weight, compared to 2500 lb for the 1985 13B-powered GSL-SE—no mean feat and a tribute to Uchiyama's and his team's painstaking efforts. The car's weight distribution has improved markedly, from the previous GSL-SE's 54% front/46% rear to an ideal 50%/50% proportion with two occupants and a full tank of fuel in the 63-liter (16.6-gal.) tank.

Mazda's performance data for the naturally aspirated models give a 0–60-mph acceleration time of 8.0 seconds, the standing quarter-mile in 16.1 sec. and a top speed of 205 km/h/128 mph. The later-appearing Turbo cuts the 0–60 sprint to 6.7 sec., covers the 1/4 mile in 15.2 sec and gains membership in the prestigious 150-mph club with ease. Estimated EPA mileages are 17 mpg city/24 mpg highway for the normally aspirated RX-7 with either manual transmission or automatic, improving on the 1985 GSL-SE's 16/23.

The body purposeful

JUST AS THE overall concept was the subject of in-house competition, so was the new RX-7's styling. That's the official version, anyway; Mazda doesn't admit it, but I suspect there was an outside element at some early stage of things—specifically a European one.

In any case, early in the design process the competition narrowed from more than two dozen candidates (in sketch form) to two leading contenders. Both were in-house designs by the Hiroshima staff, with input from their colleagues at MANA, Mazda's Irvine, California-based R&D group. One was a highly evolutionary look, readily identifiable as an RX-7: pleasant and up-to-date, with unmistakeable RX-7 features like upright B-pillars and tapering "canopy" rear-window treatment. This conservative approach eventually lost out to a bolder step toward late-Eighties sports-car idioms. The original RX-7 was admired for its agile, airy character; it had a sort of likeable cheekiness and was often described as "cute." All well and good for the clientele of an entry-level sports car, but the P747 design team didn't see the same clientele for the new car. Mazda's astute design chief Matasaburo Maeda cautioned them, "I want the car to impart a mature feel and an impression of quality. Youthful, yes, but nothing juvenile."

So it became. The P747's shape is smooth-flowing and tightly integrated. A side-by-side comparison with its most direct competitor, Porsche's 944, reveals that the German car is more curvaceous and conveys a typically Teutonic feel of mass; the Mazda's lines and surfaces have more continuity and flow.

Its profile reveals that the visual mass has been shifted forward, a sensation lent by the sharply raked windshield, large single-stamping door, forward-slanting B-pillar and huge one-piece wraparound rear window. The effect is intended to create the effect of modern performance machinery, as represented by short-nosed mid-engine racing cars, but the rakish windshield (63.5 degrees from the vertical, as compared to the previous RX-7's 59 and the 944's 60 deg) has its aerodynamic benefit too. Windshield area is up 25 percent over the original RX-7; the glass is bonded onto its frame and surrounded by a flat strip that gives a flush fit. To further ensure smooth air flow, particular care is taken in matching the windshield to the roof panel. The long dual wipers are parked half-concealed, again to keep air drag low.

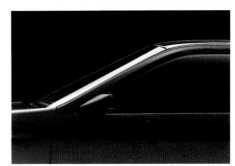

The windshield is raked at 63.5 deg from the vertical, and its surface merges smoothly onto the roof panel for efficient air flow management

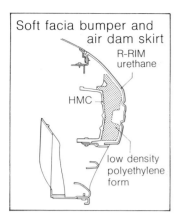

Soft facia bumper and air dam skirt

R-RIM urethane

HMC

low density polyethylene form

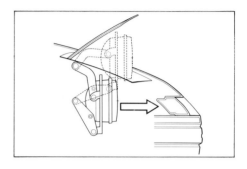

Soft-facia front end's R-RIM urethane skin is backed by energy-absorbing foam and high-strength HMC plastic beam

The nose slopes evenly down to the soft-facia front end-bumper, whose skin of reinforced reaction injection molding (R-RIM) urethane is backed by energy-absorbing foam and reinforced by a high-strength sheet molding compound (HMC) plastic beam. Fulfilling the two countries' respective regulations, the U.S. version has a 2.5-mph impact protection, the Canadian version a 5-mph protection. The original RX-7 had an aerodynamic spoiler just in front of the front wheel opening, accenting its bullet-like nose; on the new car there is a proper air dam integrated into the front end, extending downward just behind the bumper face for reduced front-end lift. The air dam leaves a practical "ramp angle" of 14 deg so that the driver won't suffer anxiety attacks when entering or exiting driveways.

Eyes that peek out

MAZDA'S DESIGNERS came up with a clever use for the retractable headlamps that they hope will create a graphic expression of their own. The lights move vertically by parallelogram linkage, so even when retracted they face dead forward. A rectangular port in front of each light provides an opening so that it can be flashed for daytime passing: the port has a lamp-like lens, and its shape was modified in the course of development to give a slight Oriental slant.

Retractable headlamps move vertically by parallelogram linkage; when retracted they face forward and can be employed as passing lights

Large single-piece rear window has compound curvature

A single-piece wraparound rear window was already on the designers' priority list when the original RX-7 was on the drawing boards, but for cost reasons they made do with a three-piece arrangement and hidden C-pillars behind it. This time around the designers won out over both the accountants and those who feared a weight penalty, and got a single-piece rear window-hatch. The huge pane is an intricate mixture of convex and concave surfaces, raked at 18.5 deg to the horizontal for smooth aerodynamics.

The designers liken the glass masterpiece to a riding saddle. Originally intended as a pure glass hatch, it eventually gained a steel frame for rigidity and tight sealing; the frame then allowed the use of thinner (5-mm) glass for a net weight saving. Like the

Large doors with single-piece outer panels offer easy ingress and egress, have flush window glass and are very rigid in construction

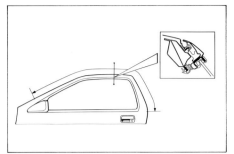

Elaborate triple sealing keeps elements out

windshield, the glass is bonded into the frame and surrounded by a flush trim strip. The hatch is supported by a pair of hydraulic struts and secured by two latches when closed. Because of the car's wedge profile, the cargo area's lift-over height is up 120 mm to 910 mm or 35.8 in..

For loading and unloading two-legged cargo, Mazda adopted large doors with single-piece outer panels (Mazda's first) and built-up inner ones. The design has three major advantages. One is flush window glass for good aerodynamics. The upper end can be very rigid, precluding "sucking out" at higher velocities: Mazda's self-imposed requirement was that the upper door stay firmly in place at the car's maximum speed (over 150 mph) in a 22-mph cross wind. And despite a hefty appearance reminiscent of the Porsche 928, the door is actually lighter than a built-up design.

To keep out the elements, door sealing is quite elaborate; there are no fewer than three separate sealing strips on its critical upper perimeter. Inside it has a fabricated HCP100 high-tensile steel reinforced beam for protection in side crashes. Sticklers for detail, Mazda located the keyhole in a bezel to preclude inadvertent scratching of the body-color painted flush door handles.

Blisters on the car's flanks won out over flares for the wheel openings. Compared to the 944's heavily arched and sharply sculptured protrusions, though, they are subdued; that Japanese width limit played a rule here too. To accentuate the large wheels and tires, only a very narrow metal surface is left between the front fender top and wheel opening. For visual impact the designers would have liked a tucked-in rocker panel, but aerodynamics dictated rolling it nearly straight down; a sculptured flare ending at the rear wheel opening recoups some of the visual effect they wanted. Like the front bumpers, the rear one is made up of energy-absorbing foam, a fiberglass beam and a RIM urethane skin. Several designers in both Hiroshima and Irvine wanted to resurrect the quad circular lamp clusters of early Mazda rotary-engine cars, but lost out to rectangular ones with rounded outer top corners.

Blisters on the flanks of the new RX-7

The quad-round proponents haven't given up yet, though, so their treatment may surface on future P747 variants. Surely everyone is happy that there are no bolted- or stuck-on emblems to mar the clean rear end; all the identification there is decals. Just under the hatch in the center is the mandatory-in-U.S. high stoplight.

Except for the bumper skins and version-specific aluminum hood, the body structure and most of its outer panels are of stamped steel sheet metal. The Turbo will have an SMC airscoop atop its alloy hood.

The structure: compact and rigid

THANKS PARTLY to relatively small openings in its compact shell, the original RX-7 body was exceptionally rigid. Given the much larger openings in the P747 body, it was a critical task for the body engineers to retain that torsional and bending rigidity. For example, the door apertures measure 1370 long × 970 mm high (53.9 × 38.2 in.), compared with 1250 × 900 (49.2 × 35.4) for the previous X605 body; this crowds the pillars and roof side rails. Too, the thin but effective rear roof pillars hidden behind the predecessor's rear-window wrapover are no longer there.

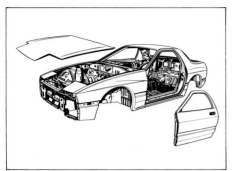
Body shell is all-steel welded integral construction. On certain models, aluminum hood panels are used

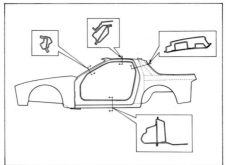
Critical body parts are strengthened by these double and multi-boxed sections

One of the solutions is that the all-steel integral shell's structural sides are single large stampings for rigidity and uniformity of fits. The perimeter surrounding the door aperture, including A-pillar, roof rail and side sill, is all double box sections; the B-pillar is two boxes in a larger closed section. The A-pillar's inner box is of 2.3-mm steel, an unusually thick gauge for this application. Together with the bumper system, the front side frames were designed and stressed for the American 35-mph crash test; same for the rear frames, which are connected to the side sills.

The sills are notably large in cross-section. Internal reinforcement of the tapering B-pillars comes from triangulated boxes; at their bases is a horizontal frame that runs along the beltline to the rear of the occasional rear seat/cargo area, forming a cage-like structure around people and luggage. The B-pillar tops also extend into the roof to form a rollbar.

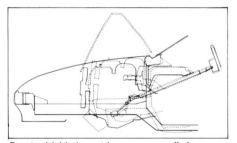
Front midship layout leaves unusually long "crush zone" in case of collision

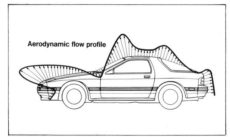
Aerodynamic forces

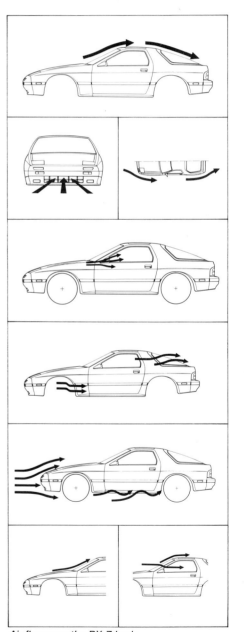
Air flow over the RX-7 body

Mazda claims a drag coefficient (C_D) of 0.31 for the base RX-7 with twin streamlined mirrors and 185/70HR-14 tries; with its small frontal area, the $C_D \times A$ figure works out to an impressively low 0.56. Composed of a front-end lift factor of $C_{LF} = 0.08$ and $C_{LR} = 0.14$ at the rear, the mean lift value is extremely favorable. Early aerodynamic development work was done at the Japan Automobile Research Institute's Yatabe wind tunnel north of Tokyo; later it was moved to the new tunnel at Mazda's Miyoshi proving ground, where these final figures were obtained. As always, there's more than meets the eye to aerodynamics. Underside airflow management was given minute attention, as were the air inlet and ducting through the engine compartment. Even the underhood structures carrying the suspension's MacPherson struts were shaped for smooth airflow around them.

An optional "aero kit" reduces the C_D to 0.29 and improves the C_{LR} to 0.07. The kit consists of soft-surfaced, foam-filled urethane add-ons designed for function, not styling effects; it may well disappoint those who want oversize wings and skirts for image. The factory rear spoiler is so short it could barely serve as a tea tray; the front air-dam extension, built up from three pieces, hangs snug and integral to the standard one. Smaller yet are deflector pieces that fit immediately ahead of the rear wheels, and hidden altogether is an extra aluminum underpan behind the standard polypropylene one to fill and streamline the space under the engine bay.

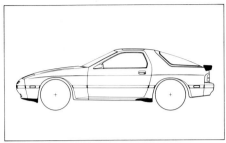

Optional "aero kit" add-on pieces

Short rear spoiler

The 13B engine: Mazda's largest rotary

THE P747'S TYPE 13B engine is Mazda's largest-displacement twin-rotor production unit to date. A Type 15A twin-rotor and a gigantic Type 21A were built experimentally, as were a number of multi-rotor ones; they are covered in Chapter Three and the Appendix. Both the 13B and the smaller 12A, the mainstay of the old RX-7 but not used in the new, are of the same family; their roots are in the Type 0810 (10A) unit that powered the company's first production Wankel-engine car, the L10A Cosmo sports coupe.

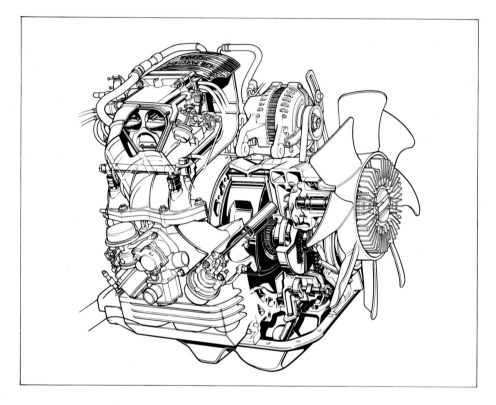

Type 13B DEI electronically fuel-injected twin-rotor engine

All these engines share the same epitrochoidal dimensions and geometry. The generating radius **R**, the radial distance from the center of the rotor to each of its apices, is 105 mm (4.13 inch). The eccentricity **e** is the offset between the centerline of the eccentric output shaft (which corresponds to the reciprocating engine's crankshaft) and the rotor centerline; it measures 15 mm (0.59 in.) in this engine family. With the generating radius, it is one of the key dimensions of the rotary engine; together they may be regarded as equivalent to the stroke of the reciprocating piston engine.

The other key element is **b**, the trochoid housing's width; it corresponds to a piston engine's bore. The smallest 10A had a 60-mm (2.36-in.) width, which gave each combustion chamber a volume of 491 cc. The Type 12A that powered RXs 2, 3 and the original 7 has a 70-mm width for a single chamber capacity of 573 cc. In the 13B, the trochoid housing is widened to 80 mm (3.15 in.) for a single chamber displacement of 654 cc; multiply by two for the two rotors and you get Mazda's figure of 1308 cc. There had already been a Type 13 engine with the rightful suffix A. It was an isolated engine type with different internal dimensions—R = 120 mm, e = 17.5 mm, b = 60 mm—so the newer 13, first used in the RX-4 series in 1973, was named 13B. Since then it has been modified internally and externally in a quest for a balance of improved performance and fuel efficiency, most recently in the course of P747 development; but because it retains the 105 × 15 × 80 dimensions it continues to be designated 13B.

New base engine: 11 horsepower more than the GSL-SE

THE LATEST 13B is a development of the fuel-injected DEI version first seen in October 1983 in the revamped Japanese Cosmo/Luce intermediates (Mazda 929) and the RX-7 GSL-SE for America. It incorporates the 6PI intake port design, refined DEI (Dynamic Effect Intake system), dual-injector fuel injection and full digital engine controls, as well as numerous further internal modifications and refinements.

Thanks to the various improvements, the naturally aspirated 13B is now rated at 146 bhp SAE net at 6500 rpm, 11 horsepower more than the previous version at the same peak speed; torque is up 6 percent to 187 Newton-meters (138 pounds-feet) at 3500 rpm. The compression ratio remains at 9.4:1.

Originally developed under the in-house code VIPS (Variable Intake Port System, which describes the arrangement aptly), 6PI refers to Six-Port Induction, with an auxiliary "power" intake port above the secondary port. The auxiliary port is opened and closed positively by a rotating cylindrical valve operated by exhaust pressure. In its early form the twin-rotor Mazda engine had two side intake ports per rotor and thus a total of four; these two additional ports make it 6PI.

A rotary engine's performance characteristics depend mainly on intake-port timing. Timing and port shape are conceived to produce the best possible compromise in low-end torque and top-end power, given the engine's maximum gas-flow volume and what is required of it in its foreseen operating environment.

For example, the intake ports of the carbureted four-port 12A engine that powers previous RX-7s open at 32 degrees after top dead center (ATDC) and close at 40° after bottom dead center (ABDC). In the lean-burn form with a three-way catalytic converter, it had good driveability and its fuel economy was improved over previous versions. But there was a tradeoff: top-end performance was sacrificed to a certain degree. So the same engine, tuned for the faster-driving European market and equipped with a thermal reactor for emission control, had its intake closing delayed to 50° ABDC at some sacrifice in low-speed flexibility and fuel economy.

Breathing: a "third wind"

WITH 6PI'S third "power" port staying open until much later, the engine is given another breathing period. In the latest fuel-injected 13B engine, the primary and secondary intake ports close at 40° and 30° ABDC; the auxiliary port stays open as late as 80° ABDC. So in effect, the engine rides on three curves of volumetric efficiency as it moves from low through middle to its highest speed range. With this variable port timing ensuring good low-end torque and fuel economy, the length of the intake passage can be set for optimum dynamic charge effect in high-speed operation. In the new 13B the individual intake tracts downstream of the air-intake

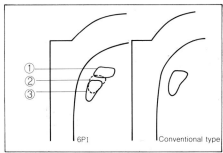

Type 13B DEI engine's 6PI auxiliary power ports are positively controlled by cylindrical rotating valves, and give extra breathing capacity at higher loads
① auxiliary port ② primary port ③ secondary port

Type 13B DEI engine in the RX-7 engine bay

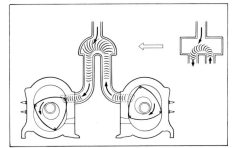

New DEI plenum chamber has rounded top corners, as compared with previous version's "box," to optimize effects of pressure waves from the two rotor chambers

plenum box are 434 mm (17.1 in.) long for the primary ports and 411 mm (16.2 in.) for the secondaries.

These long individual intake runners proceed from a box-shaped plenum chamber, or "surge box" in Mazda terminology. The box has two stories, the lower one feeding into the two primary tracts and the "mezzanine" into the two secondary/power-port tracts, and is directly attached to the three-valve (one primary and two secondaries) throttle chamber. Through computer simulation and, later, a series of test-bench experiments, Mazda engineers discovered that there was a useful pressure-increasing interaction of air between the two rotors. First, when air fed into the combustion chamber is suddenly cut off by the closing intake port, the inertia of the airflow generates high pressure. This pressure bounces back in the form of a wave in the intake manifold and travels at the speed of sound to the other intake port, where it arrives toward the latter part of the intake cycle, when the port is about to close. Pressure in the intake-port area is thus increased, which serves to charge more air into the chamber. More waves are generated just after the intake port opens, when part of the high-pressure gas in the expanding chamber is likely to rush backward into the intake manifold. This pressure travels in the form of a wave to the other intake port and works to charge additional air just before the other rotor's intake port closes.

The rotary's increase in volumetric efficiency at high speeds was found to be due to this interaction of two kinds of compression waves between the two rotor chambers. To turn the interaction into pressurization of intake air, the plenum box was given its "lower floor" for primary ports and "mezzanine" for the secondaries. These effects also bring another bonus, in the form of air resonance that further improves combustion-chamber filling. Intake air pressure, as measured just before closing, is in the order of 100 mm of mercury (almost 2 pounds per square inch), so the arrangement could easily qualify as "pulse-positive charging." The latest DEI plenum chamber has rounded top corners to direct pressure waves from the two rotors back at each other and thus optimize the pressure effects.

Electronic fuel injection with special features

DIGITALLY CONTROLLED Bosch L-Jetronic fuel injection produced by Nippon Denso feeds the 13B engine through four small injectors instead of the two larger ones used in the previous 6PI DEI 13B engine. As before, the primary injector is in the intake passage close to the primary port, an arrangement Mazda calls "semi-direct" injection. The injector is actuated by electric voltage; air and fuel mixing is promoted at low engine speeds by intake air directed to the nozzle receptacle, at higher speeds by a mixing-plate socket. This latter is an umbrella-like, open-sided plastic tube whose end plate of about 12 mm (0.47 in.) diameter has 18 small holes. The plate splashes and squeezes injected fuel, thus aiding atomization. A second injector also fitted with mixing plate injects fuel into the secondary intake tract under high-load and high-rpm conditions; switchover between the two- and four-injector modes is controlled by the central engine-management computer.

The two-injector-per chamber arrangement satisfactorily meets the uprated 13B's widely varying fuel requirements, from 700-rpm idle to 7000-rpm limit. Fuel atomization is also aided by the smaller injector size, with attendant benefits in driveability, fuel economy and emission control.

The 13B engine now employs timed fuel injection: fuel is injected once per intake cycle for each rotor chamber (alternately between the two chambers), as compared with the previous version's simultaneous injection.

Intake airflow resistance has been reduced and volumetric efficiency thus increased by a larger air cleaner, now enclosing 7 liters instead of the previous 5.6; larger throttle valve and manifold diameters; and a new Denso pendulum airflow meter.

Rotor and seals: less weight, tighter edges

THANKS TO a new thin-wall casting technique, the ductile cast-iron rotor, one of the

13B DEI now employs two fuel injectors per rotor chamber. One is in the passage close to the port opening, the other in the secondary intake tract

The primary and secondary injectors have mixing socket plates, umbrella-like, open-sided plastic tubes whose end plates have small holes. The mixing plates aid fuel atomization

engine's heavier components, has shed almost 14 percent of its weight to get down to 4.3 kg (9.4 lb). The lighter this considerable rotating mass, the less its inertia and the better the engine's response; fuel economy is thus also improved. The rotor's combustion recess is a symmetrically and centrally located MDR (medium-deep recess), inherited from the previous 13B.

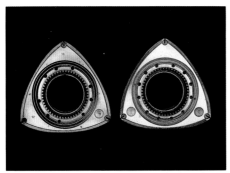
New thin-wall cast rotor on the right has shed 14 percent of its weight

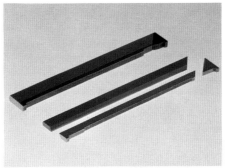
New three-piece apex seal (below) and the old two-piece design

To exert even pressure on the apex seal, two spring bars are used instead of the single-piece spring shown above

New sintered-iron side seal is 0.7 mm in thickness, as compared with the previous 1 mm. New seal and spring are shown below

New SSD (semi-surface discharge) sparkplug on the right, along with the old four-electrode type

A rotary engine's gas seals correspond to the reciprocating piston engine's compression rings and are critical to its performance and fuel economy. For the updated 13B, Mazda engineers again improved the gas-sealing mechanism significantly. The apex seals, special cast iron-alloy sealing elements at each of the rotor's three apices, are now 2 mm (0.08 in.) thick instead of 3. Their previous two-piece configuration, with a long main seal body and small triangular end piece, has given way to three pieces.

The diagonal cut facilitates the seal elements' sliding outward onto the trochoid surface, which geometrically minimizes the leakage path for gases. But pressure differences between the chambers ahead of and behind the main seal element (it separates the chambers) cause it to sway back and forth in its groove as they go through the rotary's four working cycles. Though theoretically gas-tight, both geometrically and statically, in actual operation the two-piece apex seal does leave some leakage path, however minute.

In the new three-piece design the main seal is further divided, laterally and at an angle, into upper and lower pieces; the triangular end piece is retained. The top piece that contacts the hard porous chrome-plated trochoid surface is now less likely to sway or tilt in the direction of rotor motion; instead, it slides up and down vertically on the lateral, angled contact surface with the lower element.

Tighter gas sealing is the main result; but the lighter, thinner seal also flexes and follows any surface deformation of the trochoid chamber under varying thermal loads. And the lighter apex seal exerts smaller centrifugal forces on the trochoid, reducing wear and the likelihood of scoring. A further benefit of the thinner seals is a marked reduction in mechanical friction, which again manifests itself in improved power and fuel economy. The seal's top rubbing surface is chill-hardened by an electron beam, taking on a composition similar to that of ceramics.

The side seals, another part of the analogy to piston engines' rings, are also thinner than their counterparts in the previous 13B: 0.7 mm (0.03 inch) instead of 1.0. The seal is of sintered iron, which has a self-lubricating property in running against the nitrided surface of the cast-iron side housing.

An electronically controlled high-energy ignition system with twin semi-surface discharge (SSD) sparkplugs per chamber continues; the leading plug has been moved from 23 mm ahead of the trochoid's minor axis to 18 mm (0.71 inch) ahead of it. The pressure differential between the leading and trailing chambers is smaller at this new location, so gas blowby from the trailing to leading chamber is reduced when the rotor tip goes over the plug hole in the trochoid surface; a further improvement in fuel economy is the result here.

Advances in lubrication and cooling

THE TROCHOID surface is treated by a new technique called MCP, short for micro-channel porous chrome plating; it was already used on the European 12A and Japanese turbocharged 12A engines. In the previous 13B the trochoidal chamber's working surface was porous chrome-plated; the tiny pinpoint pores retain lubricant, thus improving sealing and reliability. MCP is a refinement by which the pinpoint holes are interconnected by miniscule channels.

Thermostatically controlled valve in the eccentric shaft cuts oil flow into the rotor at low temperatures, which improves fuel economy during warmup and speeds the warmup process

In the previous carbureted engine, oil was mixed with fuel in the carburetor for seal lubrication. The fuel-injection engine has separate oil injection, with one nozzle in the primary manifold and one injecting directly into the trochoidal chamber; both are fed by an eccentric-shaft-driven pump that meters the oil in proportion to throttle opening. Oil is force-fed to the bearings by a separate trochoid pump.

Lubricant is also used to cool the inside of the rotor, whose outer flanks form combustion chambers. In this sense the rotary engine is both water- and oil-cooled; accordingly, a separate oil cooler is included just ahead of the radiator in the RX-7's nose. Overcooling the rotor when the engine is cold reduces fuel economy; so does sloshing around cold, thick oil within the rotor. Thus the 13B lubrication system now includes a thermostatically controlled valve that cuts off oil into the rotor at low temperatures. The measure reduces fuel consumption during warmup as much as 12 percent, and speeds the warmup process as well.

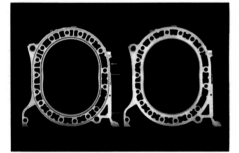

New trochoid housing on the right has smaller coolant jacket. Old 13B housing is shown on the left

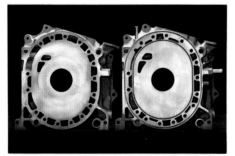

New (right) and old cast-iron side housings. Water-seal groove is now on the side housing, where it is less affected by heat. Enlarged auxiliary power port is visible

On the water side of cooling, the trochoid chamber's coolant jacket and the side coolant passages have been reduced in volume; altogether, coolant capacity is down by 0.8 liters (0.85 quart), thanks to this and the other measures, warmup is 20 percent faster. Made up of an aluminum core and plastic upper and lower tanks, the radiator weighs 5.4 kg (11.9 lb), down 1.5 kg (3.3 lb) from the previous copper core and brass tanks. It is flexibly mounted in a shroud whose shape was carefully determined to make optimum use of airflow from the small front opening, and is canted forward in race-car style to fit under the low nose. When automatic transmission is specified, its oil cooler is integrated into the radiator. Serving all this cooling apparatus is an eight-blade fan, driven by the engine through a viscous coupling that adjusts fan speed in a gradual, linear fashion instead of simply switching it in or out.

One of the rotary's less endearing qualities is its high-pitched exhaust note, attributable to the abruptness with which the exhaust ports open. A more gradual opening can reduce the harshness; to achieve this, the Mazda engineers conceived an elaborately shaped multi-chamber insert for the naturally aspirated 13B engine to replace the previous single-chamber heat-retaining port insert.

Emission control is by a closed-loop feedback system with three-way catalytic converters. The system is complex, with two monolith pre-converters and a main converter with three separate catalyst sections: two three-ways and an oxidizing one. Cleansed exhaust gas is released from dual mufflers and pipes; the main mufflers have a 10-liter (610-cubic-inch) capacity each, as compared with the previous GSL-SE's single 17-liter muffler.

The rotary engine's fundamental virtues are its compactness and light weight relative to its performance. Nothing basic has changed here; the new 13B measures just 515 mm long, 535 mm wide and 640 mm high (20.3 × 21 × 25.2 in.) and weights only 153 kg (337 lb) complete with lubricant and coolant but excluding radiator and oil cooler.

As installed in the RX-7, the engine is angled 5 deg rearward; its forefront is just over the front-wheel centerline in what is known as the "front midship" position. It is carried on three mounts, two on the engine's center housing and one on the transmission, in contrast to the previous points at the front of the engine. The relocation was done to minimize the engine resonance at about 3500 rpm, and required an elaborately shaped oil sump to make room for an aluminum mount bracket on the right side. The two cylindrical compression mounts are bolted onto the front subframe, which is rigidly bolted to the body shell and also carries the pivots for the front suspension's lower arms; the transmission mount is twin compression blocks and an abutment, the latter checking fore-aft movement.

Aluminum radiator with plastic upper and lower tanks saves 1.5 kg in weight. It is flexibly mounted in a full shroud

Multi-chamber exhaust port insert reduces harsh, high-pitched exhaust note

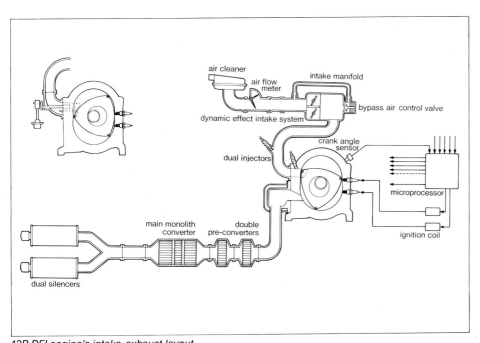

13B DEI engine's intake-exhaust layout. Emission-control system employs a multi-stage catalyst

Upping the ante: the turbo rotary

THE 13B TURBO shares most of the naturally aspirated engine's features except the 6PI. Although the RX-7 Turbo is the first turbocharged rotary model to make it to North America, it was preceded in the home market by the larger Cosmo Turbo, launched in Japan in autumn 1982, and a Turbo version of the previous RX-7. Both these models, however, were powered by the smaller 12A engine in turbo form.

Because of its inherent exhaust-port design and pulsations, the rotary lends itself well to turbocharging. Unlike the reciprocating piston engine's relatively gradual opening of poppet valves, the rotary's ports open suddenly; the exhaust gas thus strikes a turbocharger's turbine with more vehemence.

Type 13B DEI Turbo engine

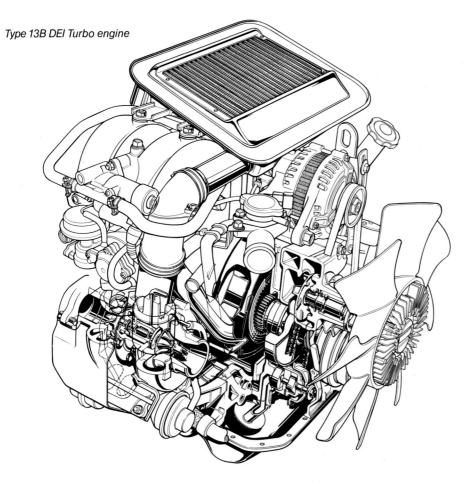

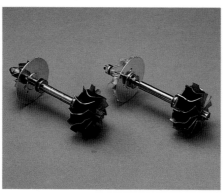

*Straight-blade impact turbine on the right;
a conventional curved-blade type on the left*

48

The first turbo 12A engine had what was essentially a proprietary turbocharger, Hitachi's HT18-BM model. Mazda engineers noted then that the rotary's exhaust force could be better exploited by a new turbine shape. They define the exhaust force that spins a turbocharger as consisting of two steps: first an "impact," when gas coming from the manifold strikes the blades, and then a "reaction" force as it continues through the blades and increases the turbine's speed.

To take advantage of this two-stage action the Mazda people devised a new turbine blade shape. In their Impact-Turbo, the part of the blade the gas hits first is straight and almost at right angles to the exhaust-gas inlet; the reaction part of the blade is curved. When the new-type turbo was introduced on the Cosmo and the Japanese RX-7, the engine's torque and throttle response improved significantly.

Unique new twin-scroll turbocharging

FOR THE new RX-7 Turbo, the bigger 13B engine has been given a turbo treatment—and a very special one at that. Hiroshi Ohzeki, cherubic and cheerful chief of the Fifth Engine Design Department, and his quiet enthusiast sidekick Tomoh Tadokoro have pulled another hat-trick of rotary wizardry: effective, ingeniously simple twin-scroll turbocharging that virtually eliminates the dreaded "turbo lag." Thus boosted and intercooled, the 13B engine has an ample spread of torque at the low end, combined with impressive power at the top. It produces 182 bhp SAE net at 6500 rpm and a torque peak of 256 Nm (183 lb-ft) at 3500 rpm; perhaps more to the point, at a mere 1500 rpm it generates 22 percent more torque than the naturally

Hitachi HT18S-2S twin-scroll turbocharger, jointly developed by Mazda and Hitachi

Turbocharger installation on the 13B DEI Turbo

Left: at low engine speeds, exhaust gas is let into the turbocharger through the open primary path. The small cross-sectional area accelerates gas speed and the scroll geometry directs gas toward the turbine blades at a close-to-right angle. Right: above 2500 rpm the trap door opens and adds its area to the total. With the turbocharger now in a more effective operating range, gas speeds need not be so fast. In this mode, the gas also strikes the turbine at a more obtuse angle

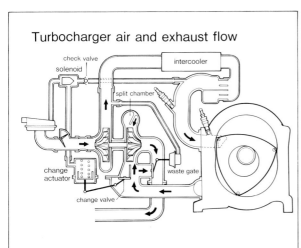

Turbocharger air and exhaust flow

check valve
solenoid
intercooler
split chamber
change actuator
change valve
waste gate

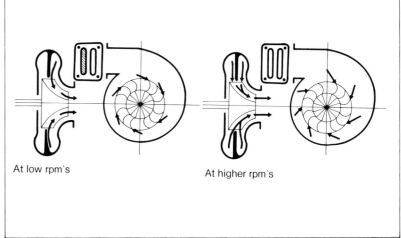

At low rpm's

At higher rpm's

aspirated 13B does at its peak of 3500 rpm. Between 1500 and the allowable maximum speed of 7000 rpm, the torque curve never falls below 145 lb-ft.

The twin-scroll turbocharger concept was developed jointly by Mazda's Department Five and Hitachi, and is manufactured by Hitachi having been designated HT18S-2S. Its turbine-side bearing area is now water-cooled, and the main body is further protected from high exhaust temperatures by a dual-skin heat shield. The 11-blade turbine, of Impact design, is 64 mm (2.52 inch) in diameter. Its scroll area, the entry path for exhaust gas, is divided into two passages separated by an integrally cast wall; one, called the secondary scroll, has a trap-door-like gate operated by intake vacuum.

The turbine thus has two cross-sectional area (**A**) factors, **A** being the scroll's smallest area as used in calculating turbocharger performance characteristics: 6.00 sq cm (0.93 sq in.) for the primary path and 9.48 sq cm (1.47 sq in.) for the secondary. The other factor is **R**, the distance between the turbine-shaft center and the center of area **A**: 59.4 mm (2.34 in.) for the primary path, 60.4 mm (2.38 in.) for the secondary. Thus the twin-scroll turbocharger has two **A/R** ratios: 0.40 for the primary path and 1.0 for the primary and secondary combined.

At low engine speeds, exhaust gas is let into the turbocharger through the open primary path. The small cross-sectional area has a throttling effect which accelerates gas speed; the scroll directs gas toward the turbine blades at a closer-to-right angle. Above 2500 rpm the trap door, made of HK35 heat-resistant cast steel alloy, opens and adds its area to the total. Now, with the turbocharger already in its more effective operating range, gas speeds need not be so fast. In fact, a decrease is desirable; this is obtained because the gas now strikes the turbine at a more obtuse angle.

This twin-scroll turbocharger acts as two turbos in one, combining the virtues of a unit designed for low-speed flexibility and response with another one designed for high-speed power. Its 12-blade compressor is 63 mm (2.48 in.) in diameter. An ordinary exhaust wastegate is included; the wastegate, actuated by intake pressure, limits maximum boost to 320 mm of mercury (0.42 bar/6.2 psi) at 2000 rpm, which is maintained up to about 5000 rpm, then tapers off to 280 mm (0.36 bar/5.4 psi) at 6000 rpm. For additional protection, fuel cut-off comes into play should the intake wastegate malfunction and boost exceed 400 mm mercury. The HT18-2S turbo's maximum turbine speed is 110,000 rpm.

Air-to-air intercooler

Another safety device is the turbo engine's detonation prevention system. Unlike the Japanese-market 12A Turbo, whose ignition control computer relies on signals from ignition-pulse, intake-temperature and boost sensors to detect the knock-prone zone, in order to adjust the ignition timing and enrich the fuel injection, the 13B Turbo employs a more positive piezoelectric knock sensor and an electronically controlled ignition retard system.

An air-to-air intercooler is mounted directly above the engine over the plenum chamber, the shortest route for pressurized and cooled air to travel to the intake system. The twin-scroll turbo mates very well with the Dynamic Effect Intake system, which might not have worked so satisfactorily with a conventional turbocharger system; its large plenum-chamber volume could hamper throttle response.

In one respect the 13B turbo engine is more conventional than its naturally aspirated counterpart; it has only two intake ports per rotor, or as Mazda calls it, 4PI. Both primary and secondary intake ports open at 32° ATDC, and close at 50° ABDC. The single peripheral exhaust port opens at 75° BBDC and closes at 48° ATDC. Also more conventional is the single-chamber exhaust-port insert instead of the non-turbo engine's multi-chamber type; the reason is to give exiting exhaust gas a clearer path.

Intercooler is mounted immediately above the engine. Large-section tract from the air cleaner has an elaborately shaped damper box to minimize intake noise

(The port insert's function is to insulate the port so that exhaust temperature is kept high for partial oxidation in the ribbed cast-iron thermal-reaction exhaust manifold.) Like the naturally aspirated engine, the Turbo has closed-loop emission control, but here the pre-converter chamber with a two-way catalyst is mounted directly on the turbocharger's turbine outlet to ensure exhaust cleansing with a cold engine. The main three-way converter is shared with the non-turbo model.

The Turbo's primary injector's mixing-plate socket has twin plates at different angle. The taller secondary injector mixing socket is similar to that of the naturally aspirated engine with single end-plate

The Turbo's fuel injection, too, is basically like that of the normally aspirated 13B engine, being digital Bosch L-Jetronic with two injectors per rotor. In contrast to the naturally aspirated engine's single-plate socket, the primary injector's mixing-plate socket has twin plates at different angles, rather like a biplane's wings, to further promote fuel atomization. Because the engine's maximum flow far exceeded the capacity of any airflow meter in manufacturer Nippon Denso's catalog, a new pendulum-flap meter—a type that deals well with widely varying flows—had to be developed by the electric-electronics specialist. Another heavy-duty item is the fuel pump, whose two-speed operation is controlled by the electronic engine-management system.

As the Turbo's specific power output and thus thermal loads are higher—the latter by some 30 percent—lubrication of the trochoid's working surface is particularly critical. As in the non-turbo engine, the surface is micro-channel porous chrome plated. Additionally, the plated surface is coated with Teflon for initial bedding-in of the trochoid and apex seals; the surface layer is eventually scraped and burned off, but Teflon squeezes into those pinpoint holes and stays there. On top of all this, the Turbo has a higher-capacity oil pump; but should the surface be starved of lubrication for any reason, be it the owner's negligence or mechanical malfunction, the Teflon will re-emerge from its holes to lubricate the sliding surface temporarily. There is a warning lamp in the instrument cluster for low oil.

The die-cast aluminum trochoid housing has an inner core of sheet steel cast in; the plating is applied to it. This process is called SIP, for sheet-metal insert process. The sheet's material was changed from HPC45 to stronger HPC50, contributing to greater housing durability.

Internal modifications shared with the naturally aspirated 13B engine include a reinforced rotor-gear assembly, now with twelve spring-loaded pins securing it to the rotor body instead of the previous nine. This close-pitched, robust positioning reduces gear loads and precludes potentially harmful sympathetic vibrations.

The 13B Turbo engine weighs 171 kg. (377 lb) including turbocharger and intercooler, 18 kg (39.7 lb) heavier than the naturally aspirated version.

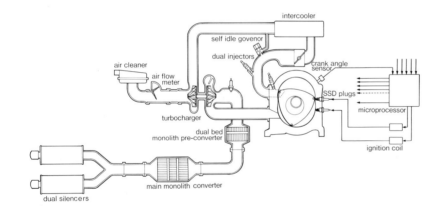

Turbocharged rotary's intake and exhaust layout. The turbo engine has a normal four-port intake system. Not shown in this drawing, the turbocharger is fitted with a wastegate

P747 drivetrain: five-speed manual or four-speed automatic

"EVOLUTIONARY" IS THE word for the P747 RX-7's drivetrain. A choice of five-speed manual or four-speed automatic transmission is available for the naturally aspirated RX-7; there is a strong new manual gearbox for the Turbo, and a new final drive unit was developed to go with the new independent suspension.

Standard fitment in naturally aspirated models is a refined version of the Type M five-speed manual transmission used on the previous 13B-powered GSL-SE model. Its clutch is a single-dry-plate type, with engagement pressure provided by a diaphragm spring with a ball throwout bearing. It is hydraulically actuated and includes automatic adjustment for disc wear; the disc's outside and inside diameters are 225 mm (8.86 in.) and 150 mm (5.9 in.).

The transmission housing is aluminum, die-cast in three pieces. Its main case houses the clutch and gear-synchronizer clusters for first through fourth gears and reverse; the center case carries the fifth-gear set, and a rear extension takes the shift linkage and shift-lever base. The gearbox is a straightforward two-shaft affair with Borg-Warner synchronizers on all forward gears, constant mesh on reverse, and internal ratios of (first) 3.475:1, (second) 2.002:1, (third) 1.366:1, (fourth) 1.000:1, (fifth) 0.711:1 and (reverse) 3.493:1, working with a final drive ratio of 4.100:1.

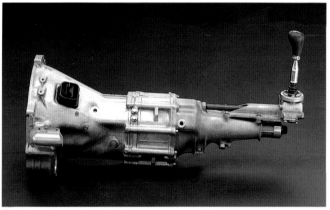

Standard fitment in naturally aspirated models is a refined version of the Type M five-speed gearbox

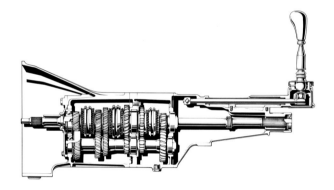

Innards of the Type M gearbox. The shift lever's base is moved back 30 mm (more than an inch) and the lever is now more upright

Improved 1–2 shifts

TO IMPROVE shifting between first and second gears, the only major source of complaint with the previous RX-7 manual gearbox, the synchronizer cone's diameter has been enlarged from 61 to 65 mm (2.56 inch). The gear modules had already received attention in the GSL-SE application, in that fine-mesh gears (smaller teeth) had been adopted to enlarge the meshing area as well as to reduce noise. The shift lever's base has been moved about 30 mm (1.18 inch) rearward, so the lever can now be more upright. With its diameter of 27 mm (formerly 24), it is also sturdier than before.

For the Turbo's 30-percent greater engine torque, Mazda unshelved the Type R gearbox design, a robust box used in the RX-3 series of rotary-powered cars, and produced a new unit on the basis of it. Unlike the Type M, it is housed in a four-piece aluminum case, with the clutch in its own housing bolted to the main assembly. The clutch, again of single-dry-plate type with diaphragm spring and hydraulic actuation, has the largest disc used in Mazda passenger cars: 240 mm (9.4 inch) outside, 160 mm (6.3 inch) inside.

All the gear modules in this box are new, second through fifth being of the so-called high-mesh type. The gearbox ratios are (first) 3.483:1, (second) 2.015:1, (third) 1.391:1, (fourth) 1.000:1, (fifth) 0.762:1 and (reverse) 3.288:1, combining with a final drive ratio of 3.909:1 (4.100 optional). Gears and synchronizer-cone splines for first, second and main drive gears, the three that handle the highest torque, are machined separately and then electron-beam welded together to get maximum tooth widths within the space constraints; this technique resulted in 3 mm of extra width. The other gears and splines are integrally machined. Synchronizer cones for the 1–2 and 2–3 shifts are also oversized: 76 and 65 mm respectively.

Automatic transmission's selector lever has an overdrive engagement-disengagement push switch on the knob side

Four-speed overdrive automatic

THE OPTIONAL automatic transmission is an updated version of the JATCO (Japan Automatic Transmission Company) L4N71B unit, with a four-speed planetary gearbox, torque converter and a converter lockup clutch. Its torque converter has a stall torque ratio of 2.0:1. An oil cooler for the transmission is integrated into the lower part of the radiator, but fluid temperature can still be critical if the car is driven at high speeds and loads; so the converter housing has its own air inlet and duct, and the converter impeller has cooling fins to help lower fluid temperature.

Working in a normal straightline quadrant, the selector lever has an overdrive engagement-disengagement push switch on the knob side beneath the park-reverse lockout button. Only in the overdrive fourth gear and above 70 km/h (44 mph) does the torque-converter lockup clutch come into action. The JATCO automatic as used in Mazda rotary-engine cars has sometimes been criticized for jerky lockup engagement or disengagement, so it is now set up to unlock the converter under conditions when jerks are most likely to occur. To smooth out 1–2 and 2–3 upshifts in the "D" range at partial throttle openings, the second-gear band servo has been given a longer working stroke. The planetary gearset ratios are (first) 2.841:1, (second) 1.541:1, (third) 1.000:1, (fourth) 0.720:1 and (reverse) 2.400:1, combined with a 3.909:1 final drive.

The single-piece propeller shaft has conventional universal joints at either end, and is 782 mm (30.8 in.) in length and has an outer diameter of 75 mm (2.95 in.) for the

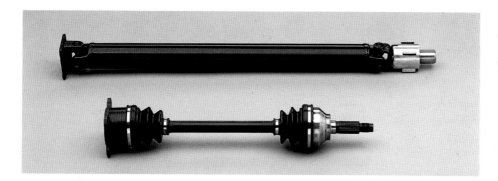

Single-piece propeller shaft with universal joints on either end is at the top, an axle halfshaft with inner and outer constant-velocity joints below it

Long-nose final drive unit with aluminum rear cover-cum-mounting bracket

normally aspirated manual transmission model, and 733 mm (28.9 in.) and 57 mm (2.24 in.) for the automatic. For the Turbo, the propeller shaft is a tube-in-tube construction; an outer tube on the transmission side encloses an inner tube on the final drive side, the two connected by three pressed-in and bonded rubber rings on the tube walls. There is a mechanical stopper in case the rubber rings should fail. The flexible construction eliminates high-speed resonance noise emission from this mass; the shaft is 774 mm (30.7 in.) long and has outer and inner tube diameters of 74 mm (2.95 in.) and 62.5 mm (2.46 in.).

Aft of the rear U-joint, the new RX-7 is very different from the old, with independent rear suspension instead of the previous live axle. The final drive unit is a new design, with a cast-iron front case, a long nose and an aluminum rear case/mounting bracket—a construction that saved about 5 kg (11 lb) over an all-cast-iron case. It is mounted at three points, with a front shear block halfway out of its nose attaching to the T-shaped rear subframe, which in turn is rubber-mounted to the body shell and also carries the rear suspension arms. The wide rear bracket has a large cylindrical rubber mount at either end, each bolted directly onto the body shell. By separating these rear mounting points from the suspension-carrying subframe, Mazda's noise-vibration engineers were able to tackle gear noise and resonance without worrying about involving the rear suspension.

Multi-plate limited-slip differential is standard on the GXL model

The driving bevel shaft is supported by two tapered roller bearings immediately in front of the gears and a third bearing at the front of the nose. For the Turbo, the gears are an oversize 8-in. combination; a multi-disc limited-slip differential is standard on the GXL, optional on the other models. The solid axle halfshafts are of equal length, with Birfield constant-velocity joints at both ends.

As usual, this final drive to independently suspended rear wheels is heavier than a live axle—altogether 35 kg (77 lb) more so than the old RX-7's axle. But even this penalty has its positive side: an improvement in weight distribution.

New suspension for a new sports car

At the front: new but evolutionary MacPherson struts

FOR THE new RX-7's front end, the Mazda chassis engineers stuck with MacPherson struts and concentric coil springs, an arrangement whose virtues include light weight, compactness and reasonable cost. Mazda's young chassis-designer prodigy Takao Kijima considers this widely used suspension type an extension of the time-honored unequal-length A-arm type in basic geometry and function, but with an invisible upper arm, and felt comfortable with its handling potential right from the beginning.

None of the new P747 RX-7's suspension components are carried over from its predecessor or shared with other Mazda models; they were specifically designed and developed for this car. The basic construction is straightforward, with the strut enclosing a tubular shock absorber and carrying a concentric coil spring. It is bolted onto the cast-iron hub carrier, and the hub itself is aluminum; the strut assembly is located by a wide-base forged aluminum A-arm via the usual ball joint. The A-arm is an open H-section forging and identical for both left and right sides. Each arm weighs 1.9 kg (4.2 lb); in steel it would have weighed 2.9 kg (6.4 lb). Its high cost, more than double that of a steel arm, is justified by the lower unsprung weight as well as the contribution to reducing overall car weight. A handsome piece of forging, the arm has two cylindrical rubber bushings at its inboard end, where it mounts to the fabricated sheet-steel, H-shaped suspension subframe. The subframe, rigidly mounted to the body shell at four points, also carries the engine mounts and rack-and-pinion steering.

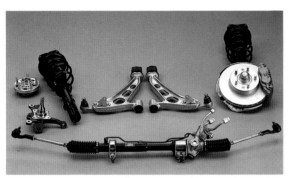

Front suspension, steering and brake components of the upper-grade GXL and Turbo models, with four-piston aluminum calipers

Front suspension, steering and brakes of the P747 RX-7

Front shock absorber-strut and spring assembly

Aluminum front hub

Forged aluminum A-arms are mounted on the fabricated subframe, which is in turn rigidly bolted to the body shell. Also seen in this view is the aluminum engine bracket

A critical element is the front bushing, which is 50 mm (2.0 in.) long and has inner/outer diameters of 40/17 mm; it is designed for high lateral stiffness, a prerequisite for precise handling. But it also provides fore-aft compliance—1.5 mm when subjected to a 100-kg longitudinal load—for reasonable riding comfort. For an anti-dive effect on braking, the A-arm is angled at 1.0 deg to the horizontal.

A straightforward anti-roll bar is connected to the A-arms with lever links; its diameter is 22 mm for the normal suspension, 24 mm with the sports package that is standard on the Turbo and optional on the GXL.

Kijima and his team claim to have arrived at a front suspension geometry that balances straight-line stability, cornering response, acceptable steering effort (without power steering) and isolation from shimmies and vibration. The front suspension allows 180 mm (7.1 in.) of wheel travel, 80 mm for jounce (upward) and 100 for rebound (downward). A caster angle of 5 degrees was decided upon after three different angles were tried in engineering "mule" vehicles. Seven degrees gave good straight-line stability but needed too much steering effort and tended to vibrate at the steering wheel; 2.5 deg reduced the steering effort considerably but didn't improve response much.

More critical was the influence of jounce travel on the wheel's toe attitude. The more the toe-out, the greater the understeer; the chassis designers' objective was to reduce toe-out to half its unchecked amount. They came close; by raising the steering-linkage knuckle mount 5 mm they were able to pare toe-out at 50 mm of jounce from 10 to 6 mm (0.24 in.). Other factors affecting steering response, including A-arm bushings and tires, also got careful attention from Kijima's group.

As mentioned earlier, the suspension is available in two calibrations. "Normal" means relatively soft springs and shocks, "Sports" a firmer set; the latter is standard on the Turbo and may be specified on the normally aspirated GXL model. Either way, low-pressure gas-filled front shocks are used to preclude fluid cavitation on rapid rebound strokes and assure stable ride and handling. The shocks' piston-rod size has also been increased, from the previous GSL's 20 mm to 22 mm (0.87 in.) for greater strut rigidity and smoother operation. Additionally, the GXL is equipped with electronically controlled adjustable shocks; American tune-it-yourself enthusiasts may lament the demise of manually adjustable shocks with external dials and eight different settings; these are still available on the Japanese-market Turbo, though.

Rear suspension: all-new, independent and innovative

MAZDA'S NAMING committee must have burned a lot of midnight oil over the P747's new rear suspension before arriving at the final set of initials, DTSS—short for Dynamic Tracking Suspension System.

This elaborate new system is a variation of the popular semi-trailing-arm type, fitted with a triad-pivot floating hub that controls the wheel's toe attitude under specific load conditions and a multi-link/pivot arrangement that compensates for chamber changes and provides anti-dive and -squat effects.

The toe-control hub has its name too: tri-axial floating hub. But several enthusiastic insiders at Mazda favor the yet-to-be-approved moniker "Kijima-Maebayashi hub," honoring the conceptual ingenuity and development efforts that the young engineers Takao Kijima and Jiro Maebayashi put into it. As mentioned earlier, Kijima designed the chassis; Maebayashi was in charge of the P747's basic mechanical layout.

The KM hub, shall we call it, is in parts. The wheel bearing is carried in a forged aluminum hub—by Mazda's nomenclature, the outer hub. A cast-iron hub carrier that grows from the trailing arm's end is called the inner hub. The outer hub is mounted to the inner hub or carrier at three points, each with a different axial phase. The forward pivot is a cylindrical rubber bushing, ahead of and below the wheel centerline, with its axis angled slightly forward from the vertical. Above and behind the wheel centerline is another cylindrical bushing, with its axis slightly inclined to the longitudinal. The solid pivot is a ball joint aft of and under the wheel centerline. Because the bushing

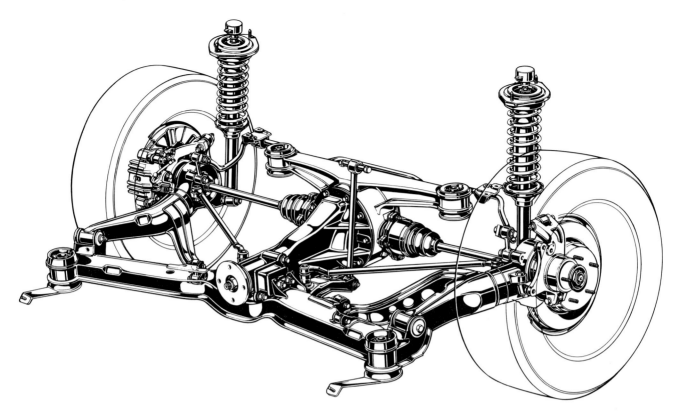

Rear suspension is new, innovative

Tri-axial floating hub outer with preloaded front bushing

allows not only axial rotation but controlled flexing, the outer hub has three dimensional freedom around the ball joint.

In an exhaustive series of studies, Kijima and his team of designers used Mazda's NASTRAN computer mathematical models to determine the phases, construction, kinetics and interactive effects of the three pivot points. Here is how the KM hub determines the wheel's toe attitude under the four major types of wheel loading:

The ingenious Kijima-Maebayashi tri-axial floating toe-control hub

THE HUB is float-mounted on the hub carrier or suspension-arm extension at three points. At points **A** and **B** are rubber bushing units; **B** being pre-loaded; bushing **A** has a near-longitudinal axis, bushing **B** a near-vertical one. Point **C** is a ball joint on which the hub can pivot in three dimensions, its movement being checked by the two bushings' geometry and kinetics. Bushing **A** and ball joint **C** form an imaginary kingpin line in the suspension geometry.

Fig. 1 Tri-axial floating toe-control hub of "Kijima-Maebayashi hub"

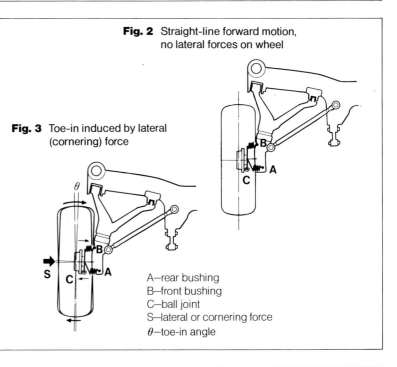

A—rear bushing
B—pre-loaded front bushing
C—ball joint

Toe-in induced by lateral force

Figure 2 shows the wheel in straight-line forward motion with no lateral forces applied to it. Bushings **A** and **B** do not deform. Figure 3 shows toe-in attitude induced by lateral force **S**, generated by the vehicle's cornering. By lever motion on ball joint **C** as pivot, an inward force is applied to bushing **B** and an outward force to bushing **A**; the wheel is turned inward at **C**. Also, load applied to the tire's contact patch exerts force on the wheel toward positive camber on the ball joint's low pivot. Between this force and the bushings' stiffness and axial inclination, the wheel assumes a toe-in attitude.

Fig. 2 Straight-line forward motion, no lateral forces on wheel

Fig. 3 Toe-in induced by lateral (cornering) force

A—rear bushing
B—front bushing
C—ball joint
S—lateral or cornering force
θ—toe-in angle

Toe-in induced by braking

Figure 4 shows braking force **R** applied in a rearward direction at the tire's contact-patch center. The upper bushing **A** has a washer-shaped abutment to restrict forward axial movement while allowing rearward as well as outward flexibility. Thus restricted by the abutment under the load imposed by force **R**, busing **A** and the lower ball point **C** form an imaginary kingpin (a real kingpin would have inhibited the hub's three-dimensional movement). The braking force turns the hub about this imaginary kingpin axis **Q**. Because there is an offset **I** between the tire's contact center **P** and the imaginary kingpin-axis extension, the wheel is toed in by the moment created by force **R**.

Fig. 4 Toe-in induced by braking

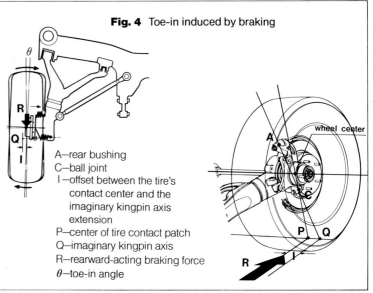

A—rear bushing
C—ball joint
I—offset between the tire's contact center and the imaginary kingpin axis extension
P—center of tire contact patch
Q—imaginary kingpin axis
R—rearward-acting braking force
θ—toe-in angle

Toe-in induced by forward driving force

Driving force **T**, as in acceleration, is applied in the forward direction to the wheel center as shown in Figure 5. Because the force is applied here, the wheel assumes a toe-in attitude by virtue of force **T**'s moment on the offset **J** between the load center and the point **N** that intersects imaginary kingpin axis formed by upper bushing **A** and ball joint **C**. In this case the upper bushing's forward flexing is also checked by the abutment.

A—rear bushing
C—ball joint
J—offset between the load center and
    the imaginary kingpin axis

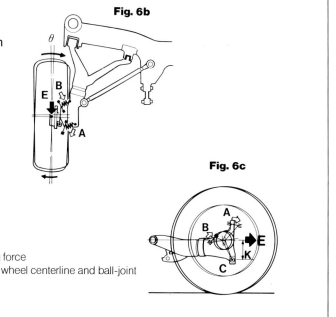

Fig. 5 Toe-in induced by forward driving force

N—point on the horizontal plane to the
    wheel center that intersects with
    the imaginary kingpin axis
T—forward-acting driving force
θ—toe-in angle

Toe-in induced by engine braking

Engine braking force **E** acts in the rearward direction on the wheel center as shown in Figure 6a. By virtue of offset **K** between the wheel centerline and the ball-joint height shown in Figure 6c, the wheel moves rearward on the ball-joint pivot, which causes it to assume a toe-in attitude by pivoting around an axis formed by bushings **A** and **B**.

Fig. 6   Toe-in induced by engine braking

Fig. 6b

Fig. 6a

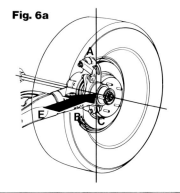

A—rear bushing
B—front bushing
C—ball joint
E—engine braking force
K—offset between wheel centerline and ball-joint
    height
θ—toe-in angle

Fig. 6c

Finite Element Module Analysis (FEM) model and load/toe-in comparison of four fources inducing toe-in

E— engine braking force
R—rearward-acting
    braking force
S—lateral force
T—forward-acting
    driving force
α— toe-in value

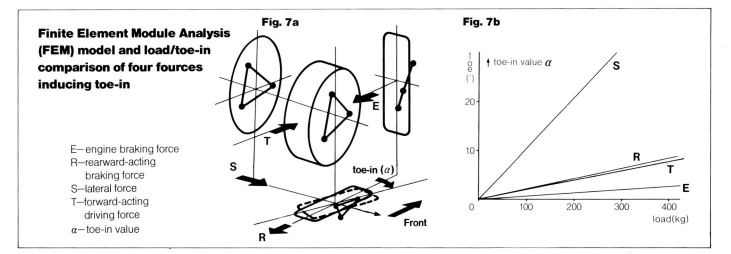

Fig. 7a

Fig. 7b

toe-in value α

IN A nutshell, the KM hub generates or augments toe-in, or compensates a decrease thereof, so that optimum cornering force is obtained and maintained by optimizing the rear tire's slip angle in a given environment.

But aye, there's the rub. That desirable stability of toe-in has a price in vehicle dynamics: in the response to steering input under low to medium lateral acceleration. Mazda chassis engineers call this "turnability," the vehicle's ability to turn quickly in the intended direction, and it's an important ingredient in sports-car handling. Neutral steering characteristics or a slight toe-out of the outside rear wheel improve "turnability."

In the course of conception and development, Mazda engineers evaluated a Porsche 944 and found that its rear suspension assumed a permanent toe-out attitude under cornering load. A pronounced and obstinate understeerer under power, the Stuttgart car nevertheless has very good turnability. Experience with their own four-wheel steering system also indicated to the Mazda people that steering the rear wheels in the opposite direction to the fronts, equivalent to a forced toeing-out of the outside rear wheel, makes the car highly responsive to initial steering input.

The KM hub incorporates such a feature, in that under low to medium load conditions (up to 0.4–0.5 g lateral acceleration), it actually produces a slight toe-out attitude. At higher lateral loads, it assumes the desired amount of toe-in. This is accomplished by preloading the front bushing. Inside the bushing's steel tube is a half-moon-sectioned bearing block of sintered iron, with Teflon-impregnated Kevlar woven sheets bonded to its two (flat and curved) contact surfaces. Kevlar has self-lubricating ability and has proved its durability in the support bearings of the F15 fighter plane's flap-actuating mechanism. The part-cylindrical bearing block exerts a preload on the bushing that resists initial load input, giving the rear wheels a slight toe-out attitude; under increased load the preload is overcome, changing the suspension's attitude to toe-in.

Cross–section of bush B

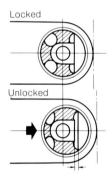

Locked

Unlocked

The half-moon-section bearing block inside the front bushing's steel tube exerts a preload on the bushing that resists initial load input, giving the rear wheel a slight toe-out attitude

Half-moon-section bearing block has self-lubricating Teflon-coated Kevlar cloth pieces on its contact surfaces

Preloaded front bushing's bearing block and abutment pieces

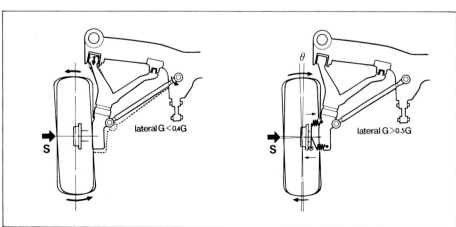

lateral G<0.4G

lateral G>0.5G

Left: because of the preload, bushing B resists initial load input, and the trailing arm's mount bushing flexes rearward, giving the rear wheel a slight toe-out. Right: increased load, the preload is overcome, changing the suspension's attitude to toe-in

Toe-control characteristics

THE CURVES in Figure 8 show toe-control characteristics of the P747 RX-7 in a test on a skidpad of 30-meter (98.4-ft.) radius, along with those of alternative geometries.

Toe-in is likened to a four-wheel steering system's steering both front and rear wheels in the same direction, toe-out to opposite steering at the two ends. The P747's initial reaction to low and medium lateral load, up to 0.4–0.5 g, is mild toe-out, which improves the car's turnability. At higher load conditions the KM hub assumes a toe-in attitude whose amount is dependent on the wheel loading.

Fig. 8

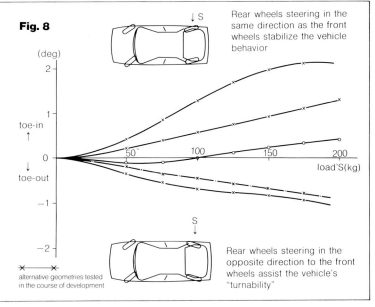

Rear wheels steering in the same direction as the front wheels stabilize the vehicle behavior

Rear wheels steering in the opposite direction to the front wheels assist the vehicle's "turnability"

✕ ─── ✕ alternative geometries tested in the course of development

THE REAR suspension's wishbone-shaped main arm is fabricated from stamped steel sheet and fully welded-up. It has box sections to ensure freedom from twisting and bending. Secure, precise mating of the arm's cylindrical end and the hub carrier, essential to the rigidity and geometric configuration, was achieved by a clever fabrication-welding method.

Because there is no workable way to weld cast iron and sheet metal directly together, a sheet-steel male tube is cast into the ductile iron hub carrier; the tube is then inserted into the trailing arm's sleeve end and the two welded together. The tube and sleeve are also mechanically secured, an additional reinforcement and fail-safe measure. Thanks to this construction method, the arm/hub-carrier assembly has great torsional and bending rigidity, is lighter in weight (by 1 kg) than a comparable built-up component and is incidentally much better-looking.

Semi-trailing-arm geometry is formed by the wishbone and a diagonal-lateral locating link. The wishbone pivots from the rear subframe on a cylindrical rubber bushing. The diagonal link is ball-joint mounted on the hub carrier at its outboard end, and on the subframe near the body centerline at the inboard end, forming a wide base. The

Camber-compensating linkage

FIGURE 9 shows the camber control linkage, consisting of the trailing arm, diagonal-lateral locating link, camber control arm and lever link. Points **A**, **B** and **D** are on the suspension subframe; **A**, **C**, **D** and **E** are ball joints, **B** a cylindrical rubber bushing.

Longitudinal and lateral location of the wheel is by the trailing arm and diagonal-lateral link, which together form the semi-trailing-arm geometry. Camber compensation is by the camber control arm and lever link.

Fig. 9 Camber control linkage

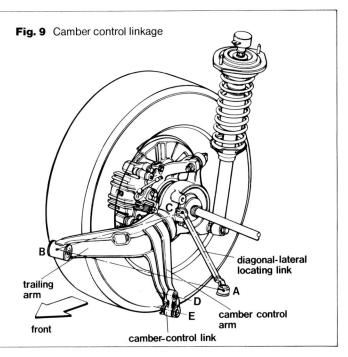

wishbone's inner arm is the camber control arm and is connected to the subframe through a short lever control link, ball-jointed at either end.

To get a 2 + 2 seating configuration, it was essential to lower the inner wishbone arm's mounting point. Adding the small-diameter diagonal-lateral link with its inner pivot point right next to the final drive unit achieved this, as well as assuring anti-dive and -squat geometry. The third bird killed by this clever stone's throw is the camber-compensating ability that has largely eliminated the semi-trailing arm's oft-criticized camber characteristics. This control linkage is designed to reduce negative camber on jounce as well as positive camber on rebound, thus maintaining the tire's contact patch virtually flat and true to the road.

The suspension is mounted to a rear subframe of a wide V-configuration, which in turn is mounted to the body shell at three points. At the front there are two large-volume cylindrical compression rubber blocks; at the rear, offset to the left to clear the final-drive nose, it is suspended from above with torque link and small rubber bushings. The final drive's nose is also attached to this subframe, via a shear-type rubber block; its main case is located by an integral wide-base arm bracket atached directly to the body shell, again by compression rubber mounts. The subframe mount rubber has three spring rates: It is vertically and longitudinally compliant, with rates of 100 kg/mm and 150 kg/mm, and stiff laterally at 300 kg/mm, the last contributing to the suspension's lateral stiffness; (the firmer Sports package's subframe mounting bushes are stiffer than the Normal's for improved suspension location).

Principle of camber compensation linkage geometry

FIGURE 10a shows the linkage in jounce, 10b in level and 10c in rebound condition.

Pivots **A** (diagonal-lateral link mount), **B** (trailing-arm mount) and **D** (camber control link body mount) are fixed points. Pivot **C** (camber control arm to hub carrier) swings on the **AB** axis, and pivot **E** (camber control arm/link pivot) swings with the **D** as axis, as well as revolving around the **CB** axis.

As the trailing arms and diagonal-lateral link move in jounce and rebound, point **E** swings in a locus **E1–E2** on the **AB** axis. Had pivots **E**, **C** and **B** been unrestricted by the **ED** linkage and moved in unison, they would have followed a locus represented by **E1′–E2′**; in actual operation, with point **E**'s motion restricted by point **D**, the locus difference between **E1–E2** and **E1′–E2′** is absorbed by angle change of the linkage formed by the diagonal-lateral link's hub mount **C** and the camber control arm's pivot **E**. The linkage **CE**'s angle change prompts axial movement of **CB**; since the wheel's camber angle is determined by the **CB** axis, camber compensation takes place.

Fig. 10 Camber compensation

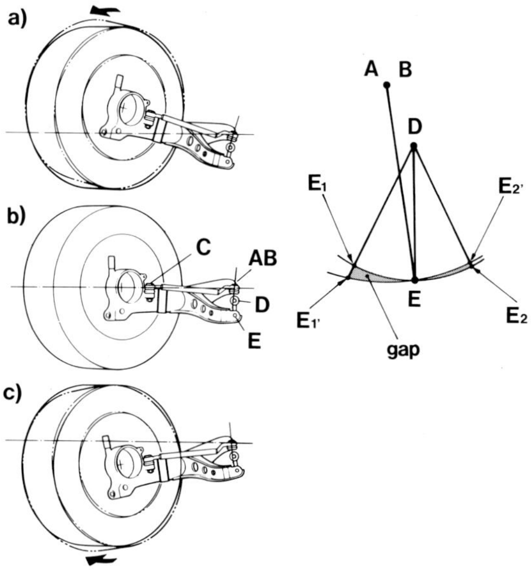

a)

b)

c)

Camber control

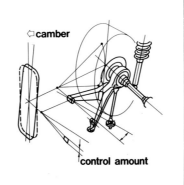

Fig. 11 Geometry of camber control linkage compensates camber changes that occur when vehicle rolls during cornering and keeps tire contact patch truer to road surface

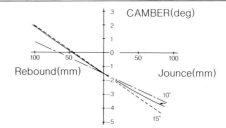

Fig. 12 Camber change is held to minimum, its characteristics similar to a semi-trailing arm geometry having the arm mount angle of 12 deg, while obtaining the lateral rigidity of a 15 deg one.

Mounting of the final drive's nose to the suspension subframe and its main case directly to the body structure is attributable to the fact that the suspension and drivetrain generate different vibration and noise frequencies and cannot be isolated entirely on the same member.

AAS—the automatically adjustable shock-absorber system

THE P747'S electronically controlled automatically adjustable shock-absorber system is a refinement of that used in the Japanese-market Cosmo series and a development of the simpler system used in the 626.

AAS consists of a central control unit, a sensor group and variable-rate shocks with electric actuators. In the P747 system the shocks have three damping settings: normal, firm and very firm. The control unit receives signals from the steering-angle sensor (for roll control), a brake fluid-pressure sensing switch (for controlling dive) and an accelerator switch (for reducing squat). From this information, it determines when damping should be altered and instructs the actuators at the shocks themselves to do so.

The new system has two operating modes that can be chosen by the driver: Normal and Sport. In Normal, the "black box" automatically checks roll, dive and squat; leaves the shocks in their softest setting for low-speed driving but the front shocks are stiffened to "firm" for added stability in high-speed straight-line driving (theory: stiffer front suspension increases understeer and therefore stability). In Sport, the shocks remain in "firm" for all straight-line, constant-speed driving but check roll, dive and squat automatically.

Rear suspension and brake components:
Wide-base semi-trailing arm is formed by the main trailing arm and ball-jointed diagonal trailing rod

Automatically adjustable shock-absorber system's actuator

AAS control switches for Normal and Sport modes

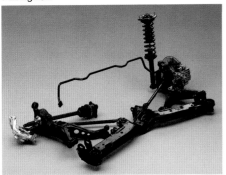

Suspension Specifications

FRONT SUSPENSION	NORMAL	SPORTS PACKAGE
Spring rate, kg/mm (lb/in.)	1.9 (106)	2.1 (118)
Spring wire diameter, mm (in.)	12.1 (0.48)	11.9 (0.47)
Coil diameter, mm (in.)	147.0 (5.79)	147.0 (5.79)
Shock absorber damping characteristics:		
Rebound/jounce, kg @ piston speed, m/sec.		
@0.1 m/sec.	35/10 (50/10*)	60/30
@0.3 m/sec.	80/25 (105/25*)	125/50
@0.6 m/sec.	140/45 (162/45*)	170/85
A-arm bushing stiffness, kg/mm:		
front bushing, axial direction	35	35
front bushing, longitudinal dir.	1250	1250
rear bushing, axial direction	50	50
rear bushing, longitudinal dir.	450	450
Anti-roll bar diameter, mm	22	24
Geometry, 680-kg weight on front wheels with two 70-kg occupants:		
caster, degrees	5	
camber, degrees	0	

REAR SUSPENSION	NORMAL	SPORTS PACKAGE
Spring rate, kg/mm (lb/in.)	1.9 (106)	2.1 (118)
Spring wire diameter, mm (in.)	9.9 (0.39)	10.1 (0.40)
Coil diameter, mm (in.)	84.6 (3.33)	84.4 (3.32)
Shock absorber damping characterstics:		
Rebound/jounce, kg @ piston speed, m/sec.		
@0.1 m/sec.	25/10 (40/10*)	40/18
@0.3 m/sec.	75/20 (105/20*)	90/35
@0.6 m/sec.	115/30 (142/30*)	142/60
Trailing-arm bushing spring, rate, kg/mm:		
axial direction	250	250
longitudinal direction	1000	1000
Sub-frame mounting block spring rate, kg/mm:		
fore-aft direction	150	300
lateral direction	300	900
vertical direction	100	300
Toe-control bushing characteristics:		
a) upper bushing, axial direction:		
preload, kg	100	100
spring rate, kg/mm	55	55
b) front bushing, right angle to axis:		
preload, kg	100	100
spring rate, kg/mm	160	160

REAR SUSPENSION	NORMAL	SPORT PACKAGE
Anti-roll bar diameter, mm	12	14

Geometry, 680-kg weight on rear wheels with
two 70-kg occupants:

caster	—	
camber	−1°30'	−1°30'

* with 14-inch wheels

AAS Shock-Absorber Characteristics

FRONT

PISTON SPEED	NORMAL kg (lb)	FIRM kg (lb)	VERY FIRM kg (lb)
m/sec. (ft/sec.)	rebound/jounce	rebound/jounce	rebound/jounce
0.1 (0.33)	35/10 (77/22)	55/35 (121/77)	60/40 (132/88)
0.3 (0.98)	80/25 (176/155)	120/55 (265/121)	125/60 (276/133)
0.6 (1.97)	140/45 (309/99)	165/85 (364/187)	170/90 (375/198)

REAR

PISTON SPEED	NORMAL kg (lb)	FIRM kg (lb)	VERY FIRM kg (lb)
m/sec. (ft/sec.)	rebound/jounce	rebound/jounce	rebound/jounce
0.1 (0.33)	25/10 (55/22)	35/20 (77/44)	40/25 (88/55)
0.3 (0.98)	75/20 (165/44)	85/40 (187/88)	90/45 (198/99)
0.6 (1.97)	115/30 (254/66)	135/65 (298/143)	140/70 (309/154)

AAS Control Modes

NORMAL	front shock absorber	rear shock absorber
low-speed zone	N	N
high-speed cruise	F	N
roll, squat and dive control	VF	VF

SPORT		
low-speed zone	F	F
high-speed cruise	F	F
roll, squat and dive control	VF	VF

N .... normal damping force
F .... firm damping force
VF .... very firm damping force

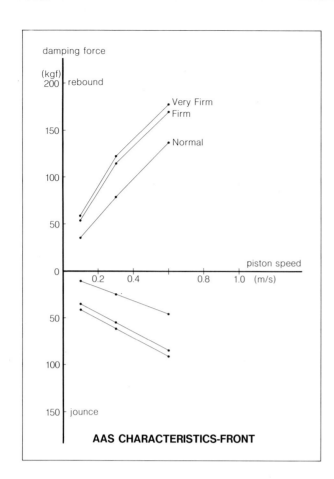

AAS CHARACTERISTICS-FRONT

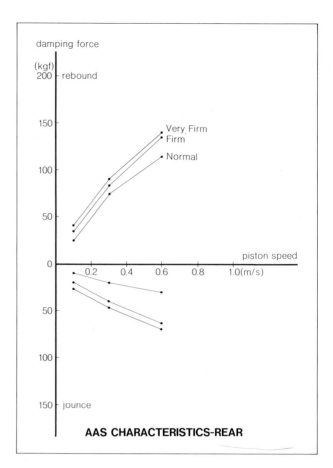

AAS CHARACTERISTICS-REAR

Manually Adjustable Shock Absorbers*

PISTON SPEED m/s	POSITION REBOUND/JOUNCE kg	1	2	3	4	5	6	7	8
Front									
	0.1	20/10	25/10	30/10	37/15	43/15	50/15	55/15	60/20
	0.3	60/20	70/25	80/25	90/30	100/30	115/35	120/35	125/40
	0.6	110/30	125/35	140/40	150/45	160/50	170/50	175/55	180/60
Rear									
	0.1	20/10	25/20	25/10	30/15	30/15	35/15	35/15	40/20
	0.3	50/20	60/25	65/25	70/30	75/30	80/35	85/35	90/40
	0.6	90/30	100/35	110/40	120/45	125/50	130/50	140/55	150/60

*For Japanese-specification Turbo only

Wheels and tires

STANDARD FOOTWEAR FOR the RX-7 is modest 185/70HR-14 tires on stamped steel 14 × 5.5JJ wheels with four studs: cast aluminum wheels of the same size offered as an option.

The GXL model with its upgraded disc brakes has fatter 205/60VR-15 tires on cast aluminum wheels of unidirectional design. Another notch upward is the Turbo's 205/55VR-16 tires on 16 × 7JJ aluminum wheels. The bodywork would accommodate 215-mm tires at the front, but Mazda engineers were unwilling to use them because they are so rare. At the rear, you can fit 225s—but be warned, skiers, that they won't accommodate snow chains.

Mazda's talented and enthusiastic development engineer Hirotaka Tachibana, of front-drive GLC/323 and 626 fame, has had a number of Japanese and European tires evaluated on his fleet of prototype and pilot-production cars. He is pleased with Bridgestone's new Potenza RE71, specifically developed for the car and, he says, at least a match for Pirelli's latest P6. For the Turbo, the choice is the Goodyear Eagle GT. Standard on the STD—yes, the base STD—, be it on humble steel wheels or the optional aluminum ones, is an aluminum spare wheel carrying a space-saving temporary tire—one of Mazda's many weight-reducing measures (models with 15-in. and 16-in. road wheels have steel spare ones, also shod with temporary tires). In addition to the 1.5 kg (3.3 lb) it saves, a German-made aluminum jack cuts another 3 lb.

Bridgestone's high-performance RE71 tire was specifically developed as original equipment for the P747 RX-7. It has a unidirectional tread pattern which is effective in expelling water in wet conditions. The two-layer polyester carcass has a truly radial cord angle of 90 degrees, topped by two layers of steel cord belts (cords running at a conventional 20 deg from the true circumferential). Tread section is further reinforced by top belts that wrap around onto the shoulders. The RE71 employs Bridgestone's Super-Filler bead filler, which adds to the rigidity of this critical area. Original-equipment RE71 differs from its over-the-counter version in that a more supple nylon bead reinforcing insert wraps around the bead and Super-Filler insert. The tread compound is a modulated Pro-Grip mix, with high-styrene SBR (Styrene Butadiene Rubber) that provides exceptionally high grip while assuring acceptable wear life

From right: Goodyear Eagle GT 205/55VR-16 tires on 7JJ × 16 cast aluminum wheels for the Turbo, Bridgestone's Potenza RE71 205/60VR-15 on 6JJ alloy wheels for the GXL, and base Bridgestone 185/70HR14 on optional 5.5JJ aluminum wheels (standard wheels are pressed steel) and the base STD's aluminum spare wheel with space saving temporary tire

Steering: rack and pinion, electronic power assist

IN AN ERA when rack-and-pinion steering was becoming the norm, the Mazda RX-7 stuck to a recirculating-ball mechanism—and was criticized for its free play around the center position. With the new P747 RX-7 comes brand-new steering, by a rack-and-pinion assembly mounted ahead of the engine on the front subframe's lateral member.

The steering gear is made by Koyo Seiko, a member of the Koyo group of companies and better known for its various bearings. Koyo answered chassis designer Takao Kijima's demand for a new manual steering mechanism that would have minimum friction and free play; cost was no object at the time, but would be negotiable if the gear was to be ordered in quantity.

Koyo's solution is an interesting one. The gearbox has an inverted cup-shaped yoke, spring-loaded and pressed against the ball-bearing-supported rack. A roller bearing enclosed in the yoke presses the rack back; the rack is machined so that contact with the roller bearing is true and the rack cannot twist. With this construction, which has

Roller-enclosed yoke and spring of the manual steering system

Slight humps (0.5 mm in height) on the rack's back keeps the roller bearing from coming into contact in the straight-ahead position. Instead, the yoke's solid surface presses against the rack on these humps

inherently less torque fluctuation in its operation, spring pressure can be increased by as much as 30 percent, which contributes to the steering gear's structural rigidity. Kijima and the Koyo engineers did agree after testing the new gearbox that it was not the rigidity alone that would translate into a precise, solid steering feel, but rather a coordination of rigidity, friction and play. A not-so-rigid steering gear could impart a feeling of precision and play-free solidity, if friction and play were minimized.

The Koyo rack has slight humps on the curved surfaces of that portion of the rack's back that is pressed against the yoke in the straight-ahead position. The humps are 0.5 mm (0.02 in.) in height, sufficient to keep the roller bearing from coming into contact with the rack back. Instead, the yoke's solid surface presses against the rack on these humps, which naturally results in more friction than the bearing itself would. This firmer support imparts the feeling of solidity in the straight-ahead position at higher vehicle speeds and prevents gear rattles and kickbacks. As more input is cranked in and steering effort increases, the humps are passed and the roller bearing now presses directly against the rack back, making low- to medium-speed maneuvers smoother and lighter.

Because of this clever variable support-area and friction feature, it was possible to adopt a 20.3:1 overall steering ratio. This takes 3.6 turns lock-to-lock and is about 10 percent quicker than the 22.4:1 of the Porsche 944's unassisted steering; and yet the effort is lighter than in the German car.

Kijima concedes that the ideal location of the steering gear from a geometrical standpoint is behind the front wheels' centerline. The P747's "front midship" engine placement dictated putting it ahead of the centerline; Kijima feels that the favorable weight distribution of this layout more than offsets the not-quite-ideal steering geometry.

The steering column has a collapsible section with ball-expanded telescopic tubes and includes a tilt mechanism for 2.5 deg of upward and 5.0 deg downward adjustment from its middle position. The steering-wheel center is offset 5 mm (0.2 in.) downward, enlarging the "window" above its center pad to the instrument pod as well allowing a larger knee clearance—one wonders if the designers weren't influenced a little too much by the Porsche 944! Two steering-wheel designs are offered depending on model and trim level; both have a 380-mm (15.5-in.) outer diameter.

Power steering: innovative solutions

EXCEPT FOR diehard enthusiasts, most drivers prefer power-assisted steering. The P747's power-steering system is a new and highly sophisticated piece of mechanical, hydraulic and electronic engineering.

The electronically controlled, hydraulically assisted rack-and-pinion system's 15.2:1 ratio requires a mere 2.7 turns of the wheel lock-to-lock and U-turns the 4.29-meter (168.0-inch)-long car in a 9.8-m (32.2-ft) circle between curbs (10.6 m wall to wall). The system was developed jointly by Mazda and Koyo Seiko on the latter's principle of reaction-force-controlled, speed-sensitive variable assist, and employs twin tandem hydraulic pumps.

Two pumps are contained in a lightweight aluminum cast-iron unit, the 8-cc-per-revolution main pump supplying fluid pressure for power assist and a 2.5-cc-per-revolution sub-pump feeding the reaction-force control plunger via a control valve. The power-steering computer receives a signal from the vehicle-speed sensor and instructs the control valve to regulate pressure accordingly to the reaction-force control plunger, which acts on the steering-input torsion bar. Compared with the more common fluid-rate control for speed-sensitive variable-assisted steering, this system allows a greater variation in power assist, from fingertip effort in parking to rock-steady feel at high speeds.

In the P747 application the system tightens the torsion bar almost solid at anything over 180 km/h (112.5 mph), turning it into virtual manual steering with a 15.2:1 ratio. ("Almost" is significant, however, as hydraulics do give, however minutely.) The

Steering wheel has a 380-mm outer diameter. Its center is offset 5 mm (0.2 in.) downward to enlarge view to the instrument panel as well as allow greater knee room

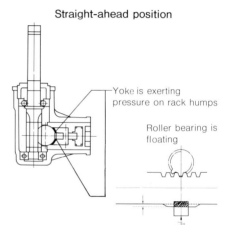

Straight-ahead position

Yoke is exerting pressure on rack humps

Roller bearing is floating

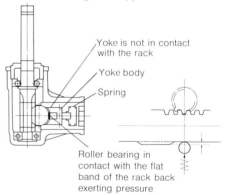

Steering lock applied

Yoke is not in contact with the rack

Yoke body

Spring

Roller bearing in contact with the flat band of the rack back exerting pressure

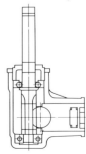

Convetional yoke

electronic control unit (computer) senses car speed every 0.3 sec. and performs instantaneous adjustment of the sub-pump output if appropriate.

Another and more important feature of the P747 power steering is that its assist is also affected by lateral acceleration ("g"). Mazda designers insist that the linear regulation of power assist according to the g-force generated is the most natural to human perception. The ECU calculates lateral acceleration from speed and steering angle, the information coming from two sensors, and instructs the control valve to adjust flow to the assist-valve mechanism.

The system also has the ability to adjust to any change in the road's friction coefficient. The sum of power assist is constant for a given vehicle speed and steering angle; if the friction coeffcient should deteriorate, a smaller amount of assist would suffice to give the steering angle. The ECU perceives the change of surface friction as a deviation from the predetermined and programmed parameter at that speed and steering angle. It then increases hydraulic assistance, lightening steering efforts as a warning to the driver of decreased tire adhesion under the deteriorated surface conditions. Its program map was written with the assistance of Matsushita Electric on the basis of Mazda's specification for optimum steering characteristics.

And what if this elaborate system should fail? If the failure is total, as with a broken pump belt, you have manual steering at the 15.2:1 ratio—heavy (25 percent heavier than unassisted steering) but still manageable. A partial failure, such as a broken connection from the vehicle-speed sensor, would fix assist at the 50-mph level, a median value for acceptable steering effort and stability up to the car's top speed. For drivers who might be insensitive to the change, a warning buzzer sounds insistently enough to prompt a trip to the nearest dealer.

Tandem hydraulic pump for the power steering

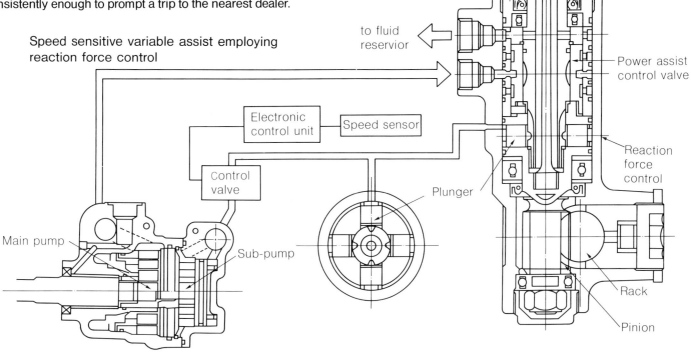

Speed sensitive variable assist employing reaction force control

SYSTEM DIAGRAM

71

Brakes: four discs in two combinations

TWO BRAKE COMBINATIONS are specified for the P747. The base model with 14-in. wheels has ventilated front and solid rear disc brakes, with cast-iron single-piston floating calipers all around and an 8-in. vacuum servo. The front caliper is attached directly to the hub carrier by two bolts. The rear caliper, bolted to the hub carrier by two bolts, is positioned at the front of the disc to facilitate installation of the toe-control hub. Disc diameters are 250 mm (9.8 in.) front and 261 mm (10.3 in.) rear, for pad areas of 86 sq cm (13.3 sq in.) front and 64 sq cm (19.9 sq in.) rear; the dual hydraulic circuits are split fore and aft and the rear circuit has a pressure modulating valve. Upper-class RX-7s, which have 15-in. wheels standard, feature four-piston aluminum-caliper front brakes with larger (276-mm/10.9-inch) ventilated discs. Each caliper weighs 3.2 kg (7.1 lb), as compared to the cast iron type's 4.3 kg (9.5 lb) or the previous RX-7's hefty 12-lb caliper—a useful reduction in unsprung weight. Each pad for these brakes has 47 sq cm (7.3 sq in.) of sweeping area, 3 sq cm more than the two-piston design. The rear brakes of this higher-performance combination have larger, ventilated discs (273 mm/10.7 in.) as well, but single-piston floating calipers; a 9-in. vacuum servo is used. The Turbo, of course, has this upgraded brake combination, as well as 16-in. wheels.

The parking brake is applied directly to the rear discs by a classic central pullup lever and cable linkage, and is adjusted automatically. To be offered optionally at a later date is a four-wheel anti-lock brake system, based on the Bosch ABS but with a Mazda-developed accumulator circuit to reduce pedal pulsations.

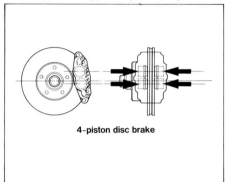

Racing type four-opposed-piston caliper

4-piston disc brake

Four-piston aluminum-caliper ventilated front disc brake for the GXL and Turbo

Single-piston floating-caliper ventilated rear disc brake for the GXL and Turbo

Single-piston floating-caliper ventilated front disc of the base model

Solid disc rear brake for the standard RX-7

The office: more space and luxury but no fads

DESPITE THE SHORTER body, the new RX-7 is somewhat roomier inside than the old. Front shoulder room is up by 40 mm (1.5 in.), maximum front leg room by 26 mm (1.0 in.) and head room by a fraction of an inch. Fore-aft seat adjustment is up from an already generous 180 mm (7.0 in.) to 200 (7.8); the forward position now enables an AF20 (American Female 20th percentile) to operate the car, the rearmost position an AM90 (American Male 90th percentile). Comparable figures for the previous model were AF25 and AM85.

A large single-piece padded instrument panel including the center console houses instruments, minor controls, heating-ventilation outlets and the audio system. The P747 RX-7 is available with analog instrumentation only: no digitals except for the clock, no electronic graphics. And it features one of the largest tachometers in captivity, sitting at dead center in the deep-hooded cluster, measuring 112 mm (4.4 inch) in diameter and showing up to 8000 rpm, of which the last 1000 rpm are a red zone. On its right is a smaller dial featuring a 150-mph speedometer with 10-mph increments and main and trip odometers. Four quarter-circular gauges on the tachometer's left indicate oil pressure, coolant temperature, fuel level and battery voltage; the last is replaced by a turbo boost gauge in the Turbo. Marks and lettering are in dark red, pointers in orange.

With these large, legible meters and gauges filling up the main cluster, warning lights—12 of them—had to find their place in a bezel at dashboard center, along with the clock. On the main instrument pod's left flank are lighting switches and the rear-window defroster switch; on its right are wiper and washer controls and a red button to turn on the four-way flasher. The main windshield-wiper dial is on a short arm, to allow operation without the hand's leaving the steering wheel; two short levers on either side of the nacelle are for directionals, headlamp flashing and dimming, and cruise control if fitted. For precision, reliability and space efficiency, most of these functions, squeezed into the narrow confines of the instrument-pod perimeter, employ integrated electronic circuits.

Heating, ventilation and air-conditioning switches and levers are in the center console's upper area, the audio controls under them. A small panel between the gearshift lever and the rear of the console accommodates auxiliary functions, such as the adjustable shock absorbers and power mirrors. The power windows' switches are on the door armrests and follow Mazda's recently adopted policy of push for down,

Lighting switches on the left flank of the pod. Short lever on the pod face is for turn signals and headlight beam change

On the right are wipe-wash control switches, on the pod face the cruise-control switch lever. Red hazard-warning switch is internally illuminated

Heating ventilation air-conditioning control panel, with stepless speed selection for the blower

pull for up, which the Hiroshima ergonomists insist is most natural to use. Storage is provided in a dash glove compartment and a rear console box with lid.

Two types of front seats are offered. The base type has integral head restraints, the premium version separate adjustable ones. In either case the seat cushion and upper backrest have thicker padding than before, 10 mm (0.4 inch) more in the cushion. The seat frame has been reinforced and now rides on rails with latch locks on both sides for firmer location. Base seating comes with the usual two adjustments, fore-aft and backrest angle; the deluxe version has cushion-height and lumbar adjustments as well, all of them manual. Cloth upholstery is standard across the board, leather optional in the upmarket models. As in Porsches, rear seating in the 2 + 2 configuration is strictly for rare occasions; the rear backrest can be folded flat to increase cargo space. In the two-seater, two storage bins replace the rear seats.

The large rear hatch is now released from the driver's side by a mechanical latch, instead of the previous magnetic one; it is supported by twin hydraulic struts, one of which carries a lamp for illumination of the loading area. A temporary spare wheel-tire is mounted vertically in a well at the rear; turning a knob on its cover releases a catch and the wheel then leans forward for easier removal. According to SAE measurement practice, luggage space in the two-seater is 184 liters/6.5 cu ft, in the 2 + 2 with the rear seatback in place 104/3.7.

Upper models' front seats have separate head restraints. Base version's restraints are integral with seats

The 2 + 2 model's rear seat is strictly for rare occasions

Two-seater's luggage compartment has two lidded bins in place of the occasional seat

Interior Dimensions

	P747 RX-7	Previous RX-7
FRONT SEATS		
head room, mm/in	949/37.2	942/37
leg room, mm/in	1109/43.7	1083/42.6
shoulder room, mm/in	1340/52.8	1305/51.4
hip room, mm/in	1380/54.3	1366/53.8
REAR SEATS (2 + 2)		
head room, mm/in	839/33.0	—
couple distance*, mm/in	507/20.0	
LUGGAGE SPACE		
two-seater, liters/cu. ft.	184/6.5	104/3.7
FUEL TANK CAPACITY		
liters/U.S. gal.	63/16.6	

* couple distance: distance between the centerline of
the front seat occupant's hip and that of the rear seat
occupant

Heating and ventilation

THE HEATER has a higher-output fan, up to 200-watt/12-volt from the previous 180W, whose 415-cubic meter/hour output (14,656 cu ft/hour) is close to that of the heater in a fullsize American car. (A rotary engine, by the way, is a generous heat source.) Fan speed is now steplessly controlled by a sliding lever; heat output is regulated electrically through a logic circuit, also by a sliding lever.

The driver selects the operational mode by a row of pushbuttons: a defrost/heat mode is included to clear the windshield while directing part of the heated air to the footwells. There are side defrosting outlets at either end of the dash, each capable of 30 cu m/h (1059 cu ft/h), sufficient for arctic northern Europe. The high center tunnel and low dash impede air circulation, so a duct tube is included in the front footwells for heated air.

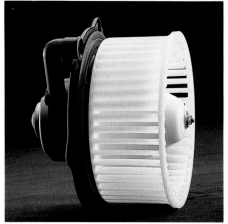

Blower fan for the heater: its output is close to that of a full-size American car

Side vent outlet on the dashboard

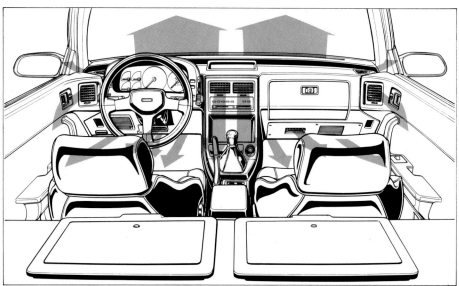

Ventilation air flow

Tilt-up and slide electric sunroof

Air-conditioning performance has also been improved. A higher-output compressor for the optional system is mounted low and closer to the engine on a short aluminum bracket; it is driven by its own belt, which reduces transmission of compressor vibrations. There is a logic circuit for the a/c, which among other things cuts out the compressor when full engine power is demanded for acceleration. On lefthand-drive versions the air conditioning does not affect normal ventilation operation; with righthand drive, however, natural ventilation is sacrificed.

A pleasant fresh-air option is the new tilt/slide electric sunroof. The metal panel's rear end lifts up and slides back, leaving a 250 × 704-mm (9.8 × 27.7-in.) opening and forming an airfoil that Mazda engineers claim contributes to high-speed stability. Its drive motor is at the rear and the roof itself is relatively thin, so intrusion into head room is at a minimum.

Audio system

THREE GRADES of audio entertainment are offered in the P747, or four if "Grade 1" is included—but then it has no radio or tape deck.

Grade 2 includes an AM/FM radio with electronic tuning. Two 12-cm (4.7-inch) speakers are under the dash, one in an enclosure under the glove compartment and the other directly in front of the driver. In the rear suspension towers are two 16-cm (6.3-in.) speakers. Grade 3 brings a higher-performance AM/FM radio with twin diversity tuning reception antennas (a main electrically raised one on the rear deck and an auxiliary thin-wire type in the windshield), AM stereo, mechanical tape deck and two rear speakers in enclosures. The top-of-the line Grade 4 replaces the mechanical tape deck with a full electronic logic-controlled one and adds a 9-band graphic equalizer.

The next logical step may be a compact disc player; another audio group at Hiroshima has already introduced one in the updated Mazda 323 (GLC) compact. Space is more limited in the sports car's low dash, and of course anything that goes into the RX-7 must be better than in the GLC. Whether or not it's available by debut time, it will eventually be an RX-7 option.

Facing today's reality: the burglar alarm system

AN ANTI-THEFT system designed and developed by Mazda is offered in the P747. Its electronic control unit with a 4-bit CPU receives signals from one or more of a group of sensors and switches strategically placed, and emits a warning by flashing the hazard lamps, sounding the horn for five minutes and rendering the starter motor inoperable.

Mazda may introduce an even more elaborate system with sensors and switches that guard against forced entry through the sunroof or a broken window.

16 cm (6.3-in.) speaker in its resonance box in the suspension tower

Grade 3 audio complement

1986 Mazda RX-7 (P747) U.S. Specifications

GENERAL

Wheelbase, mm/in	2430/95.7
Track, front, mm/in	1450/57.1
Track, rear, mm/in	1440/56.7
Overall length, mm/in	4290/168.9
Overall width, mm/in	1690/66.5
Overall height, mm/in	1265/49.8
Curb weight, kg/lb	
2-seater manual transmission	1190.5/2625
2+2 manual transmission	1190.5/2625
2-seater automatic	1225/2695
2+2 automatic	1232/2715
Turbo	not available
Weight distribution, front/rear % unladen	51.2/48.8
with 2 passengers and full fuel tank	50.2/49.8
Trunk capacity, liters/cu ft	
2-seater	184/6.5
2+2	104/3.7
Fuel tank capacity, liters/U.S. gal	63/16.6

ENGINE

	13B DEI EGI	13B DEI EGI Turbo
Type	Wankel rotary engine, 4-stroke	
Number of rotors	2-in tandem	
Generating radius, R, mm	105.0	
Eccentricity e, mm	15.0	
K factor (R/e)	6.8	
Width of trochoid chamber, mm	80.0	
Single chamber capacity, cc	654.0	
Total cubic capacity equivalent to reciprocating piston engine, cc	2616	
Formula obtaining chamber capacity	V_H (volume) = $3 \cdot \sqrt{3} \cdot \text{Reb}$	
Compression ratio	9.4	8.5
Bhp @ rpm, SAE net	146 @ 6500	182 @ 6500
Torque @ rpm, SAE net, lb ft/Nm	138/193 @ 3500	183/256 @ 3500
Induction system	6PI dynamic effect intake, electronic fuel injection	4-port dynamic effect intake, electronic fuel injection, turbocharged
Number of intake ports and location	3 in side-housings per chamber	2 in side-housings per chamber
Port timing		
primary intake port opens, deg	32 ATDC	32 ATDC
closes, deg	40 ABDC	50 ABDC
secondary intake port opens, deg	32 ATDC	32 ATDC
closes, deg	30 ABDC	50 ABDC
secondary power port opens, deg	45 ATDC	n/a
closes, deg	80 ABDC	n/a

Exhaust port number and location	1 peripheral per chamber	1 peripheral per chamber
exhaust port opens, deg	75 BBDC	75 BBDC
exhaust port closes, deg	38 ATDC	48 ATDC
Fuel injection	digitally controlled Bosch L-jetronic fuel injection with pendulant type airflow metering, twin-injectors per chamber (one in primary intake port, one in secondary manifold)	
Fuel supply	engine management computer controlled 2-speed electric pump	
Turbocharging	n/a	Hitachi HT18S-2S twin-scroll turbine inlet with exhaust pressure-operated flap-valve
turbine diameter, mm	n/a	64
A/R, low speed passage	n/a	0.4
A/R, low and high speed passages combined	n/a	1.03
compressor diameter, mm	n/a	63
maximum boost pressure, mm Hg	n/a	320
maximum turbocharger rpm	n/a	110,000
Intercooler	n/a	air-to-air
Ignition system	high energy ignition, the engine management computer controlled; 2 semi-surface discharge spark plugs per chamber	
Lubrication system	force-feed and oil jet lubrication on bearings; oil injection by nozzles to the trochoid chamber rubbing surface; trochoid oil pump and metering pump; full flow filter; aircooled oil-cooler	
Lubrication capacity, liters/U.S. gal	6.2/1.6	
Cooling system	rotor housings water-cooled; thermo-modulated viscous coupling fan; auxiliary electric suction fan with air-conditioning installation; aluminum radiator with overflow tank; rotors oil-cooled	
Water capacities, liters/U.S. gal	8.7/2.3	

DRIVE TRAIN

	13B DEI EGI model	13B DEI EGI Turbo model
Transmission type	manual 5-speed	manual 5-speed
Clutch	single dry plate, diaphragm spring; hydraulically operated clutch	
Clutch outer dial, mm/in	225/8.9	240/9.4
Gearbox	M type	R type
gearbox ratios I	3.475	3.483
II	2.002	2.015
III	1.366	1.391
IV	1.000	1.000
V	0.711	0.762
rev	3.493	3.288
Final drive type	hypoid bevel	
final drive ratio	4.100	3.909
limited slip differential	standard on GXL	optional
Automatic transmission		
Type	JATCO L4N71B torque converter and 4-speed planetary gearbox; hydraulically controlled	not available
Torque converter stall ratio	2.00	
lockup	in overdrive 4th gear	
Gearbox ratios I	2.841	
II	1.541	
III	1.000	
IV	0.720	
rev	2.400	
Final drive ratio	3.909	
Drive shafts	equal length half shafts with constant-velocity joints	

CHASSIS AND BODY

Layout	front engine, rear wheel drive
Body/frame	unitary welded steel body with front H-shaped power unit and suspension mounting subframe, and rear wide-angle V-shaped and rubber mounted suspension mounting subframe
Suspension, front	independent, MacPherson struts, lower forged aluminum A-arms, concentric shock absorbers and coil springs and anti-roll bar
Suspension, rear	independent, Mazda Dynamic Tracking Suspension; semi-trailing arms with tri-axial floating mount toe-control hubs and camber compensating linkage; coil springs, tubular shock absorbers and anti-roll bar

GXL only	AAS electronically controlled automatically adjusting shock-absorber system with variable damping rate shock absorbers
Steering, manual	Koyo Seiko rack and pinion, constant ratio
gear ratio	20.3:1
turns lock to lock	3.6
turning circle	
curb to curb, m/ft	9.8/32.2
Steering, power assisted	electronically controlled, lateral G-sensing variable assist rack and pinion; Mazda, Koyo Seiko and Matsushita Electric
gear ratio	15.2:1
turns lock to lock	2.7
Brakes, STD model	
front type	Sumitomo ventilated disc with single-piston floating caliper
front disc dia., mm/in	250/ 9.8
rear type	Sumitomo solid disc with single-piston floating caliper
rear disc diameter, mm/in	261/10.3
pad area, front, cm^2/sq.in	86/13.3
pad area, rear, cm^2/sq.in	64/ 9.9
power assistance	8-inch Mastervac vacuum servo
Brakes, GXL and Turbo models	
front type	Sumitomo ventilated disc with 4-piston aluminum caliper
front disc dia., mm/in	276/10.9
rear type	Sumitomo ventilated disc with single-piston floating caliper
rear disc dia., mm/in	273/10.7
power assistance	9-inch Mastervac vacuum servo
pad area, front, cm^2/sq.in	94/14.6
pad area, rear, cm^2/sq.in	64/ 9.9
To be offerred later date	Bosch ABS electronically controlled 4-wheel anti-skid brake system
Wheels and tires	
STD	pressed steel, 5.5JJ × 14; Bridgestone Potenza 185/70HR14
GXL	cast aluminum, 6JJ × 15; Bridgestone Potenza RE71 205/60VR15
Turbo	cast aluminum, 7JJ × 16; Goodyear Eagle GT 205/55VR16

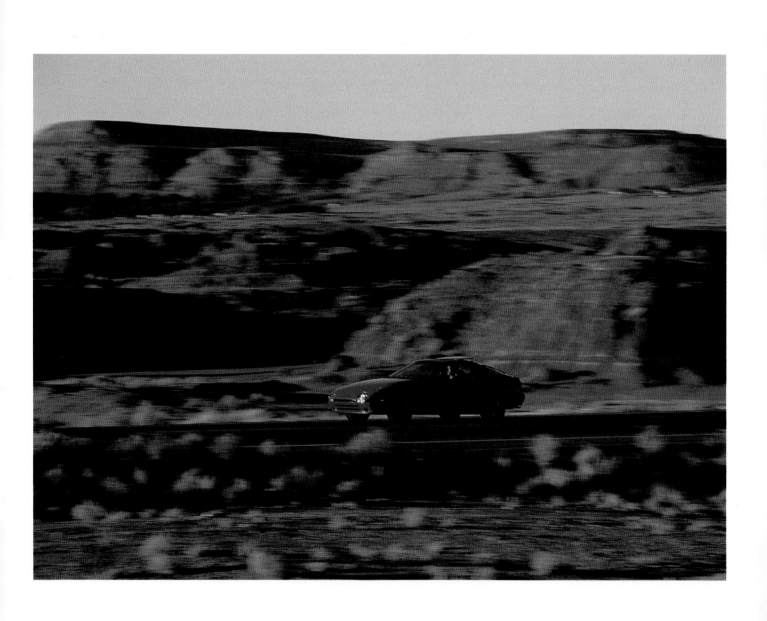

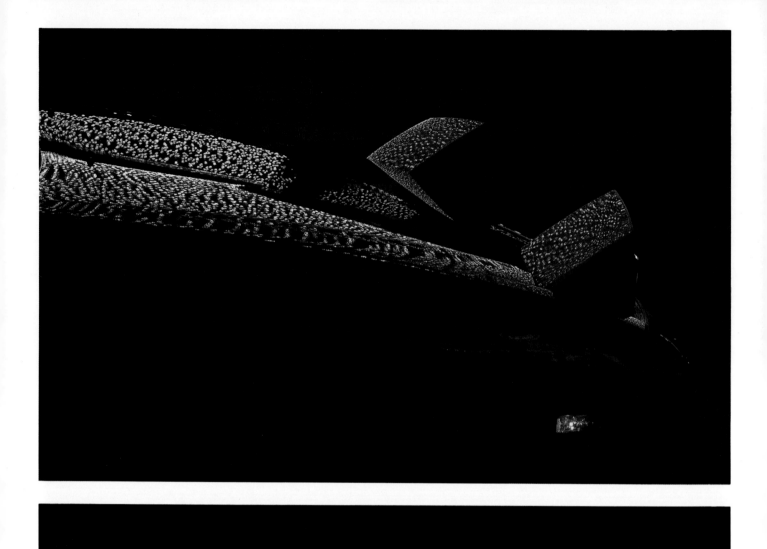

2

THE P747 DEVELOPMENT STORY

Operation feedback

CHIEF PROJECT ENGINEER Akio Uchiyama had to leave the country.
Japan had never bought many two-seaters. However, that prejudice was removed overnight, to the joy of the development group at the Hiroshima company. Uchiyama had led the group for three years up to the new sports car's launch on March 30, 1978 in Japan. The RX-7 became the hottest wheeled item on the Japanese market for the remainder of 1978 and into 1979, selling an unparalleled 9000 cars a month at its peak and setting an absolute record for sports cars that is intact to this day and probably will remain so. Sadly, the old prejudice has returned to Japan's view of sports cars; today no marque, either established or aspiring, can escape it.
In the midst of all the excitement that surrounded the original RX-7, Uchiyama was thrust into the limelight and put under heavy press demand. Senior Managing Director Kenichi Yamamoto, then head of Research and Development, was more farsighted than the press. He summoned Uchiyama and in his typically forthright, yet enigmatic manner ordered him, "Go to America. See, breathe and taste the country, which will be the RX-7's truer home in years to come. Do not mind trivia and details, but be alert. Sleep with your mind's eye open."
Uchiyama spent the next three months on the highways and byways of America, amassing more than 100 personal contacts and holding interviews with new RX-7 owners and Mazda dealers. As part of getting to know America and her people, Uchiyama asked to be shown an RX-7 owner's basement cellar and the contents of a home refrigerator! The subjects of these contacts were people happy with their new possessions, many overjoyed with a car that provided such enjoyment for the money, and dealers highly satisfied with the money they were making on it.
Uchiyama, too, returned home generally happy; but the project chief in him was uneasy. Reception and expectations seemed to have far surpassed the car's real value; after all, it was basically a conventional, straightforward design borrowing many a component from the corporation's more mundane products. Uchiyama was acutely aware of and shared Yamamoto's fierce determination that the ground lost in the precious American market by rotary-engine cars must be won back by this new rotary sports car; the way to do it properly, to retain customer confidence, would be the continuous refinement and development of the basic theme.
In fact, Uchiyama's lieutenants already had the beginnings of an RX-7 replacement project waiting for him when he returned from his American stay, or Operation Feedback as it was called. That project would be postponed and kept in cold storage for the next three years, while Operation Feedback was kept active providing information on customers' needs and desires and the ever-changing market conditions. Uchiyama and his development group devoted their efforts exclusively to detailed improvements to the original X605 (its project code) RX-7 and its evolutionary derivatives, which would acquire four such codes in the process.
By autumn 1980 they were facing the harsh reality that the plain little RX-7 couldn't be kept competitive much longer; perhaps into the mid-Eighties but certainly no later. A widening gap between its value and the price it commanded kept nagging their engineer's minds.
The original RX-7 carved its own sizable niche between the lightweight and middle-class market segments, combining a price tag near that of the former with performance appropriate to the latter. It climbed the price ladder steadily, the uppermost model now touching the middle segment contested by such potent competitors as the 924/944 Porsches and Nissan's ZX; but in this category its live rear axle, 13-inch wheels, recirculating-ball steering and three-piece quarter/rear-window treatment seemed less and less appropriate.

Chief project engineer Akio Uchiyama (fourth from left) and designer Yasuji Oda (on extreme right) were among Mazda product planners and engineers on Operation Feedback trip

Uchiyama and his colleagues amassed more than 100 personal contacts and interviews with new RX-7 owners and Mazda dealers in three months

To know America and her people, Uchiyama asked to be shown the contents of an RX-7 owner's refrigerator

RX-7 at an American race meeting. Active participation in competition was decided prior to the car's launch

In addition, the lightweight segment would soon be crowded with new entries like Pontiac's Fiero (not so much in size and weight, but certainly in price), Toyota's similarly configured MR2, the Honda CRX, Subaru's four-wheel-drive XT coupe and, according to Mazda's intelligence, a 1.6-liter mid-engine Nissan yet to be announced. Among Mazda's product planners the conclusion was foregone: the new car, to be developed under the in-house code of P747, would be an upgraded, upmarket sports car in the middle segment. An entirely new body, more powerful engines, sophisticated fully independent suspension, larger wheels and wider tires were called for to endow the car with more (but not necessarily luxurious) comfort, exceptional performance and impeccable road manners.

Mazda rotary in strange company, as discovered by Uchiyama

The basic concept was thus established, and the official development proposal was put forth in June 1981. It was then tested and evaluated within the corporate structure as well as at preliminary outside clinics. Subsequently, Uchiyama and his men drew up a concept catalog for Project P747, many of its pages exclaiming "What progress!" The catalog listed everything pertinent to the car, from the basic concept through engineering marvels to detail refinements. As the project progressed, the group kept on updating the catalog and adding new features. It was included in the presentation package submitted to Mazda's Board of Directors and "served as a constant reminder of the project's fundamental conception," as Uchiyama puts it. "It could have served as a powerful deterrent, too, should any faction in the company's hierarchy attempt to degrade or modify it," confides the project chief. "After all, it had been approved unanimously by the Board!"

Uchiyama was also fortunate in having Senior Program Manager Noriaki Yoshioka, an unassuming and enthusiastic engineer, who oversaw the design and development activities of Mazda's upper passenger car models including the RX-7, as his co-project chief. Yoshioka gave staunch support to the new RX-7 team, presenting their case well at the Board meeting.

In spring 1982 the concept was put to its first public test through a series of clinics held in the U.S. It was presented along with two alternative concepts as well as comparative data on existing sports and specialty models. Minor regional differences were noted as to the specifications preferred by clinic participants, but the upgraded mid-class sports car—Civilized Sports Car, as Mazda calls it—emerged as the clear winner in those early contests.

Three sports car proposals put forth by Mazda's product planners. Upgraded mid-class sports car—Civilized Sports Car, as Mazda calls it—emerged as the clear winner

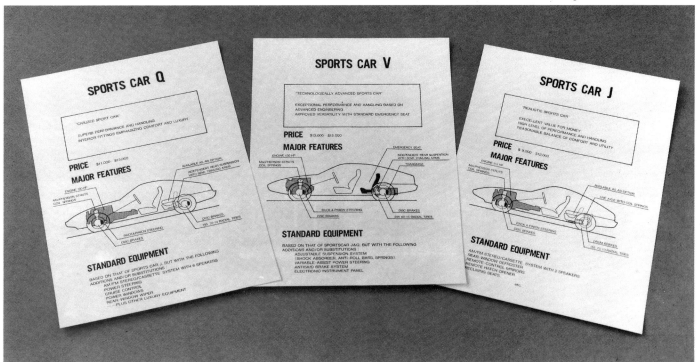

The sun is different

COLORS CHOSEN for their brightness and deep luster assume less exciting hues. Curvatures and lines thought to be exquisitely expressive are described as busy and strange. On more than a few occasions, Japanese designers were disheartened by the foreign press's criticism of their creations. Automobile design is best judged in natural environments, and the Japanese gradually learned that those environments are not the same on the expanses of the North American and European continents as in their small isles of the Far East; The sun shines differently, as it were.

With this discovery behind them, major exporting members of the Japanese auto industry moved quickly to establish design studios in California and station designers in Europe. In January 1982, Project P747's small group of young designers moved their operating base to Mazda of North America's premises in Orange County, California, where they would remain for two months to develop the next-generation RX-7's basic design theme. Their itinerary included such diverse stops as Disneyland, the Briggs Cunningham Museum, an SCCA race meet at Riverside, a motocross in Anaheim, the Art Center College of Design, shopping centers and a jaunt to Death Valley in a convoy of sports and specialty cars.

It may sound like fun, but it really was hard work. "In the second half of our stay, it was a straight 16 hours a day," recalls Takashi Ono, a promising young designer who worked on the exterior. "We did not shame the image of the workaholic Japanese." This was Mazda's first organized attempt to initiate design activities in the target country of a specific product, according to Yasuji Oda, Chief Project Designer in charge of the P747. The group produced around 20 exterior proposal sketches and several interior ones, including some full-size renderings and tape drawings; "A most efficient and productive exercise," confirms Senior Designer Shunji Tanaka. "We saw the light of the California day, breathed desert air and felt freeway jolts," contradicts young Ono, "but ah, tasting the country! We survived on take-out Japanese food—some of the sketches had license plates crying out 'Hungry' and 'Wanna go home!'"

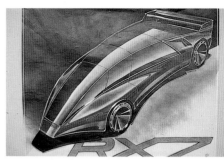

Early concept—wild ones at that—sketches done at Hiroshima

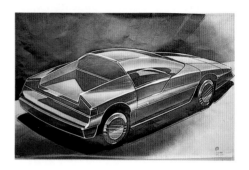

More down-to-earth sketches

Mazda designers' Death Valley tour in a convoy of sports and specialty cars, a part of their less arduous efforts to know the target country

Serious work awaited young Ono

Full-size rendering and tape drawing at Mazda's Southern California studio

Of the 20 sketches done in California, 10 were selected and shown at a series of clinics in America in March 1982, conducted separately from the product-concept clinic at about the same time. The following month saw a further narrowing-down to two main contenders at Hiroshima, which moved on to clay-model stages and then to lifelike plastic models.

One of the winning designs was an evolutionary and refined version of the original RX-7 theme, with upright and stepped B-pillars, tapering rear window and front-end graphics more reminiscent of the incumbent model. Chief designer Oda was personally fond of the design, which ".... carried over all the good things that had made the RX-7 popular."

The other model was a bolder departure, and it eventually led to the production P747 design. Both these "finalists" were flown to California and shown at another clinic in mid-October 1982, in the company of a Porsche 944, Toyota Supra, Nissan ZX, Corvette and the then-current RX-7. The two designs were not identified as Mazda, and no Japanese were allowed in the outdoor site ("Spied from a distance, in anxiety," recalls product planner Susumu Suto).

Those invited to the clinic favored the more adventurous model over the evolutionary one. But things weren't that sweet for Mazda; Stuttgart's car collected a few more points than the runner-up Mazda. "For the Porsche, it seemed to be love or hate. Porsche lovers wouldn't have it any other way," comments Suto. "But for our new shape, it was all likes, not love or hates—which we took as a very encouraging sign, as we obviously want to reach more people."

A typical criticism heard at the clinic was that the new shape's front end was too rounded and looked stubby. It was extended and reshaped as soon as the team was back in Hiroshima, but designer Ono was not entirely motivated by the popularity contests; "What ultimately shaped the front end was the wind tunnel." Project chief Uchiyama shares the view; "Clinics without the presenter's clearly defined concept are like fiscal reports without the budget specified."

The two designs were also presented to Mazda's European distributors as photographs after the Los Angeles show. Here Mazda committed a cardinal sin by admitting that "the Americans liked it." While indicating a preference of the newer shape over the evolutionary one, the Europeans were less than enthusiastic; some wanted a more radical departure—a unique design, such as a shooting brake. (Mazda had considered a sports-wagon variation in an earlier, abortive sports-car project.)

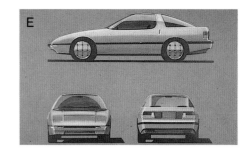

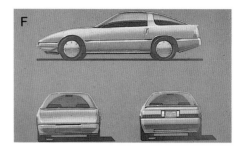

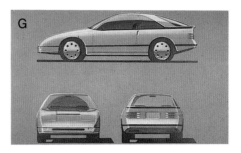

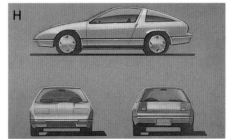

Of the 20 sketches done in California, 10 were selected and shown at a series of clinics in America in March 1982. Sketches E and F became the two main contenders

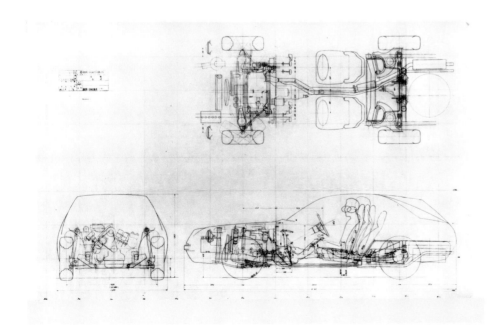

Mazda's European marketing people wanted a more radical departure, such as a shooting brake (sports wagon). Little did they know that the company had tried such a variation in an earlier, abortive sports-car project

Based on the winning sketch, this clay model was shaped in late May 1982. Note different surface treatment on either side of the model

Blisters appeared on this June 1982 clay model. Note one fully retractable headlight and one in a slit opening

This July 1982 clay model has Nissan ZX-like headlight design

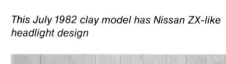

One of the main contenders for the P747 design was this "bold departure" from the original RX-7. Right side of the plastic mockup shows normal wheel-arch flares; the opposite side has blisters

The "evolutionary" contender: upright B-pillar treatment conveys heritage of the original RX-7

The two competing designs were viewed by Mazda insiders at Miyoshi proving ground's long stretch among competitors and the incumbent RX-7

They were then flown to California and presented to a clinic in October 1982. The more adventurous model won over the evolutionary one

P747 taking definitive shape, January 1983

The January 1983 clay model was put in Japan Automobile Research Institute's wind tunnel

P747 plastic mockup compared with the current RX-7 and Porsche 944, May 1983

Project chief designer Yasuji Oda (left) and exterior designer Takashi Ono (right), flanking Mazda's astute design boss Matasaburo Maeda

Outer corner of the daytime passing-beam opening assumed an Oriental slant in the model of April 1984

Quad circular taillights were favored by "old rotary guard" (R100 coupe, RX-2 and -3 had such lamp clusters)

More conventional two-piece lamps were selected in the final design. The model also had the new U.S.-mandatory high-mount braking light

The P747 design came out as overwhelming winner in the 1974 American and European clinics

In February 1983, the new-wave design was officially chosen as the basis for the P747 design; it was further developed and refined over the next few months. Running prototypes were taken to America and Europe in 1984, for road and track tests as well as probing public acceptance. This time it was the overwhelming winner in another series of incognito clinics, in both America and Europe.

Designers' shopping list

THE DESIGNING group presented the engineers a list of features they would like to see incorporated in the P747, including several firsts for Mazda:

1) Windshield rake should be as laid-back as possible, for optimum aerodynamics
2) As little metal as possible between the front wheel opening and fender top, to emphasize a look of big tires and wheels
3) Short rear overhang
4) Aerodynamic drag coefficient better than $C_D = 0.30$
5) Front-end graphics that would express the car's distinctive character
6) Front airdam to be moved forward, relieving the car of the original RX-7's "bullet" image
7) Hidden drip rails
8) Rear-window rake of about 18 degrees from the horizontal
9) One-piece glass pane integrating rear and quarter windows

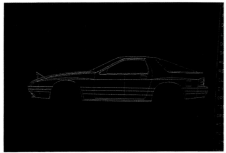

Windshield rake is as laid-back as possible for optimum aerodynamics. The P747 body contours in a computer graphic display

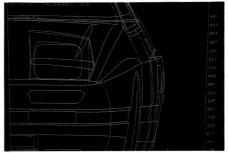

Front-end graphics that express the car's distinctive character: vertically retractable headlight and flash-to-pass window

Aerodynamic drag coefficient better than $C_D = 0.30$

As little metal as possible between the front wheel opening and fender top

A design "must" was that the front airdam be moved forward. The original RX-7 with smoothened front end and airdam in a wind-tunnel test

10) Flush door handles
11) Could A-pillars be hidden behind the windshield?
12) Soft urethane facia integrating the front bumper system

The industry's most rakish windshield angle is on the Giugiaro-designed Alfa Romeo GTV: 65 degrees. Could the P747 match it? No, that would have both functional and esthetic disadvantages. The dash top would be too expansive, instruments would reflect on the upper windshield, wiper storage could be problematical and the front end would look too stubby. The final design comes close—63.5 deg—but the front end had to be stretched 20 mm (0.8 in.) for visual balance.

Designer Ono wanted a sharply sloping nose that would suggest the engine was not there and give a bit of mid-engine look. Hard as his team and the engineers tried, though, they couldn't quite "hide" the powerplant; hood height had to be raised by 13~25 mm (0.5~1 in.) from the "no-engine-underneath" level. The fender top also had to be lifted slightly, a fact cleverly camouflaged by a subtle bead line, to clear an inner bolt head of the suspension strut's top mounting. Another thing the designers didn't get was their hidden A-pillar, which would have caused sealing problems and been too costly.

The struggle for a soft front end

THE DESIGNERS and engineers alike were determined to have the soft urethane front end. Ono's group discoverd on the Death Valley trip that sharp flying rocks played havoc with metal surfaces, and project chief Uchiyama supported them firmly. For better aerodynamics, looks and function, he wouldn't have it otherwise.

But the top engineering echelon wasn't quite convinced. A number of existing examples brought in, mostly from Detroit, were of little help in persuading the bosses; but they did allow that if the body group could come up with a facia whose surface quality and match to the surrounding metal was as good as the Porsche 928's, they would give their approval. Just the same, they also required that the working groups have a backup design ready.

Development engineer Hirotaka Tachibana staged this interesting encounter of four- and two-wheeled sports machinery to ensure the P747's visual dynamics

The designers obliged with a sketch of a half-metal, half-plastic nose. "We did our best, but could hardly be proud of it," admits senior designer Tanaka. Less enchanted with this compromise solution were the body engineers; "If we must, we could come up with engineering drawings in a couple of 24-hour shifts, so why not leave it at that? Our objective is the soft front, so let's concentrate on it," they observed. So it was left at that.

Somebody had faith that it could be done; before the front-end design was set, the body group had a test injection-molding facility installed at Mazda's Ujina (Hiroshima) plant at a cost of a half-million dollars, and produced sample facias for tests and evaluation. Eventually this test site was developed into a full-scale production facility, defeating an outside specialist firm in a quality competition along the way.

The front facia is R-RIM, fiberglass-reinforced reaction injection molded urethane—a strong, resilient material. Mazda mixes its own concoction of ingredients and catalyst, the formula being a well guarded secret claimed to assure good surface quality, durability and fit. The material is not without its problems; high temperatures and humidity cause it to expand, potentially forming ripples. To counter this, the P747 facia is mounted in a pre-stretched state in a controlled-temperature environment at one section of the assembly line; the inevitable expansion is accommodated in the fore-aft direction. Prototype cars were sent to Puerto Rico in summer 1984 and left out at 110°F and 90 percent humidity for prolonged periods; they passed with flying, er, staying colors. Mazda's quality standards stipulate that there can be no appreciable color mismatch between the different material surfaces for several years.

Soft front facia being examined by the evaluation group. A Porsche 928 is in the foreground

Going for a big rear view

LIKEWISE, THE single-piece compound-curvature rear window involved wading through technical and production difficulties as well as some vehement protests from cost-and weight-control quarters. Intended as a frameless glass hatch, it acquired a stamped steel frame (an aluminum one was also tried) in the course of development to ensure the sealing quality Mazda standards required. Along the way the glass area shrank 20 percent too, but it is still such a huge and complex piece of glass that manufacturer Nippon Glass had to install a new oven for it. Reinforced by its frame and secured by two latches when closed, the glass hatch actually contributes materially to the body's bending stiffness—which exceeds that of its predecessor's already exceptionally rigid shell in static tests.

In designing and developing bodies, Mazda engineers now rely on their new Dynamic Modal Analysis. The analytical program has been under constant development since its inception in 1979 as GNC1 (Geometric Modeling and Numerical Control), is currently at its second stage as GNC2 and will soon progress to a third phase. In DMA a test body is put on a shaker rig and put through vibrations of varying frequencies that exert bending and twisting effects; the body's stress distributions and deformations under load are observed dynamically and visually on the computer display. Such dynamic testing and analysis are more informative than static ones. The tests indicated that the P747 shell had an extremely good, balanced distribution of stress points and areas while matching its predecessor's rigidity and light weight. Body-in-white weight without doors, hood or hatch is a fraction under 200 kg (440 lb).

Compound-curvature one-piece rear window is surrounded by stamped steel frame

Solemn pledge: no digitals, no graphics

INTERIOR DESIGN development followed much the same path as that of the exterior. Three designers, two from Hiroshima and one from Mazda's American studio, began putting their ideas on paper in Irvine, California. Later, when the project moved to product design stages, the group was joined by another talented designer, Yasuo Aoyagi, who would coordinate the interior development.

"Involvement and envelopment" was the concept theme; Mazda designers like to sketch a bathtub, that most secure and personal of spaces, to illustrate the idea. Single king-size and twin-tub variations were drawn up; the California work produced four interior proposals, from a "neat and compact" scheme to a futuristic one featuring digital readouts, electronic graphics and a cathode-ray tube. All were evaluated at the April 1982 management staff meeting; the choice was the most sports car-like interior. Work then progressed to types and graphics of instruments for the large pod. Again, four designs—from straightforward analog dials with "proper" needle pointers to a full digital display—were presented to Mazda's inner circles as well as the first American clinics. Votes were 9 to 1, 90 percent favoring the classic circular instruments and the remaining 10 percent divided among three electronic displays. Project chief Uchiyama decided then and there that the instrumentation would be straightforward analog—come hell, high water or Corvette. Mazda's electronics people were wary that there might be a change of heart halfway through the project, so Uchiyama gave them a solemn no-digital no-graphics pledge so that their attention could be directed to other matters. The only digital displays are to be found in the clock and some of the optional radios.

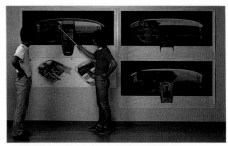
Designers evaluating more sketches

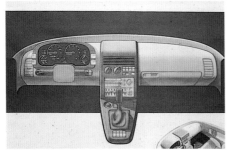 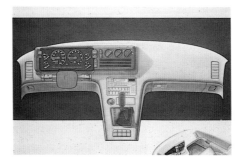 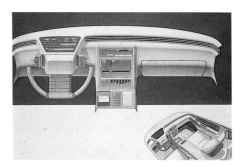

Instrument-panel design proposals

 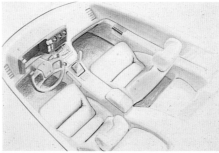 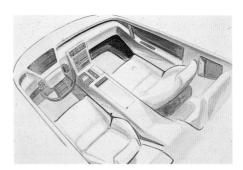

"Involvement and envelopment" was the concept theme

A more controversial issue was the control layout. Persistence is a hallmark of Mazda designers, and they had long been pursuing an ideal layout of switches. They'd had their fingers burned too; the Cosmo/929's "satellite switches" were supposed to manifest that ideal, but actually were awkward and confusing. Since then, with help from the company's ergonomic specialists and engineers, they had developed an internal design code to ensure that ergnomics precede novel looks.

But the P747 design team wanted something different and better. As in the 626, they grouped switches on the face and either flank of the large instrument nacelle. Controls relating to driver vision—headlights, auxiliary lights, instrument lighting, rear-window defroster and headlamp washers—were grouped on the left flank, wiper

Electronic digital-graphic display and straightforward analog instrument ideas. Choice was for the analog in a 9:1 vote

First "sitting buck" model on the approved design theme. This model was shown at the 1982 American clinic, criticized for its bright color contrast and strange handbrake knuckle

Basically the same design in more serious color. The handsome four-spoke steering wheel was soon to be abandoned

and washer switches on the right. An isolated item was the hazard warning switch, a red button that is lighted from within at night; it was placed over the wiper-washer controls, where the passenger can reach it if need be.

A short lever on the nacelle's left face controls directional signals and headlight beams; a matching one on the right is for the cruise control and includes a main switch and an engagement indicator lamp. Conventional twin steering-column stalks would have worked just fine, so why deviate?—that was the reaction of diehard functionalists, Chief Project Engineer Uchiyama and Chief Designer Oda among them. To convince his bosses, young Aoyagi and his group showed six alternative designs, each with their rationale and predictions of future switchgear trends.

"A time-consuming process of persuasion," he says, "but the key men finally agreed on the nacelle-mounted controls."

The instrument pod had originally been designed to adjust up and down with the tilt steering column as in the Porsche 928, but the idea was abandoned because of its complication. Sufficient instrument visibility was obtained by offsetting the steering wheel center just a trace downward; 5 mm, or less than a quarter-inch, but this increased the upper "window" area by a full 20 percent.

Interior sitting buck, circa September 1983. Lower 1/4 of the tachometer space was occupied by AAS (automatically adjustable shock-absorber system) display

Final interior, with fully circular tacho- and speedo-meters and three-spoke steering wheel

Maeda and Oda examining the sitting-buck model

Box suspension towers that housed audio speakers were replaced by cylindrical ones. Storage bin on left and an occasional seat on right

Final production instrument panel and minor switches

Rotary resurgence

AH, FOR THE good old days of the RX-2, when engines could breathe deeply of mixtures rich with inexpensive fuel and exhale freely through uncatalyzed tailpipes. The RX-2's rotary revved uncannily—a swoosh motor, it was. "Bring back the feeling" was the development theme for the P747 engine. A sort of rotary resurgence was called for, and yet all the demands and laws of a much changed world also had to be met in the process.

In early summer 1982 the planners presented a set of performance targets to the Fifth Engine Design Department, listing among other things these three engine alternatives for the P747:

1) Type 12A engine with carburetor and six-port induction for the base model; minimum power output 125 bhp

2) Type 13B DEI (Dynamic Effect Intake), either carbureted or electronically fuel injected, for a midrange model; minimum output 145 bhp

3) Type 13B turbocharged or TISC (supercharged) engine, producing 170 bhp or more, for a top-of-line model.

Rotary-engine designers searching for more power: Hiroshi Ohzeki, chief of Department 5 (fourth from left) with his lieutenants Tadokoro (second from left), Kurio (on Ohzeki's right) and young engineers

Type 13B DEI fuel-injection engine as installed in the RX-7

New "tournament" double-deck plenum chamber utilizes air interaction between the two rotor chambers for pumping in higher-pressure air

On the basis of the blossoming high-performance trend, a year later the planners elaborated further, specifying the desired performance levels of these three variants in terms of specific power (power per liter) and power-to-weight ratios:

	SAE net bhp	bhp/liter	lb/bhp
12A carbureted	120	50	24 or more
13B DEI EFI	155	60	18–20
13B Turbo	180	70	16 or less

On top of this, the engines should return acceptable fuel economy, if not superior to that of the best contemporary and anticipated future high-performance reciprocating engines; above all, they must escape the dreaded U.S. Gas Guzzler Tax. In Mazda's 1983 evaluation of the RX-7, present and future, the planners determined that the highly sophisticated 13B DEI would surpass the smaller, carbureted 12A's fuel efficiency by 1985; this led to dropping the 12A from consideration for the P747.

Mazda's rotary after 20 years

IN THE Sixties the Wankel rotary was considered revolutionary. Now it has been under continuous development by Mazda for more than 20 years—first to ensure its viability and reliability, then to meet ever-tightening emission standards in America and Japan, then to improve its once notorious thirst for fuel, and most recently for a good measure of performance with reasonable fuel economy.

The latest 13B engine's features are the fruits of this long R&D process. Several years ago, for instance, improved gas sealing cleared the way for a catalytic converter, and therefore leaner air-fuel mixtures for better fuel economy. Then an advanced project called TISC, short for Timed Induction with Supercharging, led to the Six Port Induction (6PI) intake concept. The experimental TISC engine had an auxiliary intake port into which boosted air is injected by a high-efficiency air pump, the port being controlled by a rotary valve. Development of electronic fuel injection for the rotary led to a new resonance charge system, employing a plenum chamber and tuned intake tracts to take advantage of air interference effects peculiar to the twin-rotor engine; this became DEI, the Dynamic Effect Intake system.

Along the way the smaller 12A engine was turbocharged for a high-performance RX-7 for the Japanese market. The turbocharging system then evolved into the so-called Impact Turbo with a new turbine-wheel design to take better advantage of the rotary's powerful onrush of exhaust gas.

There had been other detailed improvements in engine construction, metallurgy and material choices, and production techniques; no one could accuse the men of Department 5 of being idle. On the contrary, they were suspected of having even more eggs hidden in their little engineering basket; department chief Hiroshi Ohzeki grins and says, "They think we are doling them out." True or not, there would be no doling-out this time; it would take all the tricks in their bag to get more power, squeeze out better fuel economy and still retain the reliability and durability the rotary had come to deliver.

That last item was of particular concern to Department 5. Ever since they had had their fingers burned by high oil consumption, they had been acutely concerned with reliability; in fact, a special committee, the RE Reliability Conference, had been formed. Having licked the oil consumption some years ago with a new seal design, the group now renamed itself the RE Development Promotion Conference and set about eliciting more new ideas from the design and development engineers.

Thus when a second fleet of 10 engineering "mules" for the P747 project was built, the cars had five different sets of engine specifications, incorporating various features developed by the Conference. One was a naturally aspirated 13B with a refined version of DEI that had already been conceived when the first production DEI system was launched. The new "tournament" plenum chamber, so named for its "batting

Mazda's incumbent Mr. Rotary, Hiroshi Ohzeki, cherubic and enthusiastic chief of Department 5

Latest Type 13B DEI engine powers the P747 RX-7

back and forth" action of air charges it produced, pumped higher-pressure air into the inhaling combustion chamber; used with digitally controlled fuel injection, this arrangement would add 10 horsepower.

Reduced mechanical friction, tighter gas sealing, quicker warmup and fully electronic control of fuel injection, idling stability and ignition all contributed to markedly better fuel economy; now it would comfortably clear the 1985 Gas Guzzler limit.

An eleventh-hour power search

AFTER THAT initial target of 170 bhp, the planners had raised their goal for the Turbo to 180 bhp in autumn 1983 in the face of the emerging spate of twincam multi-valve piston engines. But this late date was time for final engine specifications, not new targets; production blueprints would soon have to be ready to meet the tight schedule.

This last-minute demand for more power entailed hard work. With a conventional turbocharger, no more than 160–165 bhp could be attained safely; above that, increased boost would lead to detonation. Enrich mixtures to head off the detonation and misfiring would set in. Exhaust pressure would hinder the freer breathing essential to more power—in short, the barrier was formidable.

The idea of a variable-geometry turbocharger had long attracted Ohzeki and his designers. A variable-nozzle scroll was tempting, but would have been too complex and costly. The team came up with a twin-scroll turbocharger with a trap door in the turbine scroll, to alter passage volume and the direction of exhaust gas impinging on the turbo's turbine blades, thus achieving the effects of variable-geometry turbocharging with much less complexity and cost; see the Engine section of Chapter One for details.

Turbocharged 13B on a test bench

Twin-scroll variable area turbocharger, jointly developed by Mazda's Department 5 and turbo maker Hitachi

Mazda's collaborator in turbocharging, Hitachi, was initially uncertain of the twin-scroll turbocharger's viability in volume production. A separator wall cast integrally into the scroll might develop hairline cracks at high temperatures, so would it stand the rigors of high-speed driving? Not until spring 1984 did Hitachi assure assistant department chief Tomoh Tadokoro that the concept could be produced with the certainty of reliability. By then, Tadokoro had already discovered that even though such cracks might sometimes develop, the pressure difference across the wall would even out through the cracks and cause no breakage or loss of performance.

Ohzeki and Tadokoro also give credit to Nippon Denso for producing a new, extra-large-capacity airflow meter for the dual-injector Bosch L-Jetronic fuel injection. And since no proprietary fuel pump would satisfy the turbo 13B, a new high-flow pump had to be developed; it has two speeds, determined by the engine's central control computer.

With all this—DEI, dual electronic fuel injection, high-energy ignition with knock-sensing timing retard, full electronic engine management and the innovative twin-scroll turbocharging—the 13B Turbo attains its targeted 180 bhp and delivers a healthy spread of torque throughout its speed range. Quite a last-minute change, I'd say.

Type 13B DEI Turbo, with twin-scroll turbocharger and intercooler

Map and labyrinth: developing the P747's new rear suspension

CHIEF PROJECT ENGINEER Akio Uchiyama believes in youth. In his younger days, he had initiated several modest but ambitious sports-car projects. Either corporate policy at the time or the time itself was not on his side; they had to be aborted one after another—until fulfillment came in the form of Project X605, the original RX-7. Jiro Maebayashi was a junior member of the X605's basic layout design team.

Mazda TTL (twin-trapezoidal-link) rear suspension of front-wheel-drive 323 and 626 models has toe-correcting ability

Uchiyama assigned Maebayashi and his group to configure the P747. The group had seen the virtues and limitations of a live rear axle clearly; no one suggested continuing this type of rear suspension for the P747. Independent rear suspension was a foregone conclusion.

It was equally clear that it couldn't be ordinary suspension, whatever form it might take. Mazda's research had shown that the direction the company had taken in developing its TTL (twin-trepezoidal-link) suspension for the company's front-wheel-drive-323 (GLC) and 626 models was a good one, right on a trend line eagerly pursued by the world's foremost chassis designers.

Specifically, a road car's rear suspension should incorporate some form of toe control for a good balance of roadholding, handling, ride quality and noise suppression. Porsche's Weissach Axle is a widely acclaimed example of this. Because of elasticity, conventional suspension with compliant mountings tends to assume an inherently

Porsche's widely acclaimed Weissach Axle also incorporates toe-control

Daimler-Benz's remarkable and complex multi-link rear suspension, whose arrival Mazda chassis designers had long anticipated

unstable toe-out attitude under deceleration or braking loads. Though they use rubber mount bushings, the TTL and Weissach concepts counter such undesirable tendencies by kinematics designed into their geometry, and assume stable toe-in attitudes upon deceleration or braking.

Mazda researchers extended their probe into recent patents and patent applications in major automobile-producing countries, particularly in the U.S. and West Germany, and confirmed that toe control was indeed sharply in focus among chassis designers. Daimler-Benz's complex and remarkable multi-link rear suspension, first seen in the Mercedes 190 series, came as no surprise; it had been anticipated at Hiroshima. The patent "map" also helped Mazda planners and designers to avoid labyrinths that could lead them to a dangerous dead end, such as patent infringements awaiting seemingly new ideas and inventions. Maebayashi and his team wanted the new rear suspension to react to and counter not only deceleration, braking, rapid acceleration and lateral loads singly, but to all these forces in any combination, always producing the right amounts of toe-in for optimum stability and maximum cornering force. Through their painstaking research, they concluded that no existing or planned suspension systems had a full measure of this multi-force compensation. Theirs must have it; must outshine them all, both on the road and in the inevitable patent contest.

Ambitious goal: ideal toe-control

THUS THE conceptual target was set; a new toe-control mechanism would be incorporated into the P747's rear suspension. The man called upon to put the concept onto paper, into the computer terminal and finally into metal was Takao Kijima, a chassis engineer assigned to the Third Chassis Design Department. There was a minor complication here, as Department 3 was primarily responsible for Mazda's commercial vehicles; but Uchiyama persisted on the assignment of this brilliant young designer to the P747. Finally, Kijima's divisional chief Ito agreed to set up a special project team within the truck chassis-design deparment to allow him to get on with the work.

Jiro Maebayashi—M of the toe-control KM-hub

Kijima and Maebayashi agree that a double-A-arm suspension, with its unequal-length upper and lower lateral arms, offers by far the most positive control of wheel movement; it's no coincidence that most racing cars have it. This type of suspension with a toe-control feature added would be ideal, an opinion later advocated by Yoshimi Katayama, a competition driver who test-drove for Mazda under contract in the first evaluation of two prototype suspension systems.

But what's good for racing machinery may not be the best solution for a roadgoing car. For one thing, part of the racing suspension's precise control is attributable to solid ball joints; in a road car, however sporting it may be, compliant rubber bushings are necessary for an acceptable ride.

Space is another consideration. A 2 + 2 on the same wheelbase as the two-seater was going to be offered; the rear suspension would have to leave space not only for the seats, but for a fuel tank, a large-capacity exhaust system, and unhindered plumbing and cabling for the rear brakes. Thus unequal-arm suspension gave way to the more compact semi-trailing-arm type; Chapman struts were retained as a backup alternative.

Toe-control element: the KM hub

MAZDA HAD been experimenting with a four-wheel steering system for some time; it was one of the advanced features of the MX-02 "idea car" shown at the 1983 Tokyo Motor Show. Four-wheel steering is the ultimate toe-control; Mazda's concept steers the rear wheels in the same direction as the front ones for high-speed cornering and lane changing, in the opposite direction to the front wheels for low- and medium-speed turning. The rear wheels steer around the kingpins much like the front ones.

In the MX-02 an electronically controlled four-wheel steering system, with a black box determining which mode to use and how much to steer the rear wheels, is combined with electronically controlled active suspension in what may be the closest thing on wheels to the fly-by-wire or configure-controlled vehicle (CCV) yet. The P747 would not go to that extreme, but Uchiyama wanted it to have CCV-like stability and maneuverability.

Mazda MX-02 experimental car features electronically controlled four-wheel steering system

Kijima's answer was a kingpin axis in the rear hub carrier—but not a real, solid kingpin, as it would restrict the hub's three-dimensional movement. Instead, an imaginary kingpin axis might be formed by two mounting points between the hub carrier and hub, behind the wheel axis. Another rubber bushing mount ahead of and under the wheel axis would induce a certain amount of toe change under a specific kinetic force. A lower ball joint and an upper cylindrical rubber bushing would form the imaginary kingpin axis, the bushing giving three-dimensional freedom.

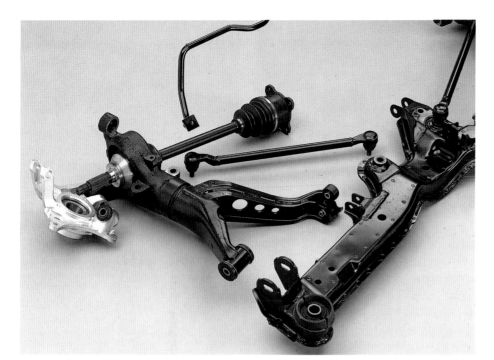

Construction of the two rubber bushings, one above and behind the wheel centerline and the other ahead of and under the wheel center, would be "tuned" to produce precise toe changes. The positions of the two bushings and one ball joint, the bushings' axial planes, rubber hardness and interaction of the bushings were determined by extensive computer analysis and simulation in Mazda's NASTRAN program.

The resulting Kijima-Maebayashi hub does not employ electronics and servo motors for direct rear-wheel steering as in the MX-02, but it can be said that it has an invisible geometrical "brain" developed by a computer.

Two engineering mules based on the existing RX-7 got KM hubs added to their rear suspension, in one case semi-trailing arms borrowed from a senior Cosmo model, in the other a Chapman-strut system located by TTL-like twin transverse links and a single trailing arm. When the mules were completed in spring 1982, they were handed over to the testing-development group.

Called X-0, these cars already had front MacPherson struts located by fabricated, welded sheet-steel A-arms—heavy hunks of metal that allowed a rack-and-pinion steering mechanism to be placed ahead of the engine on the front subframe.

Development engineer Masayoshi Nakamoto had never experienced a suspension like that which he was now confronted with; he had no established parameters by which its behavior could be judged. The car with semi-trailing arms responded sluggishly to steering inputs. Nakamoto's colleague Shuichi Mizushima was thoroughly outspoken in his evaluation of it; "Not worth further effort. Why not drop it?" They tried locking the KM hub solid, turning the rear suspension into perfectly ordinary semi-trailing arms. But soon they hit a barrier; the usual semi-trailing-arm quirks began showing up. Nakamoto did concede that the KM hub helped increase the rear wheel's cornering force under lateral loads, and lift-off oversteer—commonly called tuck-in—was milder and more manageable with it.

X-0's front suspension had these steel-sheet fabricated A-arms

Work continued on the two cars until December 1982, when three racing drivers under contract to Mazda got a chance to try them at the Nishi Nippon race track; Yoshimi Katayama, Yohjiro Terada and Takashi Yorino, all seasoned pilots known for their efforts at Daytona and Le Mans.

Katayama was not altogether taken with the semi-trailing X-0 car. It did very well in fast lane changes but had an unpredictable character change on corners and bends. "It's two different cars—one entering a bend, another exiting it," he commented.

One of the two X-0 cars using the production RX-7 body had Chapman-strut rear suspension with twin parallel transverse links to which the KM hub was attached

Two X-0s were taken to Nishi Nippon racing circuit in December 1982 for comparative evaluation by Mazda's three contract racing drivers

This is the semi-trailing arm, Type X-0, with the KM hub at Nishi Nippon

"Taming one prototype is routine work," he added, "but finding two opposite characters in one car is a bit much."

Just the same, Katayama admitted the KM hub had some merit; but he doubted the wisdom of mating it with semi-trailing arms. A Porsche 944 on hand for comparison didn't make a case for semi-trailing arms either; "Much too much understeer, but with vicious lift-off oversteer." He concluded by advocating unequal-length A-arms.

Kijima was more analytical. He diagnosed the main X-0 fault as being entirely wrong bushing chracteristics in the KM hub mountings, saying that they did the opposite to what they should do. In his opinion, that could be rectified.

He was more concerned about the semi-trailing arms' severe squat on acceleration. To accommodate the plus-2 seating, the suspension mounts had to be lowered by some 60 mm (2.4 in.), which brought them lower than the wheel axis. The resulting geometry had no anti-squat action, so the car just sat down on its haunches when

Three engineering mules and one early prototype car: X-2 in the foreground, X-0 at left, X-1 at right and S-1 in the back

122

accelerating—and dived badly on braking as well.

Apart from these faults, serious as they were, the semi-trailing arms showed more promise than the Chapman struts on the other X-0 mule. The Chapman-strut car was more stable on irregular road surfaces, more manageable at the cornering limit, and less affected by throttle changes. In all other respects of this evaluation, the semi-trailing suspension was better, and everyone agreed it could be brought up to the level of the strut system in the remaining areas. The Chapman struts were also bulkier in the wheel area, crowding brake lines and cables.

Splitting the semi-trailing arm

THE CHOICE was thus semi-trailing arms with the KM toe-control hub. But the suspension mounting points needed to be raised by at least those 60 mm, which would stick them right into the passenger compartment. For acceptable head clearance, the roof would have to be raised at least an inch—not palatable for a sports car.

Kijima found a way out in splitting the semi-trailing arms, which were single fabricated pieces from the Cosmo. He would split the arm in two, with the main part on the outer mount and a diagonal rod serving as the other half. The rod would be ball-jointed, at one end to the main arm, at the other to the rear subframe. For the desired anti-squat effect, both members' pivot points from the car structure could be higher than the wheel centerline. As the main arm and diagonal rod would form a wide-based A-arm, their effective lateral rigidity would be high, eliminating one of the designers' concerns.

Camber changes inherent to semi-trailing arms were another worry, but now a camber-control arm could be added at the main arm's inner pivot point; attached to the frame by a double-jointed link, it could be made low enough to clear the desired low floor.

A second-generation engineering mule with these split semi-trailing arms and camber-compensating links—called the X-1—was completed in May 1983. Weight had become a critical factor, so its front and rear wheel hubs were of aluminum; the front

X-1 engineering mule had cast-aluminum front A-arms

X-1's main trailing arm was mounted directly onto the body shell and caused fierce resonance

X-2 employed handsome forged aluminum A-arms

X-2's rear suspension was mounted on the subframe, which also carried the front of the long-nose final drive unit. The main trailing arm was still a three-piece-bolt-up type, not the last word in structual rigidity

suspension's A-arms were now closed-section aluminum castings, much like those of the Porsche 928.

The front suspension was found to have good structural rigidity, essential to resisting the steering shimmy that often detracts from MacPherson-strut systems; as much as 50 to 60 grams of out-of-balance failed to induce undue or unpleasant steering-wheel vibrations.

Overall, the design and development groups were satisfied with the X-1 suspension's dynamic behavior and felt it had great promise. A batch of seven X-1s was subsequently built and one of them taken to Europe in summer 1983 for tests on the Nürburgring. A team of engineers headed by Uchiyama and Project Development Engineer Hirotaka Tachibana took along an incumbent RX-7 and a Porsche 944 for comparisons.

On the Ring's long circuit the X-1 proved the most forgiving car of the trio, its toe-control and camber compensation providing tenacious grip under power but only mild, manageable oversteer on lift-off. There was a minor drama on the hallowed German course, however, when Uchiyama lost the 944 and bent it—on the first lap after switching from the X-1. Having circulated serenely and uneventfully in the Mazda experimental car, the chief engineer must have been caught off guard by the Porsche's more pronounced understeer and more abrupt lift-off oversteer in the treacherous double-bend section where things went haywire.

Tachibana, who had been responsible for such successful Mazda models as the original front-drive 323/GLC and the front-drive 626, is an astute and discerning interpreter of vehicle dynamics. The Tokyoite came to Mazda from Bridgestone, along with an engine design Mazda had bought for its "micro" runabout from this largest Japanese tire maker's now defunct motorcycle division. His efforts at taming the powerful but noisy, hydrocarbon-emitting two-stroke engine were abortive; but the enthusiast and development engineer in him prompted Tachibana to ask for an assignment in Mazda's Vehicle Test and Development Division. Tadayuki Masuda, the company's cheerful but demanding development chief, recognized Tachibana's qualifications and assigned him to these all-important projects.

Tachibana wasn't quite convinced by the X-1's handling. Though he recognized its virtues of straight-line stability and exceptional cornering forces, he did not like the connotation of "forgiving" lent by its stable behavior. "A sports car needs to be predictable and safe at the limit, but its responses and transient characteristics should deliver that all-important excitement factor. Call it 'razor-edge sharpness' if you will."

In this earlier development state, the rear suspension assumed immediate toe-in upon the first sign of lateral acceleration. This stabilized, true, but also dulled steering response. At the other end, the steering linkage was interfering with the front suspension's movement, accentuating understeer and further diluting the X-1's handling.

Then the hydra grew still more menacing heads, among them severe noise and vibration problems that were traced to the new rear suspension and final drive. The main trailing arms were now mounted directly to the unit body shell by a pair of brackets; the diagonal rods and camber-compensating links were hung from a short V-shaped subframe member that also carried the short-nose final drive unit.

The trailing arms were found to transmit noise and vibration directly into the body; the other links produced atrocious wind-up vibrations. Noise-vibration specialist Yoshiaki Nakano recalls, "It was no mere drumming. At 100 mph and about 4500 rpm it was like being inside a madly pounded drum!" He adds that "In the X605 (the original live-axle RX-7), about 30 percent of the noise was attributable to the rear suspension and final drive. In the X-1 it was almost 80 percent." It would turn out that the suspension and final drive would have to be located separately and mounted more elaborately.

In autumn 1983, immediately after the European trip, a few X-1 mules were modified to an X-1′ stage to test the effectiveness of a long-nose final drive unit. Hastily fabricated with an extension of 20-mm-thick steel plate that was flexibly mounted to the subframe, the long-nose final drive was expected to prevent the problematical wind-up.

Development proceeded to the X-2 stage in the late autumn of 1983; at almost the same time, construction of the first full P747 prototype, the S-1, began. This was the real thing, with P747 styling and all the mechanical components that had by now been designed and developed for the new car.

The X-2 was yet another engineering mule for further suspension development; both were in metal by early spring 1984.

The quest for quietness: isolating the final drive and suspension

LIKE THE X-2 engineering mule, the S-1 prototype had a long-nose final drive, the nose housing an extended pinion shaft supported by three bearings. The final drive's rear mounting arms were cast integrally with the aluminum rear case. Mounting at the front was by a shear-type rubber block onto a subframe member, which had taken on a T-shape with a short center bar.

All suspension members were now pivoted from the subframe; in turn, the subframe (including the final-drive nose mounting member) was attached to the body shell through cylindrical rubber blocks with different spring characteristics, tuned to absorb varied vibration frequencies from the suspension and final drive. At the rear, an additional sub-link to the body helped steady the subframe. This separate and elaborate mounting of the suspension and final drive reduced noise and vibrations to an acceptable level, and further improved the car's dynamics as well.

The rear trailing arms (themselves part of the multi-element semi-trailing-arm

On the other hand, Kijima's styrenefoam rear suspension model had always had a single-piece main trailing arm....

Kijima explains the old built-up and new integral trailing arms

assembly) were now single pieces instead of the three-piece built-up and bolted ones of the X-1 and X-2.

Kijima had concluded that the three-piece arm, though expeditious for the engineering mules, would have difficulty meeting standards for structural rigidity and dimensional accuracy—both critical to his toe-control hub—in volume production. He overcame the inherent difficulty of welding the ductile cast-iron hub carrier and the fabricated sheet-steel trailing arm by casting a male sheet tube into the hub carrier; this tube would then be inserted into the trailing-arm body and welded to it.

At the front end, a pair of aircraft-quality forged aluminum A-arms replaced the X-1's cast ones. The forged arms had been developed in parallel with the cast ones, which had a 99-percent chance of being the ones used. But the cast arms could not be made open-sided and were therefore bulkier than the forged ones for the same strength; the design team preferred the forged arms not only for their compactness but for their good looks as well.

Of two supplier candidates, Kobe Steel won the Mazda contract to produce the arms because of its experience and expertise in forging aircraft components with an 8000-ton press. The initial problem was quality assurance in such large-scale

Male tube is cast into the cast-iron hub carrier, which is then inserted into the main trailing arm's end and welded together, making a distortion-free integral arm unit

production. For the more usual aircraft order the maximum production run would be around 1000 units; Mazda would need 10 times as many of the interchangeable left and right arms every month. The challenge was met with a new magnetic test facility which would check every A-arm for cracks.

After testing 2.5 and 7 degrees, Kijima and the chassis design group chose a 5-deg caster angle for a good compromise between straight-line stability and acceptable steering efforts with the non-assisted steering. To minimize interference of the steering linkage with suspension geometry in cornering, the knuckle-arm point height was altered. Kijima had no qualms about the basic MacPherson-strut suspension; he felt that, given careful choice of geometry and tuning, it could perform as well as the much admired unequal-A-arm type advocated by race driver Katayama and development engineer Tachibana at the earlier stages of the project. Low unsprung weight was also vital; it was achieved by the light alloy A-arms, hubs and (on the upmarket models) brake calipers.

The S-1 prototype also had new steering systems, both manual and power-assisted, developed jointly with Koyo Seiko. Called "G-sensing," the power system incorporated electronic control of the hydraulic assistance according to lateral acceleration, whereby automatic adjustment to varying road-surface friction was a welcome by-product.

When shown a drawing of the toe-control hub, it occurred to brake designer Shiro Yoshioka that he might have difficulty finding space for large enough brakes. Having been a designer of final drives, he secretly designed a final drive unit that could take inboard disc brakes just in case. As it turned out, it was possible to accommodate adequate brakes outboard, but only by moving their calipers to a position ahead of the axles; this unusual solution brought a bonus in the form of lower unsprung inertia.

For the front brakes of premium models, the brake group designed four-piston aluminum calipers. Cast-iron calipers would have weighed 5.3 kg (11.7 lb); the aluminum ones, cast by Hiroshima Aluminum, scaled just 3.2 kg (7 lb) for a saving of 4.2 kg (9.5 lb) per pair. The brakes are made by Sumitomo Electric.

S-1 prototype on test at home on the Miyoshi proving ground, avoiding a couple of recklessly driven Mazda vehicles

Four-piston aluminum brake caliper is used on the GXL and Turbo for optimum stopping power

Rear brake caliper ahead the axle lowers unsprung inertia

One more elusive goal: "turnability"

IN TERMS of stability, high-speed handling, quality and noise-vibration isolation, the S-1 prototype satisfied the engineering team. But one goal had remained elusive; the traditionally contradictory combination of good straight-line and high-speed cornering stability with responsive low-speed maneuvering or "turnability."

For cornering stability at high speeds, understeer is desirable; roll steer, bump steer, compliance steer (all forms of toe-in) and something called "camber thrust" are all in the engineer's bag of tricks for obtaining it. On the other hand, for responsive low-speed cornering you want toe-*out*. With conventional suspension it is difficult if not impossible to reconcile the two; the best engineers can do is compromise.

The ultimate solution: four-wheel steering

FOR SOME time Mazda had been experimenting with an electronically controlled four-wheel steering system conceived to circumvent this traditional compromise. Mazda's four-wheel steering has two modes. In the first, all four wheels are steered in the same direction to stabilize high-speed maneuvering. In the second, they are steered in the opposite direction for a tighter turning circle—the MX-02 idea car utilizes the latter advantage to maximize its wheelbase length.

One day project development engineer Tachibana was toying with an experimental four-wheel-steered car that had a mode selector switch. Tachibana inadvertently flipped it into the opposite-steering mode and was met with a sharp reaction. The light came on; Induce toe-out for initial steering input for quick response, then bring on toe-in at higher cornering forces for high-speed maneuvering stability.

Chassis designer Kjima had also been aware of the attributes of four-wheel steering, and he was able to incorporate the principle into the P747's rear suspension without resorting to actual mechanical rear-wheel steering or electronic controls. The toe-control hub's front bushing is "locked" by a preloaded half-moon-section block. At low cornering forces the preload prevents the hub from functioning; the compliant trailing arm bushing gives and turns the outside rear wheel outward for toe-out, or opposite-steering effect; the result is quick response to steering input. At a lateral force of about 100 kg, the preload neutralizes and the toe-control hub's front bushing begins to "unlock," which then turns the outside rear wheel inward for toe-in, or same-direction steering effect. This occurs somewhere between 0.4 and 0.5 g; the bushing has an abutment that precludes toe-out movement under braking, engine braking and rapid acceleration, allowing only toe-in for best stability.

S-1 on an American test trip

Chassis designer Takao Kijima, fifth from left in dark glasses, confers with development engineer Hirotaka Tachibana on the American trip with S-1 prototype

Prototype RX-7 in the Nürburgring paddock

Amply instrumented prototype RX-7

This rear suspension was installed in a later S-1 prototype, built in spring 1984, as well as the S-1.5 (summer 1984) and S-2 (the final prototype, late 1984); it is the system adopted for the production 1986 RX-7. The development team took several overseas test-evaluation trips; with the S-1 to America in July 1984, to Europe in November of the same year, and to Canada in the winter for extreme cold-weather tests. Two cars taken on the Canadian trip, which included a prolonged "park and freeze" period, caught the attention of an enterprising photographer, who to the chagrin of Mazda then marketed his pictures to several auto magazines. The S-2 stayed home in Japan for final refinement, pinning down the final design and serving as the basis for production blueprints.

Freeze the P747

MAY 1983 was the most critical month for Project P747 and its men. By then, the exterior and interior design had been set and basic development of major mechanical components was almost complete. The one barrier that appeared insurmountable was weight, the perpetual enemy to sports-car performance and vehicle dynamics. Mazda management ordered a freeze on the project for one month, during which weight and cost would be restudied and the project's viability would be given a hard look. Crisis was upon the P747 team; criticism poured in from various quarters of the company. All new and advanced features of the car and its design were subjected to persistent attacks. "Why accept the complication and weight penalty of the complex rear suspension? Go back to a live rear axle," said some; "Retain the three-piece rear window," said others. "Reduce the wheels to 13-inch ones," and ultimately, "Our investment in the X605 (original) RX-7 is amortized. Let's continue building it." Uchiyama confesses that his team was pushed to the wall. The managing directors' meeting on final product approval, scheduled for June 1983, was postponed to November—a serious threat to the project's progress. If the debut was to take place as planned in late 1985, it was time to place orders for production dies and presses for major components. Senior Managing Director Takushi Mitsunari, then in charge of Mazda's R&D activities, took it upon himself to give the go-ahead signal—which could easily entail an initial expenditure of $80 million—without waiting for his co-MDs' concurrence.

Prototype RX-7 was taken apart in search of weight reduction by grams and kilos

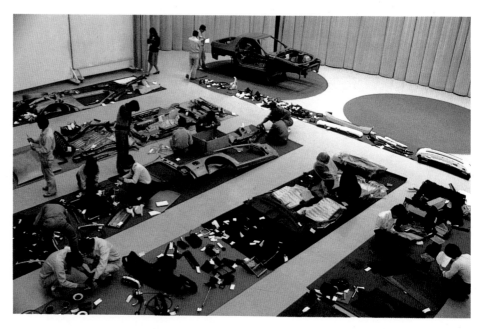

Given Mitsunari's grace, Uchiyama organized a weight-reduction campaign he called "Operation Gram Per Head," suggesting that all designers and engineers on Project P747 come up with an idea to save one gram of weight. A prototype car was taken apart in the design center's auditorium, its components and parts spread out on the floor so that they could swarm over them in search of expendable grams and kilograms.

In the end, considerable weight was saved by liberal use of light alloy components—albeit at considerable cost penalties. A pair of alloy front-suspension

Forged aluminum front A-arm

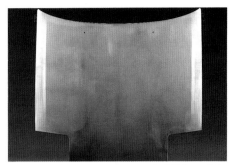
Aluminum hood panel on certain RX-7 models

Aluminum final drive rear cover/mounting bracket

Aluminum jack, imported from Germany, is standard equipment in the RX-7

Aluminum pedals

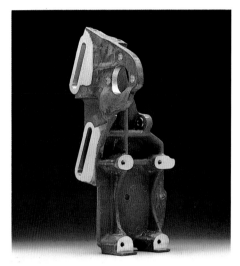
Aluminum power-steering pump mounting bracket

A-arms weighing 1.9 kg (4.2 lb) save 2.0 kg (4.4 lb) each, but cost 140 percent more than fabricated steel ones would have. Alloy front wheel hubs save 3.3 kg (7.2 lb) per car and cost twice what iron ones would have. Other major aluminum parts include rear hubs (3.4 kg/7.5 lb lighter), engine-mount bracket (1.1 kg/2.4 lb lighter) and final-drive case/mounting arms (2.0 kg/4.4 lb lighter). Uchiyama's hunt for a lighter jack (saving 1.4 kg/3.1 lb) has already been documented, and a cast aluminum space wheel is fitted in certain RX-7 models even if they have steel road wheels.

The spirit of Operation Gram Per Head spread through the individual design and development divisions, departments and sections. Their endeavors and results are too numerous to list, but a few more examples deserve mention. Engine design chief Ohzeki's Department 5 men were more acutely aware than anyone else that an extra ounce robs a precious fraction of a horsepower, so they went on an all-out weight hunt. The external-accessory group shaved 4.1 kg (9 lb) off various items; internally, the two rotors lost almost 1.3 kg (3 lb), which brought doubled rewards by reducing frictional losses and cutting engine inertia.

We often find that the whole is more than the sum of the parts. That was certainly the case with Operation Gram Per Head: The sum of all these little savings was not only a considerable weight reduction for the new Mazda, but its very salvation as well. Soon the new RX-7, with even better dynamics and performance thanks to its reduced weight, would be on its way to dealers' showrooms and into its new owners' hands.

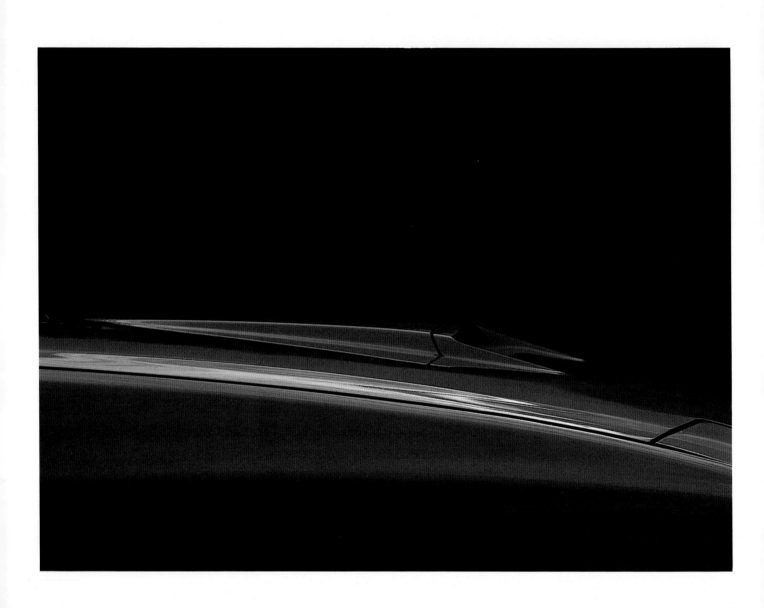

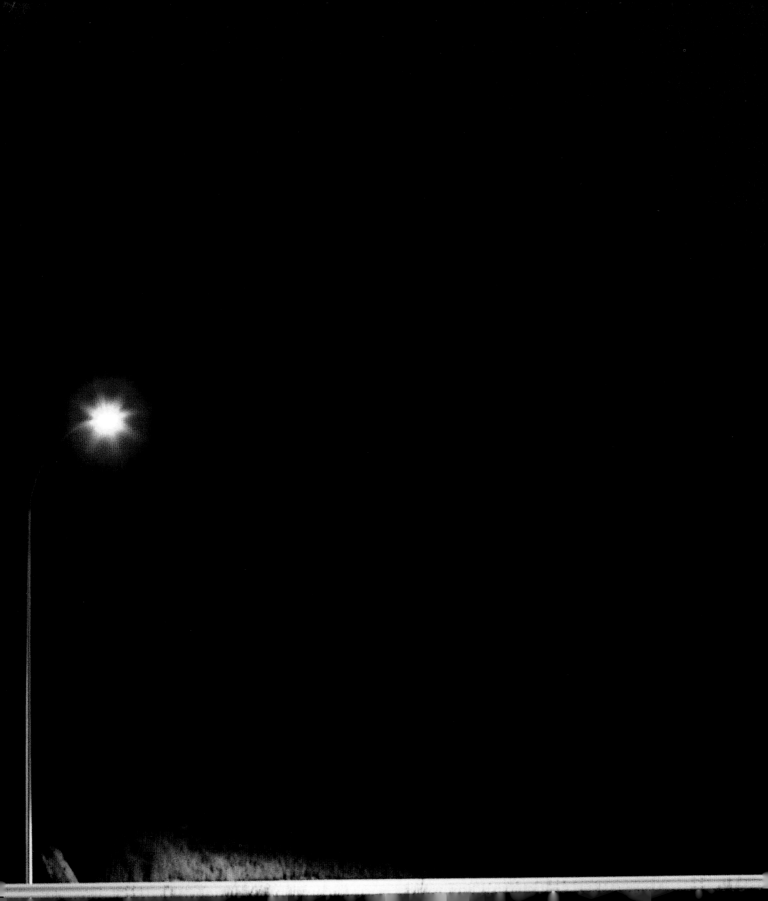

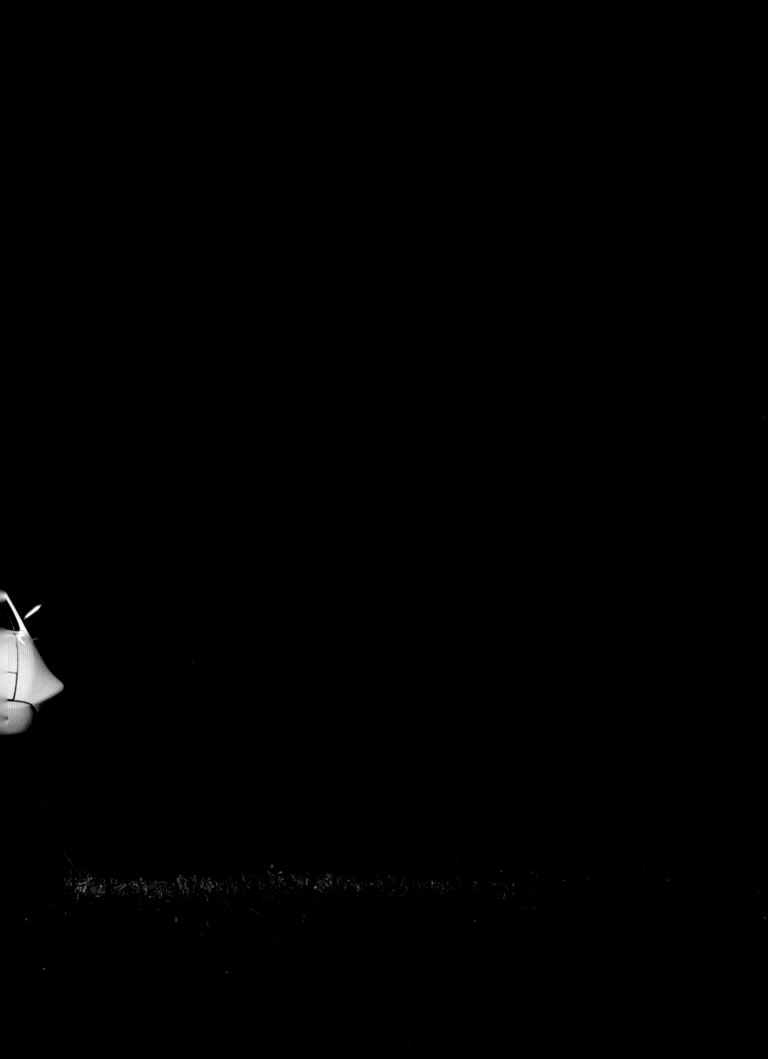

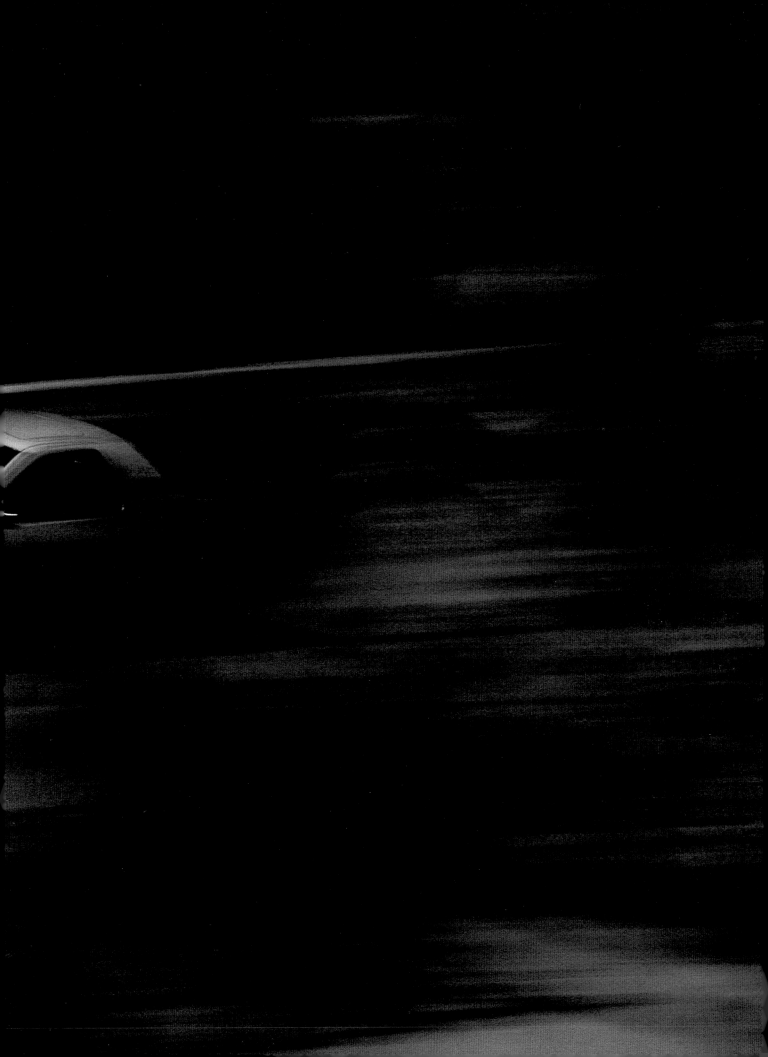

3

**MAZDA
ROTARY ENGINE SPORTS CARS**

Cosmo Sport 110S

TOYO KOGYO KAISHA of Hiroshima (hereinafter referred to as Mazda, for its new official corporate name Mazda Motor Corporation adopted in May 1984) launched the Cosmo Sport 110S coupe on May 30, 1967. Six years of intensive research, development and testing of its Wankel rotary engine under West German NSU license had occupied a 47-man engineering team, headed by Kenichi Yamamoto, before the introduction. The Cosmo Sport 110S was the world's first twin-rotor engine production car, preceding NSU's own Ro80 sedan by three and half months. Mazda's Rotary Engine Research Division had completed its first prototype twin-rotor engine in July 1963. Work on a new sports car to be powered by the twin-rotor engine, on which Mazda was pinning its hope, had commenced in the previous year; by December 1962, the basic layout and styling of Project L402A had been decided upon, and actual design work began in early 1963. Prototype cars were built in record time: by August of that year they began serving as running test beds for several variations of the twin-rotor engine.

Mazda displayed two prototype Wankel engines at the 1963 Tokyo Motor Show in October: a single-rotor engine with a single chamber of 398 cc and a twin-rotor version with the same displacement per chamber. The late Tsuneji Matsuda, heir to the founder and then president of the company, surprised show visitors one day when he drove up to the show site in one of the two prototype Cosmos brought to Tokyo, whose existence had not been known until then. After the show Matsuda rode all the way back to Hiroshima in the prototype. Accompanied by Yamamoto and several rotary engineers, he called on Mazda distributors and dealers en route.

For the following three years a Cosmo Sport prototype was displayed at the then-annual Tokyo Show. The 1966 version was a final prototype, powered by a new twin-rotor engine with its chamber displacement increased to 491 cc. This was the forerunner of the production type 0810 unit: it had two side intake ports and two sparkplugs per rotor chamber (the original-398 cc × 2 unit had peripheral intake ports and single plugs.)

A fleet of 60 Cosmos was then consigned to Mazda's distributors and dealers

Fleet of prototype cars on Miyoshi's high-speed banking, with rollbar-stainless loop bands on their quarter panels

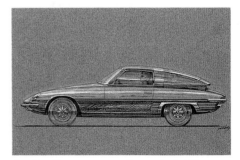

Another Cosmo proposal: an oriental Disco Volante?

Winning image sketch of a new rotary-powered sports car

A suggested racing roadster conversion

This competing design showed strong Italian influence and made it to the 1/5 clay-model stage

Rear-end sketches. Number ① won. Full-width lamps depicted in No. ② made it to full-size clay, but eventually lost out (it would surely have met with an official veto, anyway, as Japanese law stipulates "individual taillamps")

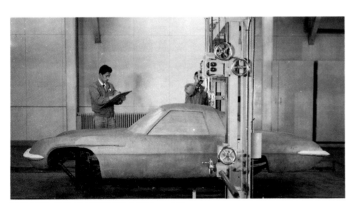

Full-size clay model being measured

Cosmo clay model being measured

throughout Japan in January 1965, to undergo real-life evaluation programs advocated by President Matsuda. Except for a few cars involved in accidents, they accumulated some 600,000 kilometers (375,000 miles) on the highways and byways of the far eastern isles without major incidents. Yamamoto and his engineers put the rigorous tests to good use, specifying three different engine types of the same twin-rotor theme in these cars according to geography and climate of the consigned areas, to help narrow down the alternatives and choose the best compromise for the production Cosmo, slated for debut in 1967.

L10A is identified by its narrow airintake

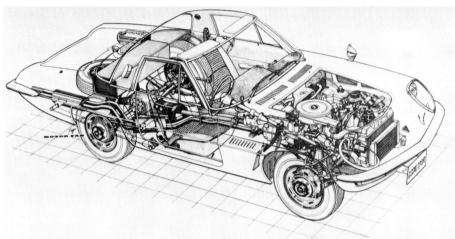

Type L10A Cosmo Sport

THE COSMO Sport was offered in one body style only, a closed 2-seat coupe with an integral steel body-chassis, although the design group had a roadster version in mind. Since then there have been numerous sketches and drawings of roadsters and convertibles in Mazda's sports car projects—the first fruition is likely to be in the new P747 RX-7.

A lean and hungry look must have been the designers' objective: the car measured only 1165 mm (45.9 in.) in height, 4140 mm/163.0 in. long and 1595 mm/62.8 in. wide. Its wheelbase was 2200 mm/86.6 in., its tracks 1250/49.2 at the front and 1240/48.8 at the rear. The production 1967 Cosmo weighed in at a moderate 940 kg/2070 lb and looked very much like the first wooden mockup of 1963.

Its twin-rotor engine was designated Type 0810 and would later evolve into the Type 10A that powered the first Mazda rotary model sold in North America, the R100 coupe. In contrast to the 10A's aluminum and cast-iron housing, this unit had an all-aluminum housing. It also departed from NSU practice, which used free-breathing peripheral inlet ports, by having side ports for low-speed tractability and better fuel economy. The 0810 was fed by a Zenith-Stromberg four-barrel carburetor and fired in sequence by twin sparkplugs per chamber.

Its dimensions of shaft eccentricity $e = 15$ mm and major rotor axis $R = 105$ mm remained unchanged through three sizes of Mazda production engines; the other

The Cosmo has an aircraft-like instrument panel with a full complement of meters and gauges. The woodrim steering wheel was standard

For other drivers, a view of the L10A

The L10A's engine bay is uncluttered, its Type 0810 engine buried deep beneath the pancake air cleaner

Shallow trunk of the L10A Cosmo

dimension making up the rotary's displacement, the trochoid chamber's width **b**, was 60 mm for a single chamber capacity of 491 cc. As installed in the L10A Cosmo Sport, it produced 110 bhp at 7000 rpm and thus acquired the export designation 110S; its maximum torque was 13.3 kg-m (96 lb-ft) at 3500 rpm on a 9.4:1 compression ratio. The engine was placed well aft of the front wheels' centerline, in what Mazda likes to call a "front midship" position. Power was taken out through a hydraulically actuated single-dry-plate clutch with diaphragm spring and a fully synchronized four-speed gearbox. The box was shifted by a short-throw lever in the best sports-car tradition with internal ratios of (first) 3.379:1, (second) 2.077:1, (third) 1.390:1, (fourth) 1.000:1 and (reverse) 3.389:1. Carried by a T-shaped member mounted to the body shell with large rubber block, the final drive had a ratio of 4.111:1.

For its time in Japan, the Cosmo chassis was quite sophisticated. Its front suspension was by unequal-length A-arms, the upper ones fabricated of tubes and the lower ones stamped, with coil springs, tubular shock absorbers and a link-actuated anti-roll bar. At the rear the Cosmo had a 51-mm dia. solid De Dion axle on semi-elliptic leaf springs, tubular shocks and a pair of upper trailing links; the axle halfshafts had ball-bearing sliding splines. Unassisted rack-and-pinion steering with an overall ratio of 16.6:1 maneuvered 14 × 4.5-in. stamped steel wheels carrying either Bridgestone cross-ply tires of 6.45–14 size or the same make's 165HR-14 radials. The brakes, discs at the front and drums at the rear, were unassisted too.

The interior of the pure two-seater coupe was all black except for checkered cloth seat inserts. Its dash was well padded and carried a matt-black panel with a full complement of aircraft-like instruments; the steering column was telescopically adjustable over a range of 60 mm (2.4 in.). For natural ventilation—there was no provision for air conditioning—there were air extractors in the rear quarter panels as well as the then-customary swiveling front windwings. Storage was possible in a shallow trunk, a shelf behind the seats and a locking glove compartment. The fuel tank held 57 liters (15 gallons) of gasoline.

Mazda had created a quick little car. The company claimed a top speed of 185 km/h (115 mph) and a standing-start quarter-mile time of 16.4 seconds for the L10A Cosmo. The Japanese magazine *Motor Fan*, which runs the most comprehensive road tests in the country, reported this performance data in its August 1967 issue:

An L10A on the dynamometer

Standing-start acceleration through the gears:

0–50 km/h (31 mph)	2.5 sec
0–80 km/h (50 mph)	5.8
0–100 km/h (62 mph)	8.8
0–140 km/h (87 mph)	18.0
0–400 m (1/4 mi)	16.3

Top speed (measured on Mazda's high-speed track at Miyoshi) 200 km/h (124 mph)*

Fuel economy at steady speed:

50 km/h (31 mph)	33.8 mpg
80 km/h (50 mph)	28.4
100 km/h (62 mph)	24.1
120 km/h (75 mph)	20.0

*Mazda explained its 10-mph more conservative claim as a "guaranteed top speed," also safely attainable on the standard cross-ply rubber.

The L10A Cosmo Sport was priced at 1.48 million yen, about $4100 at the official exchange rate of $1 = 360 yen at the time; this was about $2800 less expensive than the exotic Toyota 2000GT. In the single year it was produced, ending in July 1968, 343 L10A Cosmos were built; after that the L10B model took over.

Cosmo production trickled at the rate of 20 to 30 cars per month

L10B has a larger grille opening than the L10A

Type L10B Cosmo Sport

THE IMPROVED L10B was released on July 13, 1968, and produced at a trickle of 20 cars a month until September 1972; 1176 units were built.

For the B, Mazda stretched the wheelbase 150 mm (5.9 in.) to 2350/92.5 but trimmed its overall length a bit to 4130/162.6. It had a larger, mesh front air intake, and 15-in. wheels with 155HR-15 radial tires.

Redesignated the 0813, the two-rotor engine got revised port timing to tweak it to 128 bhp at 7000 rpm and a maximum torque of 14.2 kg-m (103 lb-ft) at 5000 rpm. Even more welcome was the addition of an extra cog in the gearbox, an overdrive of 0.841:1. The brakes were now vacuum-assisted to relieve the driver of his or her Herculean efforts. And now the Cosmo Sport could be ordered with air conditioning. Naturally, performance was up; Mazda was now bold to claim a full 200 km/h (124 mph), and gave a quarter-mile time of 15.8 sec with two aboard. A few L10Bs were exported as the Mazda 110S Sport. The upgrading was accompanied by a price hike to 1.58 million yen (about $4390), from which the manufacturer would refund 5000 yen if the customer took delivery in Hiroshima.

L10B dashboard with grab handle: the layout remained unchanged

L10B interior with cloth-covered bucket seats

179

Cosmo Sport Specifications

GENERAL	L10A	L10B
Wheelbase, mm/in	2200/86.6	2350/92.5
Track, front, mm/in	1250/49.2	1260/49.6
Track, rear, mm/in	1240/48.8	1250/49.2
Overall length, mm/in	4140/163	4130/162.6
Overall width, mm/in	1595/62.8	1595/62.8
Overall height, mm/in	1165/45.9	1165/45.9
Curb weight, kg/lb	940/2072	990/2183
Weight distribution, front/rear %	50/50	
Fuel tank capacity, U.S. liters/gal	57/15	

ENGINE		
Type	0810	0813
Number of rotors	2	2
Single chamber capacity	491	491
Compression ratio	9.4:1	9.4:1
Bhp @ rpm	110 @ 7000	128 @ 7000
Max. torque @ rpm, lb. ft.	96 @ 3500	103 @ 5000
Induction system	Zenith Stromberg 4-barrel carb.	

DRIVE TRAIN		
Transmission type	manual 4-speed	manual 5-speed
Clutch	single dry plate diaphragm spring	
Gearbox ratios I	3.379	3.379
II	2.077	2.077
III	1.390	1.390
IV	1.000	1.000
V	—	0.841
rev	3.389	3.389
Final drive ratio	4.111	4.111

CHASSIS AND BODY		
Layout	front engine, rear wheel drive	
Body/frame	unitary welded steel body	
Suspension, front	independent, double wishbones, coil springs, tubular shock absorbers, anti-roll bar	
Suspension, rear	de Dion axle, semi-elliptic leaf springs, trailing radius links, tubular shock absorbers (half shafts incorporating ball splines)	
Steering	rack and pinion, unassisted ratio 16.6:1	
Brakes, type	front disc, rear drum brakes	
brake servo	not available	vacuum
Wheels and tires	pressed steel wheels	
	6.45-14	155HR15
	(165SR14 opt.)	

R16A (1965 four-rotor prototype)

THE R16A WAS a one-off built to test the early four-rotor engine, one of a family of experimental engines with a single chamber displacement of 400 cc, peripheral intake ports and dry-sump lubrication. There were also one-, two- and three-rotor versions; Mazda set targets of 160 bhp at 6000 rpm and a 7000-rpm maximum engine speed for the four-rotor unit.

Rotary-engine research chief Kenichi Yamamoto would not have been content to have

An R16A image sketch depicting a racing two-seater

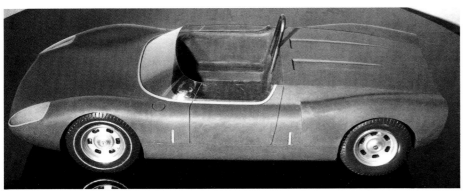

The open 2-seater as a 1/5 clay model. The "legal" size license plate shows the locality (Hiroshima) and the year the car was to make its debut

his new pride and joy tested merely in the engineering laboratories. So he asked Masataka Matsui, then head of the Layout and Styling Department (and now the Senior Managing Director responsible for Mazda's recently established Technical Center) to provide a car suitable for on-track evaluations. Matsui obliged by assigning a team of three young designers, headed by Makoto Kinutani, to the project. Two body styles were proposed—an open two-seat racing car and a closed coupe—and 1/5-scale clay models of both were made in May 1964. Because it was easier to build, the open version was chosen for the prototype. The R16A (400 cc × 4 rotors = 1600 cc = 16) made its debut at the opening of Mazda's new Miyoshi proving ground in June 1965, leading a pack of L402A (Cosmo) prototype cars on the high-speed track.

The sole R16A in Mazda's experimental shop. Its low height is accentuated by a production mini pickup

Cast magnesium wheels with knock-off hubs were intended, but pressed steel bolt-on ones had to do. Smooth flow of the front end is reminiscent of the Porsche 904 GTS

Spartan cockpit of the R16A, with a whippy long shift lever for the Lancia transaxle

Essential instrumentation includes a 12000-rpm electric tachometer, showing more than five thou' over the four-rotor's attainable limit

Although the car's design closely followed regulations for two-seater racing cars of the time, Mazda had no illusions about racing it. Instead, it was built on a shoestring budget as a running test bed, using as many available production components as possible. The Miyoshi run was its sole semi-public appearance. Riding on a 2300 mm (90.6 in.) wheelbase, the R16A had a steel tubular space frame whose lower half was reinforced with bolted inner aluminum paneling and triangular stiffeners. Its lower outer body panels were of aluminum, upper ones of fiberglass.

The front suspension was racing-type upper and lower A-arms, fabricated from steel tubes and carrying a cast-iron hub carrier, with concentric coil springs and tubular shocks as well as an anti-roll bar. Rear suspension was pure racing too, locating the hub carrier with twin trailing links, a triangular lower A-arm and the driveshaft as an upper arm. There too, tube shocks were concentric with coil springs and an anti-roll bar was included.

Rack-and-pinion steering provided a quick 12:1 overall ratio. The brakes were discs all around, with Sumitomo-Dunlop Mk 31 calipers, 258 mm/10.2 in. front discs and 234/9.2 rear ones. The tires and wheels remind us of those days' modest sizes: Dunlop 5.50L-14 or Bridgestone 5.60-14 cross-ply racing rubber fore and aft on 5.5-in. wheels. The wheels were supposed to be of cast magnesium alloy with knock-off hubs, but a set of off-the-shelf bolt-on steel wheels had to do.

A lone R16A leading a pack of L402A Cosmo prototypes at the opening run on the Miyoshi Proving Ground's high-speed track, June 1965

In more scrounging, one of the company's test cars, a front-drive Lancia Flavia with a 1.8-liter flat-four engine, was cannibalized for its four-speed transaxle. The Lancia must have been a Zagato coupe, for that model's unique wrap-up rear quarter windows were repeated on the clay model for the coupe; at any rate, the gearbox was reinforced for its new task.

A more roadworthy coupe version of the R16A theme, featuring gullwing doors

Bird's-eye view of the R16A coupe, showing gullwing doors, wrap-up rear quarter windows and buttress rear quarter panels. Influence of the cannibalized Lancia Flavia Zagato is strong

Although the 16A did run at Miyoshi, Matsui doesn't recall its ever going full chat at 7000 rpm. He recalls suspecting that the built-up, Hirth-jointed eccentric shaft was warping at high rpm; this eventually discouraged the engine group from pursuing multi-rotor engines for years to come.

Following the R16A venture, Mazda's planners and designers entertained a number of mid- and rear-engine configurations for a "Cosmo MC" (model change). One of the drawings preserved at Mazda shows an "R15A" circa November 1968, intended to carry a twin-rotor engine in its rear overhang. Footnotes listed more cons than pros for the configuration. There is also an undated blueprint of a single-seat racing car with a midship three-rotor engine. An insider hints that an assault on Formula 2 racing may have been contemplated, perhaps with the optimistic view that a three-rotor engine with 491 cc per chamber might have been allowed under the formula's 1.6-liter production-block rules!

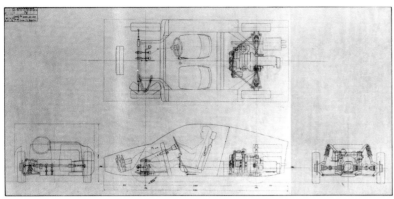

This engineering drawing of a midship road car powered by a twin-rotor engine was called Cosmo MC (model change) and dated September 10, 1968. The car has a semi-monocoque perimeter frame housing side fuel tanks

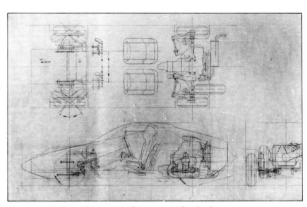

An undated engine-over-the-rear-axle design, with down-to-earth suspension by stamped A-arms at the front and semi-trailing arms at the rear

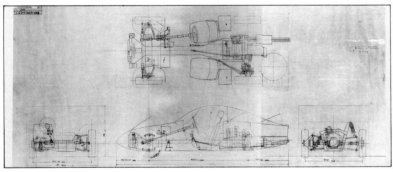

Another Cosmo MC midship proposal, on a spine frame with split tanks behind the seats. R16A-type suspension was contemplated

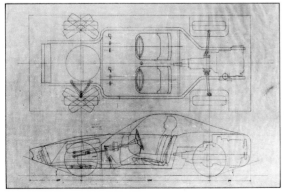

The R15A, circa November 1968, envisioned a twin-rotor engine mounted in the rear overhang

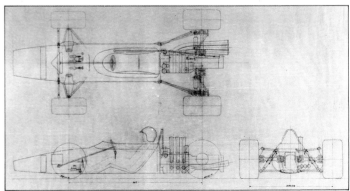

A monoposto powered by a three-rotor engine, supposedly aimed at Formula 2 racing

X810/RX500 (1970 Tokyo Show prototype)

DREAMS OF A midship engine wouldn't die at Mazda. A project coded X809 was begun in November 1968, evolved into X810 and finally became the mid-engine RX500 experimental car shown at the 1970 Tokyo Motor Show—which also commemorated the company's 50th anniversary.

The project's development proposal read like this:

"One car to be built and shown to the public as part of the 50th anniversary program. It is to demonstrate the company's wealth of technology and engineering, specifically:

1) Development of the plastic body.
2) High-performance rotary engines, two and three rotors.
3) Aerodynamic design.
4) Performance and stability at very high speeds.
5) Styling and layout befitting the rotary's image."

The RX500 on its first outing at Miyoshi. Its color scheme changed twice-subsequently, first to monotone lime green and then to two-tone blueish silver and charcoal gray

The RX500 was completed on July 17, 1970. At the homely viewing ground in the main factory premises, its bread-van rear end makes the car look heavy. Indeed, it was a heavy car for its type, scaling 850 kg (1874 lb)

Huge scoops on the rear flanks let ventilating air into the engine bay. The hood air duct has no grille at this stage

A more important purpose of Project X810 was to work toward a successor to the Cosmo 110S: the planners had a production car very much in mind. Alternative engine choices were listed:

Base model, RA engine	two-rotor, 500 cc × 2
Performance version, RS	two-rotor, 650 cc × 2
High-performance version, 3RS	three-rotor, 500 cc × 3

With a completion target date of July 1970, Project X810 got under way. From the outset a midship engine was assumed, although it was understood that this would not necessarily be true of a future production model.

The X810 was Mazda's first serious attempt to design cars in a wind tunnel, in those days a modest 1/5-scale one in the main R&D complex.

Three clay models were sculpted: Type A with a high rear roof, Type B as a pronounced wedge and Type C with buttress rear quarter panels.

Type A recorded the best drag coefficient: 0.37, not sensational by today's standard. This was subsequently reduced to 0.31 for the final shape, which featured a long, smoothly tapered tail and served as the basis for the X810.

The hood air ducts are now fitted with grilles

Rear and rear-quarter visibility is not an RX500 strong point. The finned center section is a muffler. Exhaust is let out through the left pipe; the right pipe is dummy for symmetry

A bevy of happy designers and engineers around the RX500 on its first airing

The swing-up door is spring-loaded for easy opening. Ingress and egress through small and high opening are not easy, however

Interior is fully trimmed. The seam under the dashboard on left is a fresh-air inlet. Steering wheel is all-leather

Short lever shifts Mazda-designed four-speed gearbox. Behind it are AM/FM radio switch and tuning dials

Half-moon shaped instruments are grouped in a thin cluster

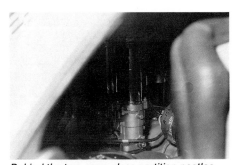

Behind the two-pane glass partition nestles a tweaked type 12A engine fitted with a two-barrel Nikki Weber carburetor. The original engineering drawing specifies, "If a three-rotor is to be fitted, a new rear end must be designed," so it must have been a tight fit

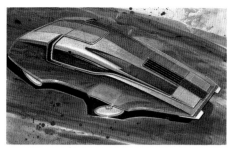
Mazda artist's impression of Project X810

Image sketches that led to the RX500

Three aerodynamic shapes proposed for X810, in 1/5-scale wind-tunnel models

The Type B "wedge" on the left has a drag coefficient value of $C_D = 0.410$. At center, Type A has the lowest value, $C_D = 0.370$, as well as the lowest lift of three. Type C, with vertical stablizer-like buttresses, has a C_D of 0.434

The Type A with smoothened and stretched rear end and smaller air-intake area improves to a C_D of 0.314. The shape served as the basis for Project X810/RX500

To facilitate construction, the new car had a tubular steel space frame which, like that of the R16A, intruded into the cabin and hampered ingress and egress. Shotaro Kobayashi, Editor-in-Chief of *Car Graphic* magazine and the only outsider allowed in the driver's seat after the lone prototype's show appearance, suggested that a more space-efficient platform frame be considered. Indeed, Mazda's original proposal had considered a perimeter frame.

The body's lower outer panels were of fiberglass, the upper ones of ABS plastic. Mazda engineers took the rotary engine's high running temperatures seriously and allowed ample space around it for heat dissipation—the explanation for the RX500's bread-van rear end. The body engineers also wanted the car to feel solid, so they made the outer panels thicker than was absolutely necessary and thus added considerable weight. Upward-opening doors lent extra character to the body; access to the powerplant was through two gullwing-style hatches.

Front suspension was by straight upper and lower links, each located longitudinally by a trailing radius link. The coil springs wrapped around Kayaba adjustable racing shocks. At the rear, racing-type four-link suspension with coil springs and adjustable shocks completed the picture. Brakes were ventilated discs all around, 277 mm/10.5 in. in diameter at the front and 279/11.0 at the rear. An elaborate warning system was included to detect any malfunction of the dual hydraulic circuits and a vacuum booster lightened pedal efforts; steering was by unasissted rack and pinion. The wheels were of die-cast aluminum, with 8-in. front and 9-in. rear rims carrying Bridgestone RA200 racing tires in 5.10/9.50–15 and 5.50/10.80–15 sizes.

The original plan was to fit the X810 with a tuned version of the 10A engine used in the R100 coupe. But the RX500 that evolved from the project was powered by an over-the-counter racing conversion of the bigger 12A, with two chambers of 573 cc fed by a Nikki two-barrel carburetor. Mazda made a transaxle specifically for the car and quoted these maximum speeds in its four ratios: first 80 km/h (50 mph); second 120 (75); third 200 (124); fourth 250 (155).

A 1/2-scale model of the RX500

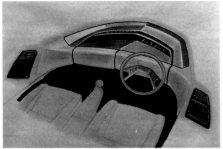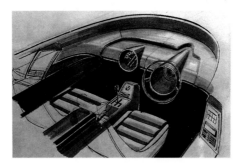

Examples of interior-design image sketches,
all showing wraparound dashboard trims

Mazda designers at work on RX500
development. Head of the Layout and Design
Division Masataka Matsui and designer
Uchida, both standing, appraise interior theme
sketches, while designer Matasaburo Maeda
(now Mazda's design chief) ponders in the
foreground

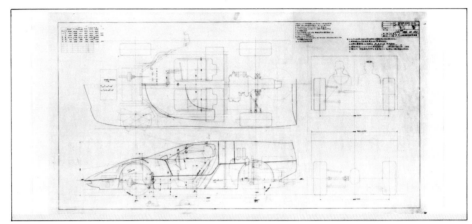

X810 engineering layout, circa March 1969

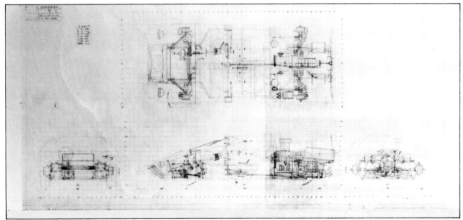

Final engineering drawing of February 1970

The final engineering drawing showed these dimensions:

Wheelbase, mm/in.	2450/96.5
Length	4330/170.5
Width	1720/67.7
Height	1065/41.9
Track, front & rear	1400/55.1
Fuel capacity, liters/gal.	100/26.4
Weight distribution, f/r, %	50/50

Editor Kobayashi recalls his impressions:
"The cockpit was cramped for a GT of this size, particularly the minimal head room.
I could not stretch my legs freely either. Breathing deeply and trying to calm myself
under the unnerving anxious gaze from the spectators—including Director Matsui and
his design and engineering staff—I pushed in the deep clutch, engaged first gear,

RX500 in the latest livery

With all four wings open

revved the engine to about 5000 rpm, and eased up my left foot. Unexpectedly, the car moved off smoothly, just like an ordinary family car."

"The tuned RX-2 engine right behind my ears was quieter than that of any mid-engine GTs I had driven to date (Lotus Europa, Porsche 914 and 914/6, a Matra and Isuzu's experimental MX1600). And it was surprisingly flexible at lower speeds, although obviously lacking the production engine's refinement below 4000 rpm."

"Having traversed the designated course in the factory compound twice at a leisurely pace, I now accelerated to 75 mph using first and second gears. The engine revved freely, and at 6000 rpm it suddenly began delivering real punch. And what a smooth engine!"

"High-speed stability was outstanding (the remark refers to the suspension's work, as the car's aerodynamics are unknown as yet). Give the steering a light input and it responded sharply, and yet for a car wearing wide racing tires (Bridgestone), the steering was exceptionally light. Even more unexpected was a lack of kickback from surface irregularities, something you usually get from suspension with solid metal joints. The ride was firm but still acceptably comfortable, more like that of an exotic and heavy GT. The body's stiffness also felt on a par with that of a passenger car. Let loose, I could have driven it back to Tokyo—that was how practical this car felt.

The four-wheel disc brakes provided exceptionally powerful retardation and were well balanced as well as light at the pedal. They were like a powerful, invisible arm grabbing the car from behind. My only complaint was the gearshift, which was very stiff and uncertain; perhaps the clutch was sticking."

RS-X to X020A

WHILE THE X810/RX500 project was well on its way to producing a one-off experimental show car, Mazda's management and planners were aware that it could not be put on the assembly line, even at a very small volume. Thus Executive Vice President Kohei Matsuda, the President's son, issued a directive to further develop the X810 theme along these lines:

1) Monthly production of 300 cars
2) Carve a niche in the American sports-car market
3) Meet all safety and emission regulations
4) Meet a price target of $5800–$7000 in America

The project in this form was begun in late 1969 under the code X810-II and renamed RS-X early the following year. Its planners had in mind utilizing existing Mazda components, such as 10A and 12A engines from the volume-production R100 and RX-2 models, unequal-length A-arm front suspension from the Mazda 1000/1200 small pickup, semi-trailing-arm independent rear suspension from the Bongo rear-engine van, the Cosmo 110S's final drive unit, and so forth. The X810-II car would be on a 2400-mm (94.5-in.) wheelbase, have tracks of 1350–1400 mm and ride on smallish 13-in. wheels.

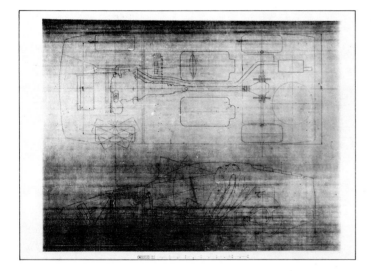

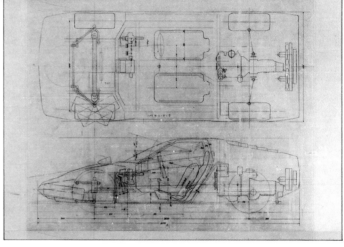

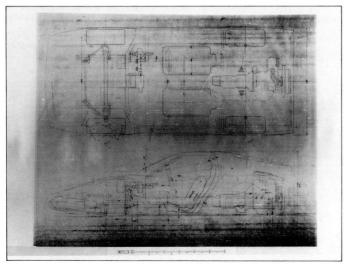

Three power-unit configurations in the same shell. Simplified comparative drawings are included in Uchiyama's presentation to the management to emphasize the front midship advantage afforded by the compact rotary

Project planner Akio Uchiyama, who would later head the two RX-7 projects, prepared his case well for presentation to VP Matsuda Junior. He cited the pros and cons of two basic layouts the X810-II (temporarily called RS-100 in his presentation) could take: a mid-engine grand tourer developed from the RX500 and a conventional front-engine/rear-drive sports car. Uchiyama emphasized how the rotary engine's compactness would allow its installation in a "front midship" position (behind the wheel centers) for favorable weight distribution and vehicle dynamics. A true midship car would have entailed heavy investment in tooling for a new drivetrain and driven up the car's price.

The front-engine/rear-drive layout would allow liberal use of existing components. Uchiyama's concept included several such concessions in the X810-II's specifications: Rear suspension would be a live axle located by five links, borrowed directly from the RX-2, and the steering gear would come from the same source. On the other hand, he included the idea of an optional high-performance engine, coded X706RAC and producing 238 bhp at 8500 rpm!

Other engine options mentioned were a 12A-based M122B RSS rated at 130 bhp at 7000 rpm, and an M122B EMS (presumably short for "emissions") with 102 at 6500. The same paper gave the car's base weight as 1100 kg (2420 lb). With the RSS engine, the car was projected to accelerate from 0 to 100 km/h (62 mph) in under 8 seconds and cover the standing quarter-mile in 15.8 sec.; with EMS power the figures would be 9.3 and 16.7 sec..

Uchiyama was encouraged by a survey of owners of Datsun's 1600 and 2000 roadsters (pre-Z models) published by the American magazine *Road & Track* in

Road & Track's owner survey of Datsun's 1600 and 2000 roadsters led to Mazda's own entry-level sports car projects

February 1970. Having asked why these owners had bought a Datsun, the magazine concluded, "Obviously anyone who buys one of these roadsters is in the market for a sports car. But why a Datsun in preference to the traditional names like MG, Triumph or Austin-Healey? Clearly the main reason is value for money." The report continued, "Next on the list of reasons for purchase came performance or engine, mentioned by 51 percent of the owners … Furthermore, 48 percent of the 2000 owners were influenced by its standard five-speed gearbox."

Uchiyama concluded from the R&T survey that it was not brand loyalty or image that would sell an entry-level sports car. The American buyer would decide on the basis of price, value and performance; this was why Datsun, a latecomer to the American sports-car scene, was able to penetrate the segment. He believed that Mazda, altogether a latecomer to the American market, could also carve a niche: with a high-performing, stylish and yet inexpensive sports car fully utilizing the rotary engine's size and performance virtues.

In October 1969 Nissan launched the Datsun 240Z in America. Offering brisk performance from its 150-bhp inline six-cylinder engine and priced at an extremely competitive $3500, it took the American sports-car market by storm. Witnessing its

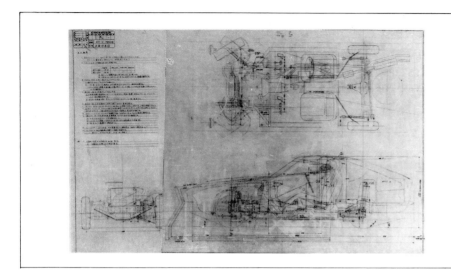

The RS-X project derived from X810-II, as presented by product planner Uchiyama. He suggested heavy borrowing of existing components. The base version was to have the RX-2's link-located live axle and a choice of Types 10A and 12A engines

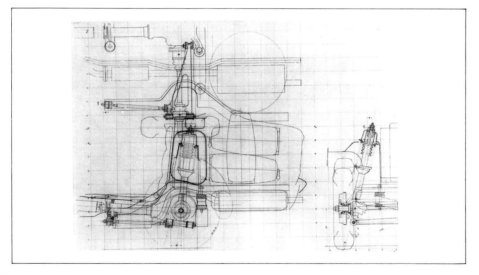

For the upper-model RS-X, a Chapman-strut independent rear suspension was specified

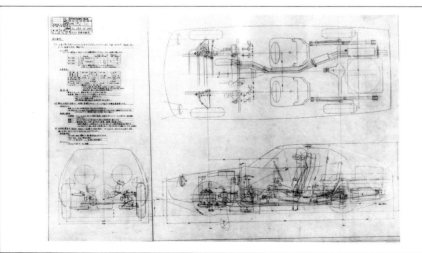

This X020 Z50 had a live rear axle on semi-elliptic leaf springs. Three performance levels were suggested: RS-100 (10A engine), RS-120 (12A side-port and peripheral-port), and RS-130 (13B). The upper models were again to have i.r.s. This drawing is dated November 1970

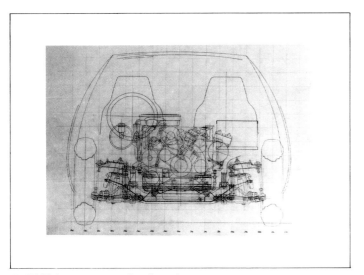

An X020 front cross-section, featuring
unequal-length A-arm suspension borrowed
from Mazda's small pickup

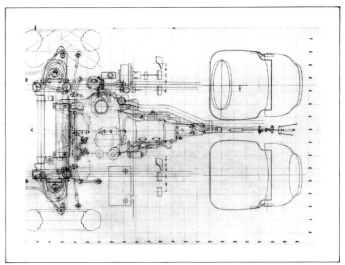

X020 has its two-rotor engine behind the front
axle

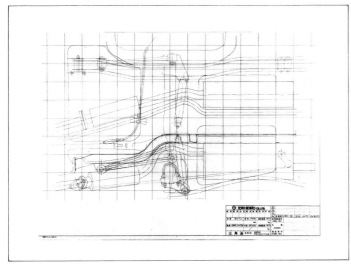

A simple live axle on a pair of semi-elliptic
springs was checked by upper torque rods on
X020Z

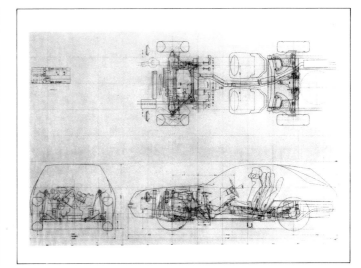

X020A, circa November 1971, suggested three
body contours. Front suspension was now
MacPherson-strut type, and semi-trailing arms
was used at the rear

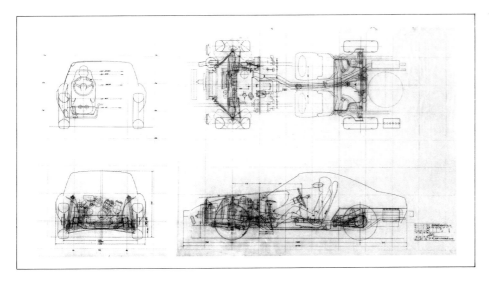

Another X020A plan, with semi-trailing-arm
rear suspension

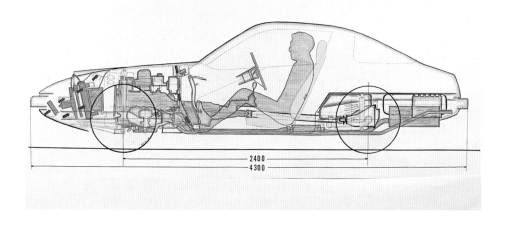

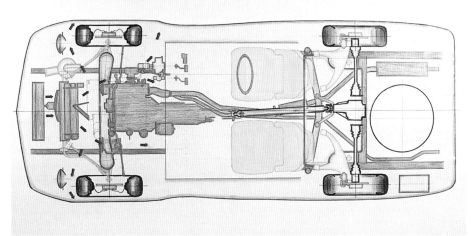

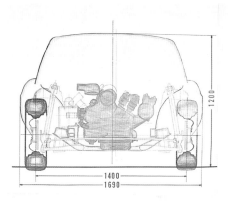

X020A layout with i.r.s.

$X020Z$

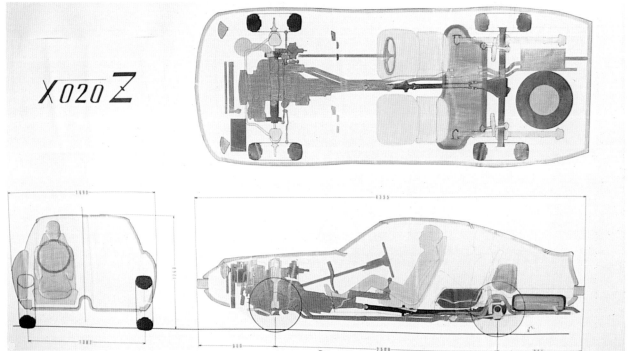

Base X020Z, with live-axle rear suspension

194

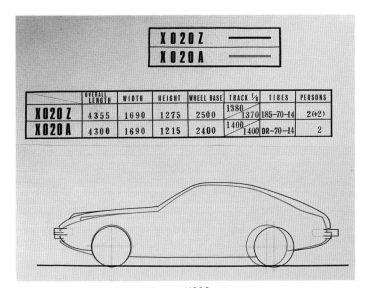

	OVERALL LENGTH	WIDTH	HEIGHT	WHEEL BASE	TRACK F/R	TIRES	PERSONS
X020Z	4355	1690	1275	2500	1380 / 1370	185-70-14	2(+2)
X020A	4300	1690	1215	2400	1400 / 1400	DR-70-14	2

	OVERALL LENGTH	WIDTH	HEIGHT	WHEEL BASE	TRACK F/R	TIRES	PERSONS
X020A	4300	1690	1215	2400	1400 / 1400	DR70-14	2
240Z	4140	1630	1285	2305	1355 / 1345	175 SR-14	2

Dimensional comparison of the two X020 types

Dimensional comparison between the X020A and the Datsun 240Z

success, Mazda changed the course of the RS-X; Uchiyama submitted another extensive report titled Project X020 on August 24, 1970. He now described the planned model as "a competitively priced sports car for the masses."
It would offer three engine options and two chassis:

	RS-100E	RS-122E	RS-122S
Engine	10A	12A	12A
Bhp @ rpm	82/6500	97/6500	170/8000
Top speed, km/h / mph	190/118	200/124	235/146
0-1/4 mile, sec	17	16.4	14
Curb weight, kg/lb	927/2039	940/2068	950/2090
Wheelbase, mm/in		2500/98.4	
Track, front		1400/55.1	
Track, rear		1360/53.5	
Length		4250/167.3	
Width		1680/66.1	
Height		1235/48.6	

Independent rear suspension would be standard, but a price-leader version would have a live axle.
October 1970 saw another change in the X020, which was now planned as both a low-cost two-seater and a 2 + 2. Two prototypes were foreseen: one with a live axle from the X908 sedan (to become the RX-4), the other with an independent rear end for comparative handling studies. For production, however, the decision was already in favor of the live axle. This became Project X020A.
None of these projects, from X810-II through the RS-X to the X020A, ever got even to the clay-model stage.

X020's target performance was compared to some of rivals (data on other makes from Road & Track road tests).

195

Front-end proposals by sketches. The X020G was to have 240Z-like fixed headlamps

Soft urethane-covered front end is contemplated in this profile study

Alternative designs with separate bumper pieces

Tail-end proposal

Z-like front end of the alternative design. Width is over 70 inches

X020G—rotary behemoth

A DERIVATIVE OF the X020 was considered as a concept car to be shown at the 1971 Tokyo Motor Show. The American Department of Transportation was very concerned over safety. European and Japanese government agencies as well as several major industry members likewise expressed concern, willingly or otherwise, so it was prime show time for a number of experimental safety vehicles, widely referred to as ESV at the time.

Thus the Tokyo Show X020 became more of an ESV than a sports-car prototype. A hideous-looking clay model was built; President Kohei Matsuda, succeeding father Tsuneji after his death in November 1970, decided to shelve the show project and concentrate his engineering resources on a lower-price (target $3000) 2 + 2 for the American market that subsequently became the X020A.

Project X020 took another sharp turn, this time upward, in early 1972. Mazda now set its sights on challenging the world's premium GTs and sports cars, the likes of Corvette, Porsche 911 and Jaguar E-Type, with a new big rotary sports, code-named X020G and targeted exclusively at America. The planners and designers threw their inbred caution and reserve about size to the winds: with its width of over 1800 mm (70 in.), the X020G would not qualify for Japan's small-car tax break. It would be a sizeable 4360 mm/171.6 in. long and scale a hefty 1350 kg/2979 lb—still 300+ lb lighter than its chief competitors, though, thanks to the rotary engine.

The suspension would be all-independent, by unequal-length A-arms at the front and semi-trailing arms at the rear. Mazda's performance goals were ambitious: 0–60 mph in under 7 sec., the standing quarter-mile in 14.8 sec. and a top speed of 220 km/h/137 mph. The project got under way in February 1972 and quickly progressed to exterior design sketches, then full-size clay models, mechanical layout

Massive integrated front end, as expressed in full size clay

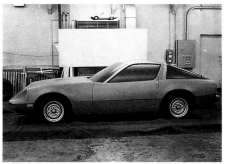

The profile is clean and pleasant

Inverted L-shaped tail lamp clusters

X020G was intended for the American market, so it would have to clear the standards of the Clean Air Act. A huge cast-iron thermal reactor is included on the 15A engine

Corvette-competitor from Hiroshima

Different tail-end treatment and three-piece rear glass area

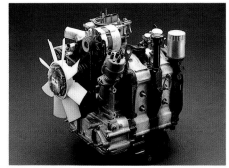

Sleeping giant of an engine: the Type 21A in a corner of Mazda's Engine Development Division storage room

and finally preparation for building a prototype.

The Rotary Engine Research Division built a number of potent two-rotor prototype engines for the project. Besides those based on production units there was a Type 15A, with its trochoid housing widened to 90 mm for a single chamber capacity of 750 cc; it was targeted to produce 135 bhp at 5750 rpm.

A real monstrosity was the Type 21A, with entirely new trochoid dimensions and a chamber displacement of no less than 1050 cc. It was to put out 180 bhp, and could be enlarged further to a 22A size with a target of 200 bhp. A 15A and a 21A were built and ran on the test bench, but neither ever went into the X020G car; it fell victim to the Great Oil Crisis of November 1973.

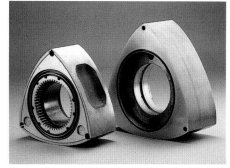

Comparison of a 21A rotor and one from a 13B engine

Sports specialties

X110

IN A mid-1971 lull between the RS-X/X020 and X020A, the styling group undertook another concept study. Called Project X110, it was to be a sporty specialty coupe—much along the lines of Toyota's Celica, which had been launched in late 1969 with immediate success. A similar product, the Mitsubishi Galant GTO, was introduced in Japan and Nissan was eyeing the segment with a coupe based on the 710 sedan: wearing the revived name Silvia, it would become the first 200SX in America.

The X110 got no further than a concept and styling exercise, but a number of sketches were done.

X110 sketches done by Hiroshi Zaima, a brilliant young designer who has since moved to Honda and styled such successes as the Civic and Integra

X110 ideas included an airy coupe and a sports wagon

X208A Cosmo RX-5, 1975–81

THE OIL crisis put an end to the Corvette-beating X020G, but Mazda still believed in significant marketing opportunities in both America and Japan for sporty specialty cars, such as the Ford Mustang, GM's H-specials (Chevrolet Monza et al) and the Toyota Celica.

X208A was a crash project directed by chief project engineer Yoshiou Mizobuchi (now in charge of quality control at Mazda), with Akio Uchiyama doing the basic chassis layout. Another familiar face was Yasuji Oda, who shaped the car's exterior.

Uchiyama and Oda would join forces again in the two RX-7 generations to come. The mechanicals and floor pan were straight from the X908 sedan (RX-4), which made the Cosmo RX-5 a rather big 2 + 2 coupe by Japanese standards: 4623 mm/182.0 in. long, 1676/62.0 wide and 1268 kg/2795 lb heavy in U.S. form. Senior Managing Director Masataka Matsui reminisces with a grimace, "Not the essense of space efficiency. There was an absolutely useless space about 4 in. deep between the pedals and the floorboard." The car did have some significant refinements, though; its live rear axle was better located by four links and a Panhard rod, and sprung by coils instead of the RX-4's semi-elliptic leaves. And it had both a five-speed gearbox and four-wheel disc brakes. Engine options included types of 12A and 13B rotaries, the former for the Japanese market only, with a thermal reactor for emission control.

Although the RX-5 was quite successful in its home country, it did poorly in the "primary market," the U.S. The consummately American-looking coupe simply disappeared into the scenery, doing little to bolster buyers' egos. Too, America still had a number of potent V-8 compacts, so its performance didn't stand out either.

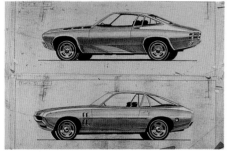

X208A image sketches. Predominant profile theme is the wind-down center window flanked by thin twin B-pillars

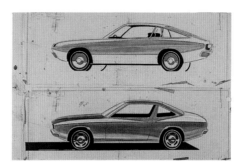

Final image sketch of the X208A, which was to revive the name of Cosmo

The very American Cosmo RX-5, with the Goodyear blimp and a couple of indigeneous competitors

Mizobuchi recalls that at $5800, it was overpriced to boot; and Mazda's skills at promoting specialty products in this highly competitive market were meager at best in those bleak days.

In its February 1976 road test, *Road & Track* magazine summed up the American enthusiast's reaction to this Japanese dazzlemobile: "We find the styling antiquated and unappealing. It's as though the top people at Toyo Kogyo, Mazda's parent company in Japan, are trying to design a car *they* think Americans will like rather than just building a car they like and selling it in America. Or maybe they like it." The editors' observation was not far from right: the Japanese indeed liked it. In the year after its introduction in October 1975, over 55,000 cars were sold in Japan, bringing in much-needed cash flow to the Hiroshima company's drained coffers. The great oil crunch's aftereffects, in fact, had brought Toyo Kogyo perilously close to annihilation.

Road & Track was not entirely unkind to the Cosmo. The magazine praised its road manners and reported lively performance; the detoxed and economy-tuned 13B engine accelerated the coupe from zero to 60 mph in 11.2 sec. and through the quarter-mile in 18.1 sec.. Mazda quoted EPA economy figures of 18 mpg in the city cycle, 29 on the highway for the five-speed version.

The X208A's failure in America was probably one of the major stimulants for renewed sports-car activity at Mazda, so its role wasn't a total loss. R&T concluded its test report this way; "We feel that the most salient point of the rotary engine is its smooth performance. A new Mazda sports car built to compete with the Porsche 914 and Fiat X1/9, with either a single or double rotor, would have been much more to our liking and would improve Mazda's fortunes in America much more than the Cosmo will..." President Kohei Matsuda and his staff took the criticism seriously, learned from the Cosmo debacle, and proceeded with Project X605—which would become the RX-7.

The X208A Cosmo in its 1976 guise, with blackwall tires

Innards of the X208A Cosmo, a thoroughly conventional chassis with major components from the RX-4. The drawing shows a Japanese version

P128 (1981–83) and P144 (1983–   )

THE X208A Cosmo RX-5 was replaced by the third-generation series P128 in September 1981. Curiously, the new car lacked rotary-engine options at its launch. Not that Department Five of the Engine Design Division had been idly standing by; in fact, it had been working overtime on further improving the 12A engine's fuel economy; a changed post-crisis world demanded that. The bigger 13B engine was temporarily shelved so that the department's resources could be concentrated on the smaller engine; once the 12A with the new 6PI (six-port induction system) was ready, it went into the aerodynamic coupe and the four-door sedan.

The P128 Cosmo was conceived and designed according to the same basic formula as its predecessor, sharing the mechanicals and floor pan of sister sedan project P938. It had two new features for rear-drive Mazdas: independent rear suspension by semi-trailing arms and rack-and-pinion steering. Mazda designers had also gone all-out on aerodynamics, achieving a drag coefficient of $C_D = 0.32$ with the Cosmo coupe.

In August 1982 a Turbo version was added. The 12A engine acquired a Hitachi turbocharger and electronic fuel injection, and for a while this Cosmo was Japan's fastest production car. A group of Japanese journalists took a stock example to the Japan Automobile Research Institute's high-speed banked track one summer day and ran it for 24 hours at an everage speed of 125 mph-plus.

In October 1983 the Cosmo got a fairly extensive facelift to become Type P144. Gone was the strange wind-down center window flanked by twin B-pillars; the big 13B engine was revived and fitted out with Mazda's new Dynamic Effect Intake System (DEI) as well as electronic fuel injection. The top 13B-powered model could be ordered with AAS, a system of automatically adjusting shock absorbers that checked dive, squat and roll by stiffening the shocks according to a computer program.

The 12A Turbo and 13B DEI engines first seen in the revised Cosmo later found their way into the existing RX-7's engine bay: the former for a Japanese performance model, the latter for the exclusive-to-America GSL-SE model.

The turbocharged and fuel-injected rotary engine of the Cosmo Rotary Turbo, which would eventually find its way into the incumbent RX-7

P128 Cosmo Rotary Turbo, circa August 1982: the fastest Japanese production car of its time

The Type 13B DEI engine was revived for the P144 Cosmo; it would soon power the American RX-7 GSL-SE

Revamped P144 Cosmo coupe. Wind-down center window is replaced by a thick B-pillar. The car may still be ordered with retractable headlamps

RX-7 revisited

X408 and X516: toward a sports car

AT THE 1978 press introduction of the X605 RX-7, President Yoshiki Yamasaki, who succeeded Kohei Matsuda to become the first person outside the Matsuda clan to head the Hiroshima company, observed that "The history of the sports-car market is a study in frustration and compromise."

That it was, but the sports-car market also had tremendous growth potential. To auto manufacturers throughout the world, the formula for success was only too obvious: a good measure of performance, respectable road manners, modern comfort and convenience features, and obvious sports-car clothing—all at a reasonable price. This is precisely what the Datsun 240Z offered. European marques plunged in too. The VW-Porsche consortium's mid-engine 914 made its debut about the same time and was technically sophisticated and ambitious. Fiat put the front-drive 128 powertrain behind the driver in the pretty little X1/9 and later followed it up with the larger X1/20, which became the Lancia Montecarlo/Scorpion. British Leyland developed a new two-seater, the Triumph TR-7, on the Triumph Dolomite sedan chassis. But none fared as well as the indomitable Z.

Not all the frustration was in the marketplace, either. A small group of enthusiastic designers and engineers at Mazda believed that the rotary engine's real forte was powering a sports car. Veteran Makoto Kinutani of the R16A prototype design team believed it so fervently that even in the dark days following the oil crisis he still harbored a desire to develop a rotary sports car.

Kinutani enlisted a young, talented chassis designer, Jiro Maebayashi (later responsible for the P747 layout and the **M** of the KM hub) to help him draw up plans for just such a car. At first, the project was not officially recognized and didn't even get a code number; later, in early 1974, the unauthorized project won recognition and became X408. It was "really an elementary study of configuration to get a low center of gravity and 50/50 weight distribution using RX-3 components," recalls Maebayashi,

A faction of enthusiastic marketers at Mazda Motors of America commissioned an artist to draw a rotary-powered sports car they would like to see in America. This "bait" photo was cleverly slipped to certain automotive writers

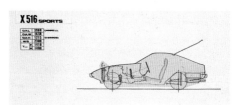

X516 was one half of the "dual" project from which a sedan and a sportscar were to be derived. Akio Uchiyama was assigned to do the sports car layout. This project led to X605, the RX-7; the sedan half of it, X517, to the X606, the original rear wheel drive 626

X408 SPORT (B)

O.A.L.	3990	(4190) U.S.A.
O.A.W.	1630	
O.A.H.	1215	(LOADED)
W.B.	2370	
Tread F	1410	
Tread R	1400	

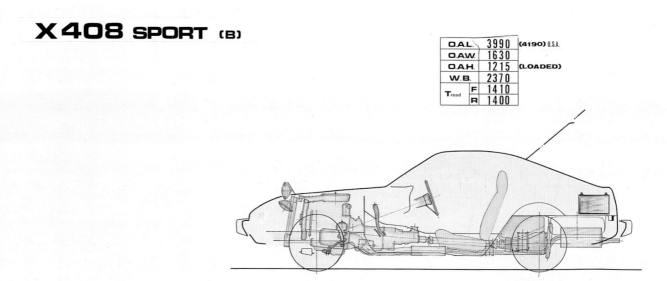

X408 was an unofficial project by veteran Makoto Kinutani and upcoming Jiro Maebayashi in their quest for a real and affordable sports car

"and a clumsy one at that—as you see from the battery's high location in the luggage compartment."

Mazda planners didn't think a sports-car project could stand on its own feet in the prevailing economic climate. Thus Project X516 came into being as half of a dual project. The X516 would be a sports car with a rotary engine. The other half would be

Project X517, to be done with a reciprocating engine; this was later to lead to Project X606, the rear-drive 626 series.

The X516 had a clever, cost-saving feature: it would share the same floor stampings as the X517. To obtain two wheelbases, the front suspension assembly was designed so that it could be turned 180 degrees. Facing one way, it would suit a sedan; the other way, a sports car with 5 in. less wheelbase. Two versions were foreseen: X516S and X516A, the latter an entry-level, volume-production model.

We Japanese do things differently. In the doldrums of post-oil-crisis economics, Mazda sent an army of its staff engineers and designers to distributors and dealers throughout Japan to help clear huge stocks of unsold cars. After his eight-month stint at a dealership, Akio Uchiyama returned to Hiroshima and was assigned to the X516 chassis layout.

During his dealership tenure in Tsu, not far from the Suzuka racing circuit, Uchiyama frequented this mecca for young enthusiasts. From his talks with spectators and amateur racers he got the impression that Mazda and the rotary engine were inseparable; that for better or worse (in those days, more of the latter), the ground lost by rotary-powered cars must be regained by a new one. A sports car.

Higher up in the company's hierarchy, another man discovered the same tenet: a different breed altogether, banker-turned-marketing-executive Sinpei Hanaoka. Appointed by Sumitomo Bank to Mazda's board of directors a year earlier, Hanaoka toured America in late 1975; upon his return, he flabbergasted the board by recommending that Mazda develop and launch—in America—a sports car powered by the rotary engine. This in spite of the fact that the rotary had been widely blamed for Mazda's woes in America!

Project X605: the RX-7 is born

PROJECT X605 replaced an unfinished X516 in summer 1976, but was given independent status with no connection to the X606 sedan.

Before documenting this all-important project and the car it produced, I want to give

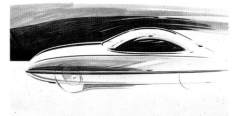

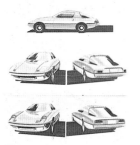

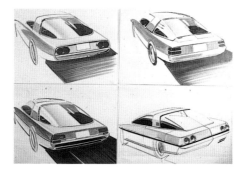

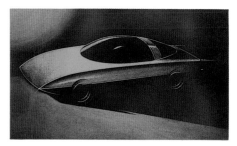

This model features a one-piece wraparound glass hatch. The drawing was translated into one of four 1/5 clay models

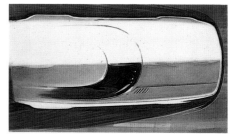

Front-end graphics reminiscent of the aborted X020G

Rear-end proposals

An airy light-aircraft-type canopy is the theme of these styling concept sketches

credit where it is due. The X605 was conceived, designed and developed under the engineering regime headed in person by former President Kohei Matsuda. Directly responsible for actual day-to-day activities was deputy chief of R&D Moriyuki Watanabe, now Chairman of the Board. Sumio Mochizuki was the Chief Project Engineer, assisted by Akio Uchiyama, who was also responsbile for the chassis layout. Heading the styling group was Matasaburo Maeda, aided by exterior designer Yasuji Oda.

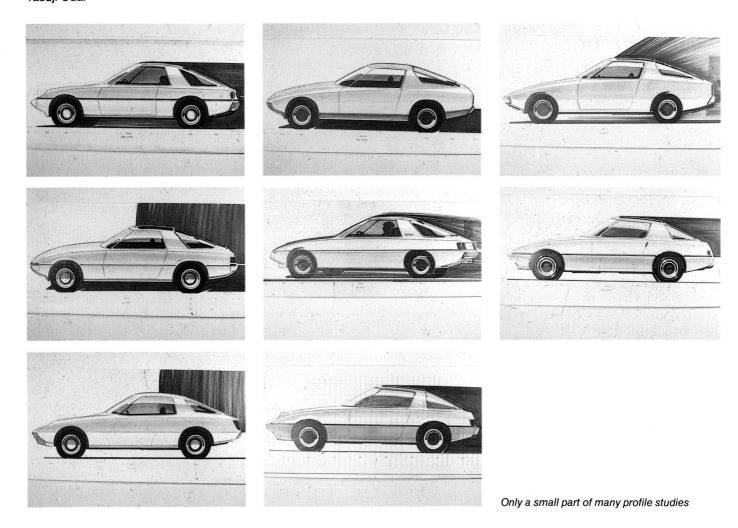

Only a small part of many profile studies

Interior design sketches

The alternatives were narrowed down to two candidates

Variations of front-end graphics. Retractable headlamps have been finalized at this stage

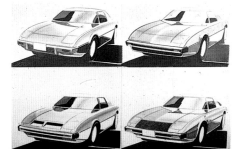

Lower center drawing shows a Targa proposal

Cockpit layouts

The planning and design teams aimed at creating a clean, functional, unostentatious sports car. Its shape might be described as a stereotype modern-classic sports car. Wisely, the Mazda men avoided the trap they had fallen into with the RX-5 Cosmo, this time avoiding gearing it too specifically to the tastes of a single market—or to what they thought were the tastes of that market. To borrow a line from Mazda of America, it was to be "a car of international flavor that would look equally at home in Stuttgart, Arkansas or Stuttgart, Germany."

Only two elements of X605's styling created any great controversy. One was the headlights, which on the early prototypes were fixed "frog eyes" in the manner of the original Austin-Healey Sprite. Abetted by the engineering group, the styling team

Four exterior design proposals in 1/5 clay. Second from right is an ambitious model with integrated soft front facia and single-piece wraparound glass hatch, features that would have to wait until the P747 RX-7

Winning design in full-size clay. Headlights are still fixed "frog-eyes," reminiscent of the original Austin-Heale Sprite

Final full-size clay model with retractable headlamps

Mockups of the winning interior design

doggedly insisted on retractable lights until finally Director Watanabe gave the nod. The other was that the designers wanted a single-piece wraparound rear window like the Porsche 924's; here cost and weight considerations prevailed and the three-piece solution was chosen. The more elegant single-piece window would have to wait until the P747 RX-7.

The first prototype was completed at the beginning of 1977; production started in March 1978. April 24, 1978 was the launch date in America. Here is how the first production RX-7 looked from an engineering standpoint:

Birth of the RX-7, Type X605

2 + 2 seating for the Japanese RX-7, with tartan checks

Production RX-7 interior

The powertrain

AN UPDATED version of the 12A two-rotor engine was chosen. The 1146-cc unit (2 × 573) produced 100 bhp SAE net at 6000 rpm and 105 lb-ft of torque at 4000 rpm on a 9.4:1 compression ratio, 5 bhp and 3 lb-ft more than the RX-3 engine.

This engine adhered to Mazda's established arrangement of two side intake ports and one peripheral exhaust port per chamber. Mixture was supplied by a compound four-barrel carburetor. To promote oxidation of pollutants despite leaner air-fuel mixtures, the exhaust system included a heat exchanger to warm secondary air injected into a thermal reactor. A number of modifications to housings, seals, rotors and ancillary equipment added up to considerable improvement in the engine's performance, fuel economy and reliability.

Four- and five-speed manual transmissions were offered; they shared their first through fourth gears (3.674, 2.217, 1.432 and 1.000:1) and the five-speed added an overdrive fifth of 0.825:1. Optionally available was a JATCO-designed and -produced three-speed automatic; the final drive ratio for both transmissions was 3.909:1.

Body and chassis

FOR THE American market the RX-7 was purely a two-seater; for the home market it was a 2 + 2 by virtue of elimination of a pair of heavy sheet-metal frame extensions needed to meet the American government's rear-end crash standard. The compact unit body-chassis had exceptional torsional rigidity: 6780 lb-ft per degree, a figure so good that it also became the target for the new P747.

MacPherson-strut front suspension was chosen, located by stamped lower lateral arms and trailing links and including a 23-mm (0.91-in.) anti-roll bar. The coil spring

Type 12A engine on the bench at wide-open throttle

Type 12A engine as installed in the X605 RX-7

X605 prototype in JARI's wind tunnel. The car attained a drag coefficient of $C_D = 0.36$

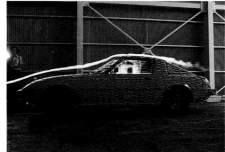

Airflow over the body top is being studied

was concentric to the strut and tapered at the bottom to bring the tire center and kingpin axis close. This small steering offset (38 mm/1.50 in.) helped minimize steering vibrations and stabilize handling and braking under certain conditions.

At the rear, a live axle was located fore and aft by four trailing links and laterally by a Watt linkage. This type of linkage had been used on the factory-sponsored RX-3 racers in Japan; Uchiyama and his chassis designers chose it over a Panhard rod because it gave a more favorable rear roll center. The linkage was located ahead of the rear axle, offset to the right of the final drive unit; this helped keep rear overhang short. (If a Panhard rod had been used, the RX-7 would have been some 3 in. longer.) Coil springs and gas-filled Kayaba shock absorbers were mounted separately at the rear, and an 18-mm/0.71-in. anti-roll bar was included.

Mazda designers and engineers were pragmatic about the RX-7's steering, brakes and wheel size, none of which was exactly *de rigueur* sports car stuff. Cost, space and time constraints had dictated recirculating-ball steering, drum rear brakes and 13-in. wheels, but the feeling at Mazda was that good end results would offset the humble means.

Steering rigidity was an area where detail changes from RX-3 components lent the new car a more sporting feel. The steering shaft's diameter was increased from the RX-3's 25.5 mm to 33 mm and the bearings relocated to increase rigidity. Typical rack-and-pinion steering would distort 7–16 deg when 1 kg-m (7.2 lb-ft) of torque is

President Kohei Matsuda had to be convinced of rectractable headlights' absolute reliability in adverse conditions. Lamp lids were frozen solid in the cold test room and pushed open by the activating motors

Heavily camouflaged prototype surrounded by development engineers while a yellow Porsche 924 flashes by. Deputy project chief Uchiyama looks on at right

Prototype car on a transcontinental jaunt in America

RX-7 at the press preview at Miyoshi's high-speed track

Mechanical layout of the X605 RX-7, showing how the rotary engine sits well aft of the front-wheel centerline

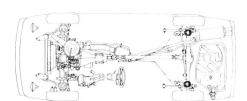

applied to the steering wheel; the RX-3 system would distort 19–33 deg. The changes brought this down to 15 deg, reasonably competitive with a rack-and-pinion system. Disc brakes of 226-mm/8.9-in. diameter were used at the front, 200 × 33-mm (7.9 × 1.3-in.) drums at the rear, with vacuum assist and front-rear hydraulic split. Tires were 165HR-13 for the base model, 185/70HR-13 for the GS, both on 13 × 5J steel wheels; 13 × 5.5J cast-aluminum wheels were offered optionally.

•Dimensions, weight and price
RIDING ON a 2420-mm (95.3-in.) wheelbase and front/rear tracks of 1420/1400 mm (55.9/55.1), the RX-7 measured 4285 mm long, 1650 mm wide and 1260 mm tall (168.7 × 65.0 × 49.6 in.). Curb weights given by Mazda were 1065 kg (2350 lb) for the base model, 1080 (2385) for the GS with five-speed gearbox.
The GS's American base price in 1978 was $6995, substantially less than either the Datsun 280Z ($8495) or the Porsche 924 ($11,995).

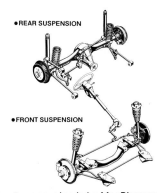
Front suspension is by MacPherson struts. The rear live axle is located by a set of trailing links and a racing-RX-3-inspired Watt linkage, which reduced rear overhang

Old and new: an L10A Cosmo Sport and an X605 RX-7 at the Hiroshima preview

The RX-7 was publicly launched with a gala event at the Mark Hopkins Hotel in San Francisco on April 24, 1978

Press test day at California's Sears Point Raceway

•Performance
WHEN *ROAD & TRACK* tested the RX-7 for its April 1978 issue, its performance figures matched Mazda's claims closely:

	Mazda	Road & Track
Acceleration to speeds, sec.:		
30 mph	2.8	3.0

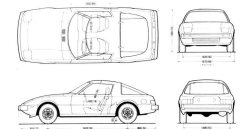
Outer dimensions of the X605 RX-7

40 mph	4.3	4.7
50 mph	6.3	6.7
60 mph	8.7	9.2
80 mph	16.0	15.8
0–1/4 mi, sec. @ mph	16.7 @ 82.0	17.0 @ 83.0
Stopping distance from 60 mph, ft	155	151
Lateral acceleration, g	0.80	0.78
Speed in 700-ft slaom, mph	59.1	59.3

Rear spoiler exerts downforce and improves the RX-7's high-speed stability

EPA fuel-economy estimates for the 49-state GS with five-speed transmission were 17 mpg city/28 mpg highway (by the more optimistic rating method used then); for the California version the figures were 16/29 mpg.

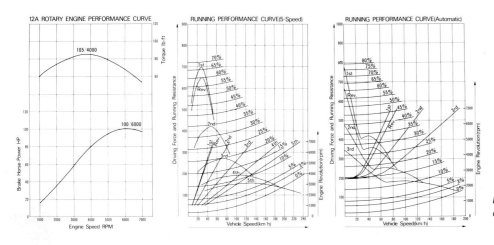

Performance data of the 12A engine and the car it powers

First improvements: P642 and P815 RX-7

THE FIRST production changes came in October 1979, when upgraded interior materials were phased in for the 1980 model year. This otherwise unchanged version was internally coded P642.

P815 (the P stands for "production") appeared in August 1980 with extensive styling changes. A new urethane-covered front bumper/airdam helped lower the drag coefficient to 0.34, equivalent to a gain of 5 horsepower, and reduce the front-end lift coefficient from 0.18 to 0.12. At the rear, the taillights and license plate were rearranged for a much cleaner look. Inside, leather seats were now optional on the upmarket RX-7 versions.

The 12A engine got a new emission-control system: a catalytic converter replaced the thermal reactor, enabling the twin-rotor engine to burn leaner air-fuel mixtures and thus improving fuel economy. For the 1982 five-speed model, the EPA mileage

P815 RX-7 (August 1980) with integrated front bumper-airdam.
The aerodynamic drag coefficient improved to 0.34 with the cleaned-up exterior introduced in August 1980

Mazda's styling director Matasaburo Maeda was pleased with Werner Bührer's styling analysis of the original X605, but blushed at the artist's criticism of "Baroque depression" on the rear end. One metal skin change he is determined to carry out on the P815 modification is to fill that depression (Road & Track)

Gone is the Baroque depression!

estimates were 21/30 mpg (49-state) and 20/30 (California), up very substantially from the original 1978 figures.

To tame the original RX-7's rear-end twitchiness, a thinner (16-mm) rear anti-roll bar was fitted; rear disc btakes were now used on the premium GSL model, and stickier Bridgestone RD204 radial tires replaced the earlier RD116s.

Interesting rotor-inspired aluminum wheel for the Japanese P815

A leather seat option was introduced on the P815 RX-7

More upgrades: P130 and P132 RX-7s

IN JULY 1982 an interim version appeared. Called the P130, it featured an improved lean-burn 12A engine that achieved still better fuel economy through detail refinements.

The interior received atention too. By then the RX-7's market price had hit $10,000 and more luxury-convenience equipment was in demand. A high-output audio system

Mazda dubbed Black Dynamite was offered: it proved its desirability within three hours of landing in America by disappearing from the car parked in Mazda Motors of America's lot.

American specification GSL RX-7

American RX-7 has an upgraded instrument panel

Leather seat option of the American RX-7

211

The final round of improvements came in October 1983 with the P132 series, a new higher-performance version called GSL-SE. Exclusively for the American market, it brought back the 1308-cc 13B engine last seen in the failed Cosmo, this time with the new Dynamic Effect Intake system, Six-Port Induction and electronic fuel injection. Fully 135 bhp (at 6000 rpm) and 133 lb-ft of torque (at a moderate 2750 rpm) were at the disposal of GSL-SE buyers.

Mazda's planners had wanted to introduce the turbocharged 12A version, but decided instead to offer it only in Japan, where factory services were available in the remotest corner of the country. The more conservative approach of boosting displacement would be a safer way to preserve the rotary's now excellent reputation for reliability in America.

The Japanese-market RX-7 Turbo was powered by a turbocharged, fuel-injected 12A, and introduced in 1983

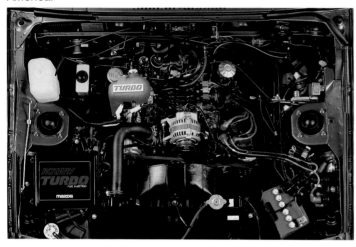

Turbocharged 12A engine as installed in the Japanese RX-7, rated at 165 bhp JIS at 6500 rpm (equivalent to about 135 bhp SAE net)

One omission from the Japanese RX-7 Turbo is the upgraded interior of the American GSL-SE

Power steering was offered in the P132 for the first time, and the chassis was modified in detail to handle the big engine's performance. Also new was an automatic transmission with overdive fourth gear. The GSL-SE got 14-in. wheels that could be shod with Pirelli's excellent P6 tires in size 205/60VR-14. Inside, a more luxurious interior featured a new instrument panel and improved controls. All this had its price: the 1984 GSL-SE listed at $15,095, a figure that moved it into a decidedly bigger league.

Road & Track tested the GSL-SE in a March 1984 comparison of six two-seaters and reported performance figures almost on a par with those of the much bigger-engined Nissan 300ZX:

0–30 mph	2.6 sec.
0–60 mph	8.5
0–80 mph	14.4
0–1/4 mi	16.4 sec. @ 84 mph
Top speed	126 mph

The first generation RX-7, from X605 through P132, saw an aggregate production of 474,565 cars (from 1978 through to the end of July 1985), of which 377,878—almost 80 percent—were exported to America.

Optional eight-position manually adjustable shockabsorbers on the P132 series

First Generation RX-7 Specifications

	X605 1978 (US GS)	P815 1982 (US GSL)	P132 1984 (US GSL-SE)	P132 1984 (Japan. Turbo Ltd.)
GENERAL				
Wheelbase, mm/in	2420/95.3	←	←	←
Track, front, mm/in	1420/55.9	←	←	←
Track, rear, mm/in	1400/55.1	←	←	←
Overall length, mm/in	4265/168	4320/170.1	←	←
Overall width, mm/in	1650/65.0	1670/65.7	←	←
Overall height, mm/in	1260/49.6	←	←	←
Curb weight, kg/lb	1080/2385	1066/2345	1200/2640	1035/2270
Fuel tank capacity, ltr/gal	55/14.5	←	←	←
ENGINE				
Type	12A	←	13B DEI	12A Turbo
Number of rotors, position	2 in tandem	←	←	←
Single chamber capacity, cc	573	←	654	573
Compression ratio	9.4:1	←	←	8.5:1
Max power SAE net @ rpm	100 @ 6000	←	135 @ 6000	165* @ 6500
Max torque lb ft SAE net @ rpm	105 @ 4000	←	133 @ 2750	166* @ 4000
Induction system	4-barrel compound carburetor		DEI EFI	EFI Turbocharged
Exhaust emission control system	Thermal reactor heat exchanger secondary air injection	Catalyst — ←	Catalyst — ←	Catalyst — ←

*JIS gross rating

	X605 1978 (US GS)	P815 1982 (US GSL)	P132 1984 (US GSL-SE)	P132 1984 (Japan. Turbo Ltd.)
DRIVE TRAIN				
Transmission type	manual 5-speed	←	←	←
Clutch	single dry plate, diaphgram spring, hydraulically operated			←
Gear box ratios I	3.674	←	3.622	←
II	2.217	←	2.186	←
III	1.432	←	1.419	←
IV	1.000	←	1.000	←
V	0.852	←	0.760	0.791
rev	3.542	←	3.493	←
Final drive ratio	3.909	←	4.080	3.909
Optional, automatic	3-speed	3-speed	4-speed	n/a
CHASSIS				
Front suspension	independent, MacPherson struts, concentric coil springs, tubular shock absorbers, lower lateral arms, trailing locating links, anti-roll bar			← 8-position adjust·shocks
Rear suspension	live axle, lower trailing links, upper torque rods, Watt linkage for lateral location, gas filled tubular shock absorbers, anti-roll bar			← ← 8-position adjust·shocks
Steering	recirculating ball	←	recirculating ball power assisted	← ←
Brakes, front	ventilated disc	←	←	←
Brakes, rear	drum	←	disc	←
Servo	yes	←	←	←
Wheels	13 × 5J	13 × 5.5J	14 × 5.5J	14 × 5.5J
Tires	185/70HR13	185/70HR13	205/60VR14	205/60HR14

MX-03 (1985 engineering concept car)

"IT'S ALMOST TOMORROW" would have been an appropriate slogan for the experimental MX-03 car, which made its first public appearance at the 1985 International Automobil-Ausstellung (Frankfurt Show) in September. A sister car was displayed at the biennial Tokyo Motor Show a month later.

"Almost," because the low "four-seat" (more of 2 + 2) coupe was no far-fetched show car laden with features that might or might not become reality sometime far down the road. Instead, it was a running prototype, and the design and development group headed by Chief Project Engineer Masaaki Watanabe intends to prove its performance potential as soon as it has completed the auto-show rounds.

Its concept is a Nineties grand tourer accommodating four people—two of them obviously only for shorter trips—and their luggage. The MX-03 includes several advanced features Mazda has been developing seriously, among them four-wheel drive, four-wheel steering, anti-skid braking and, most importantly, an advance version of the new three-rotor engine with many components of fine ceramics. The project began in July 1984 and was completed in just one year.

The MX-03 measures 4510 mm/177.6 in. long on a 2710-mm (106.7-in.) wheelbase; at 1800/70.7 it exceeds the usual Japanese small-car width limit by 4 in.. Its front and rear tracks are wide at 1540 and 1510 mm (60.6/59.4 in.), and it is a mere 1200 mm/47.2 in. high. Curb weight is given as 1150 kg/2535 lb.

Mazda's sleek MX-03, which the Hiroshima company describes "engineering concept car"

An in-house team headed by Yujiro Daikoku designed the conventional coupe body. A full-size plastic mockup of it has returned a drag coefficient of $C_D = 0.25$ in Mazda's Miyoshi wind tunnel; flush surfaces and an elaborate cooling system contributed to that low number, which incidentally has become the norm for Japanese experimental cars. The water and oil radiators are mounted on a slant in racing-car fashion, enclosed in a duct box and cooled by an electric fan; hot air is exhaled through hood louvers.

The chassis-body is a welded steel unit with outer panels of the same material except for the carbon-reinforced fiberglass trunklid-rear fender/wing panel. Its steel panels were hand-formed by Mazda's prototype artisans, whose superb craftmanship is a source of pride for chief designer Maeda. The fiberglass rear body piece opens wide to reveal a trunk slightly smaller than that of the current Cosmo coupe, still quite adequate in size as well as accessiblity. An alligator-style hood, rather like that of the

Upper rear fender, rear wing and trunk lid are integral and of carbon reinforced plastic material. Other outer panels are hand-formed sheet steel

Aerodynamic profile of the MX-03 that has a low drag coefficient of $C_D = 0.25$

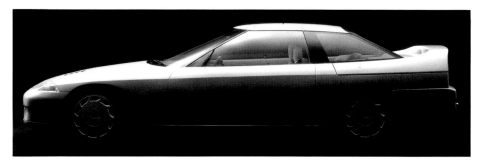

Sharply sloping nose with flush head and corner lamps

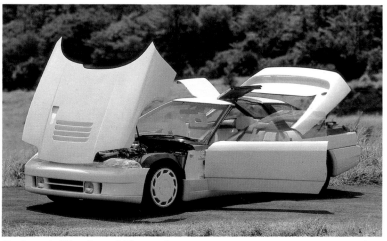

MX-03 rear end with integrated rear spoiler and dual exhaust pipes

Mazda pretends the MX-03 is a "four-seater"

Over-hood louvers let out cooling air and a NACA duct lets in air to the air-to-air intercooler

Roof panels tilt up to assist ingress/egress. They are also removable for a T-bar effect

old Jaguar E-Type, gives access to the power unit and has a NACA duct to an air-to-air intercooler for the turbocharged engine. Almost 58 in. in length, the doors open conventionally, but roof panels over them tilt up mechanically when they are opened to ease entry and egress—particularly to the rear seat. The panels are also removable for a T-bar effect.

The three-rotor engine is remarkably compact—actually smaller, outwardly, than the current 13B two-rotor. Thanks to this, it could be mounted deep and snug between the front-wheel centerline and the firewall. It retains the 13B's trochoid dimensions and thus displaces $3 \times 654 = 1962$ cc, but most of its components are newly designed and the very latest materials are used. For the MX-03, the engine is boosted by a twin-scroll Hitachi turbocharger, similar to that of the new RX-7 but having a ceramic (instead of metal) turbine.

On its 8.5:1 compression ratio and with the aid of electronic fuel injection, this impressive powerplant develops a (calculated) 320 bhp at 7000 rpm—a rating which, by the way, is quite realistic because the JIS (Japanese Industrial Standard) has been made more conservative.

If you simply multiplied the new RX-7 Turbo's power (182 bhp) by 1.5, you would come up with only 273 bhp. The additional 47 bhp will come from higher turbo boost, higher allowable rpm and the better thermal efficiency made possible by the ceramic turbocharger and aluminum rotors with ceramic combustion recesses. The maximum torque target quoted by Mazda engine people is 393 Nm (290 lb-ft), which seems realistic in view of the 13B Turbo's output. A top speed of 300 km/h (186 mph) should be possible for the slippery MX-03.

The ceramics are used for the trochoid chamber's sliding surfaces. A trochoid shaped ceramic core is pressure-fitted into a heat-expanded aluminum housing.

Rotors are of aluminum alloy, with cast-in ceramic combustion recesses similar in shape to those of the 13B Turbo's MDR (symmetrical medium deep recess). Apex and corner seals are also of fine ceramics.

The apex seals are in two pieces, as in the pre-P747 13B engine; this was dictated by the material choice. Also "old" in design are the solid corner seals (to the production 13B's spring seals) that keep the apex seals in place, but the leakage path in the apex-seal area is held to a minimum by the ceramics' small rate of heat expansion. The apex and corner seals are accommodated in the grooves of heat-resistant iron pieces cast into the rotor's apices.

The side seals sit in grooves cut directly into the aluminum rotor's sides—a less exotic measure allowed by the lower thermal and kinetic loads here. But because the ceramic engine runs hotter, various seal springs and sealing elements must have greater heat resistance: The gas-seal springs are of silicon-treated molybdenum alloy, probably the first such application of the material, and metal bellows O-rings are considered in the oil seals instead of the usual rubber ones.

The new ceramic material could readily be used for other important components in the rotary engine; for example, the side housings (cast-iron in the MX-03 engine) and side seals. Such components are being developed at Mazda, although the MX-03 engine does not includes them.

In the rotary engine, mixtures are always taken in at one side of the engine, then moved in the rotating combustion chamber to the other side, where combustion occurs. There are thus distinctive cold and hot zones of the engine. The ceramic housings have excellent heat-insulation capability, raising allowable limit of temperature difference between the extreme zones to almost three times that of all-aluminum housings. Coolant is still circulated in the trochoid and side housings for even cooling, and the rotors remain oil-cooled.

One remarkable feature of the ceramics is that they can be machined: port openings, sparkplug holes and seal grooves are machined into the inner core and housings. The exhaust port is also fitted with a heat-retaining ceramic insert—a natural application for the material.

Equivalent to a reciprocating piston engine's crankshaft, the eccentric shaft is a more complex built-up assembly. On Mazda's previous multi-rotor engines, toothed Hirth-type couplings (also called Curvic couplings) were used but were found lacking in torsional rigidity. In the new three-rotor engine, two-piece shafts are connected by a tapered coupling between chambers 1 and 2; a solution found to provide the

Phase I advanced three-rotor engine that powers the MX-03. It is a turbocharged intercooled DEI three-rotor unit that shares the internal dimensions of the production 13B. In this form, the engine still has cast iron side-housings. Phase II engine under development will have more ceramics and light alloy components

required shaft rigidity and yet be simple to manufacture. The eccentric shaft is supported by three main bearings.

The three-rotor could be described as a 2 + 1; chamber 1 (starting at the front) is built up with tension bolts that attach the front cover, trochoid housing and first intermediate housing. Separate tension bolts connect chambers 2 and 3 from the first intermediate housing rearward. This unique construction imposes less strain on the assembly as a whole, according to Mazda engineers.

A computer system manages the engine's fuel injection (Denso-Bosch L-Jetronic with twin injectors per rotor) and ignition timing.

The three-rotor also employs DEI (Dynamic Effect Intake), but relies on secondary pressure waves rather than the two-rotor's primary charge interference and resulting positive pressure pulses. The three-rotor has reverted to the the original two-side-intake-ports-per-chamber configuration, without positively controlled auxiliary power ports.

The dry-sump three-rotor measures 860 mm long, 670 mm wide and 500 mm tall (33.9 × 26.4 × 19.7 in.). Its short length was achieved by packing accessory drives tightly into the front engine cover, the low height by dry-sump lubrication.

A four-speed automatic transmission with lockup torque converter and partial electronic control, similar to a Mazda production unit, takes power to a central differential; here the torque split between front and rear wheels can be varied by hydraulic pressure to the multi-disc wet clutch. The rear final drive is equipped with a multi-disc limited-slip differential that can be manually disengaged.

Steering is by power-assisted and electronically controlled rack and pinion with vehicle-speed-sensitive variable *ratio*. An aircraft type steering "wheel" turns only 120 degrees to steer the car on all four wheels. The rear wheels are steered by servo-motor-actuated hydraulics, electronically controlled, giving a maximum wheel angle of 8-deg either direction. The four-wheel steering incorporates a fail-safe provision that mechanically locks the rear wheels in the straight-ahead position should it detect any system failure.

It seems that of the MX-03's engineering, only the suspension and brakes are conventional; but they are also first-class. Suspension is by unequal-length upper and lower arms at both ends, with longitudinal torsion bars at the front and coils at the rear, tubular shock absorbers and anti-roll bars. Brakes are ventilated discs with conventional vacuum assist and Bosch ABS (anti-skid brake system). Drive to either the front or rear wheels is also automatically cut off by the torque-split system (which adjusts the split ratio between 0/100 and 100/0, zero actually being "very close to zero") when ABS comes into play.

The accommodation is thoroughly conventional; no space-ship decor or gadgetry. Individual front seats slide and recline in the normal manner and have belt-in-seat restraints (no airbags, thank you). The rear seats are adequate in size for two adults but limited leg space precludes the car being a true four-seat as Mazda would like to call it. The seats are upholstered in homely beige cloth. Instrument displays are EL (electro-luminescent), with highly legible yellow lettering and green graphics against a black background; the panel lights up by crimson LCD (liquid crystal display) to give overrevving and failure warnings. The driver can choose between seeing the MX-03's speeds on a jet-fighter like "head-up" display on the lower windshield, or in the main instrument pod. Instrument readout selection switches as well as lighting control buttons are in the steering wheel center pad. The graphic display includes a circular tachometer and a four-wheel drive torque-split ratio indicator.

Steering wheel pad has lighting control buttons as well as switches for changing instrument displays. Speed (0 km/h) is shown in a head-up display on the lower windshield glass

Steering "wheel" turns only 120 degrees to steer the four wheels

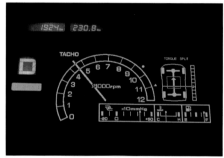

Torque split ratio of the four-wheel drive system is shown in graphic display

4

THE ROTARY PEOPLE

Mazda P747 RX-7 with the key designers and engineers responsible for its creation.
In the foreground with the car are : from left to right, Kenichi Yamamoto, President,
Takashi Kuroda, General Manager R&D, Michinori Yamanouchi, Deputy General Manager
R&D, and Akio Uchiyama, P747 Program Manager (see page 277 for other names)

Four men responsible for Mazda's Rotary movement. From left, Yasuo Tatsutomi, head of the Engine Design Division, President Yamamoto, Managing Director Takashi Kuroda, who had suceeded Yamamoto as the head of the then-Rotary Engine Research Division and now in charge of Mazda's R&D, and Hiroshi Ohzeki, manager of the Fifth Engine Design Department

Techno-romanticist

"I HAVE ALWAYS been a romanticist and I found my early romance in the wedding of the sea and the sky—the amphibious airplane," reminisces Kenichi Yamamoto, who was "Mr. Rotary" of Mazda for two decades until November 1984, when he was appointed President of the Hiroshima based company.

Yamamoto was born in September in the 11th year of the reign of Emperor Taisho, or 1922, in Kumamoto in the southern island of Kyushu. After graduating as a mechanical engineer from Imperial University (now Tokyo University) in 1944, he sought employment with Kawanishi Aircraft, a famed amphibian builder. This was during World War II; young Yamamoto, or for that matter, Kawanishi could not devote efforts and resources to that type of aircraft. Instead, he found himself assigned to the design office developing the landing gear of a non-amphibious naval fighter. Toward the end of the war, he was commissioned as a naval technical lieutenant and supervised the production of a special attack plane, daintily named Wild Orange Blossom—a deadly device for its pilot as well as for its target because it was designed with only enough fuel capacity for a one-way trip—and no landing gear.

Yamamoto's short aeronautical engineering career came to an abrupt end when Japan surrendered. Luckily, his home in Hiroshima was spared the devastation of the atom bomb, as was the Toyo Kogyo Kaisha (TKK), then a local manufacturer of three-wheel trucks and sundry machine tools. "I joined Toyo Kogyo not because I

The late Tsuneji Matsuda, third President of Mazda (then Toyo Kogyo). Matsuda's insight and determination in engineering excellence brought the Wankel rotary engine to Hiroshima

really wanted to," muses the President, "but because it was the only employer left in the city." Realizing that neither his diploma nor his naval commission would earn him a bowl of rice, Yamamoto had to take what was available at the factory: a line worker's job in a transmission plant. Day in and day out he toiled, assembling gearboxes and differential units for Mazda three-wheelers. Physically, it was hard work; mentally, the isolation was painful. He was surrounded by machinery, yet so far removed from engineering work.

One day he found a heap of engineering plans and blueprints piled on a corner desk of the plant chief's office. Young Yamamoto sought the chief's permission to examine and study the documents and was granted permission. Yamamoto studied the oil-stained papers, checking the tolerances and materials of the transmission he assembled. This went on for a year and a half before a senior engineer from the engine design department strolled into the transmission plant and noted this young worker diligently checking engineering plans. Yamamoto jumped at the casual offer of a job in the design department from the engineer.

Senior executive Tokinosuke Murao, in charge of Toyo Kogyo's engineering in the immediate postwar period, never hesitated in giving important tasks to young up-and-coming engineers, often much to the dismay of older hands. He was acutely aware of the urgent need for a new and more powerful engine for Mazda's bread-and-butter three-wheeler trucks, which were still powered by old-fashioned side-valve engines. Murao gave the assignment to 25-year-old Yamamoto, ordering him to design an overhead-valve engine, the first of its kind at Mazda. Yamamoto designed a new 1157-cc air-cooled 60-degree V-twin; the powerplant was installed in a brand-new chassis, the Type CT truck, which was introduced in 1950. It became an overnight success.

Kenichi Yamamoto was now firmly established in the engineering sanctum of Mazda. He was promoted to the post of Deputy Manager of the Engine and Vehicle Design Division in 1959 and undertook several important Mazda projects that launched the company as a passenger-car producer in Japan. One was Mazda's first production passenger car, the diminutive R360 two-seat coupe that weighed a mere 870 pounds and was powered by a rear mounted 356-cc aircooled V-twin. The R360 engine was noteworthy for its use of light alloys, including aluminum and magnesium components. The car, however, could best be described as a four-wheel motor scooter, and the late Tsuneji Matsuda, son of the founder of the company in whose honor Mazda automobiles were named, wanted to have real cars. Yamamoto's answer was the Carol 360, with a 358-cc water-cooled inline four-cylinder engine. Mr. Matsuda proudly proclaimed at the car's press preview, "Gentlemen, the car sounds like the real thing. Our song of joy!" It was followed by a more conventional vehicle, the Familia 800 van, a forerunner of the GLC and 323 cars.

The late Tokinosuke Murao, Executive Vice President of Toyo Kogyo, in charge of engineering, did not hesitate to give important assignments to younger engineers. He chose Kenichi Yamamoto to design a new overhead-valve V-twin for three-wheelers

Yamamoto's early masterpiece, an air-cooled ohv 1157-cc V-twin, circa 1950

President Tsuneji Matsuda at the launch of the company's first passenger car, the R360 coupe, in 1960. In the background is a bronze bust of the founder and his father, Jujiro Matsuda

Yamamoto was ready to embark on a project for a bigger car when President Matsuda summoned him to his office. It was toward the end of 1962 and Yamamoto's new assignment was to select staff and form an independent division to research and develop the Wankel rotary engine, on which Matsuda had concluded a licensing agreement with NSU-Wankel of West Germany. TKK's experimental department had already been testing a minivan with its prototype single-rotor engine. It was infamously noted for its fierce vibrations on deceleration and emissions of huge clouds of white smoke.

Even with the aid of 47 designers, engineers and metallurgists, Yamamoto's job was a difficult one. Yamamoto likens it to a railroad. "We had been running on the rails that had already been laid. During this tremendous growth period the company moved up the product ladder, from three-wheelers to four-wheel trucks, then on to passenger cars. There were plenty of good examples and precedents. We could easily follow them, chase them and try to overtake them." But the rotary had no equal in the world. Yamamoto's reaction to his new assignment was a mixture of apprehension and expectation. Prototype engines were running, but could they be made practical for automotive application? On the other hand, Yamamoto found the development of a brand-new powerplant an irresistible challenge.

When the decision was made to put the Wankel engine into production, Yamamoto's task took on an entirely different perspective. "Little did I realize the truth about this industry. For the first time in my career, I asked myself the fundamental question: 'Why had the automobile industry been almost totally devoid of technical revolutions?' There had been nothing like the transistor or the jet engine. The chilling answer was, you see, that this was structurally a very conservative industry. It had to be. Consider the vast investment in production facilities, supply industries, marketing organizations and service networks all geared to the automobile we had known for decades. They could not be changed overnight."

Now, Yamamoto was off the established and relatively smooth road, and had to lay new rails. And his railroad had to prosper. It was a momentous decision that could be made only by the owner-manager, not by a committee of executives and directors. Tsuneji Matsuda believed that only by superior engineering could his company remain independent at a time when industrial reorganization looked inevitable. Yamamoto was deeply moved by Matsuda's philosophy and pledged to fulfill his expectation of the Wankel rotary engine. "If I fail to meet my commitment to this great man, I told myself, I would not be man enough to face the world."

Light of the Orient

JUJIRO MATSUDA WAS born on August 6, 1875 in a small fishing village in the prefecture of Hiroshima. The 12th son of a poor fisherman, he lost his father when he was three years old, and had to work with his brothers on a fishing boat through his childhood. At the age of 13 Jujiro, always mechanically-minded, took a worker's job in a small blacksmith shop in Osaka, the second largest city in Japan and the country's western center of commerce and industry.

The hard-working and enterprising Matsuda opened his own metal-working business in 1894 in Osaka, employing some 50 workers. But the times, a recession after the Chino-Japanese war, were not on the side of the 20-year-old, and in one year the iron works had to be disbanded.

Matsuda returned to western Japan, where he sought employment in the country's burgeoning military-industrial complexes. At the age of 31, he came to Osaka again and opened his own machining and blacksmith shop in a converted cowshed. Small Tsuneji Matsuda, eldest son of Jujiro, helped his father by pumping air to the furnace. Jujiro's patented invention, the Matsuda-type pump, brought prosperity to the modest enterprise, which led to the formation of the Matsuda Pump Partnership Company. Jujiro was more of an engineer than a manager, and was delivered a severe blow when he had to part with his company in a takeover bid because of his lack of legal knowledge.

Undaunted, Jujiro reorganized the Matsuda Works in 1912 with a loan from five friends, and promptly landed a contract with the Czar's Government for four million pieces of artillery fuses. The Matsuda Works, employing some 4000 workers, successfully completed the order in one year's time, and it soon changed its name to the Japan Armament Manufacturing Company. Matsuda wanted to expand the company's production facilities, and recommended a site in his home prefecture, where land and labor forces could be readily acquired. But his co-directors were against his plan, and jointly opposed it. Nonetheless, Jujiro went ahead, concluded a contract for a land space, and left the company to establish the new Matsuda Works there, which was later absorbed by the steel maker Nihon Steel Manufacturing Company.

"I treaded on nothing but thorny and rocky paths. The paths were full of difficulties and agony. I walked straight. Hurting, breathing hard, sometimes blinded, I walked straight. What made me do it was "trust," trust in myself and others. My life is a life of trust; therein lies my profound gratitude," narrated Jujiro Matsuda in his autobiography, *Seventy Years of Factory Life.*

Mazda's first motorized and wheeled endeavor was this Toyo Kogyo motorcycle, circa 1930. A batch of 30 machines was actually produced and sold

Fagaceous Abemaki trees are indigenous to the mountainous terrains of the Chugoku region of Japan's main island. The tree's thick bark was an acceptable substitute for cork. A privately owned enterprise in Hiroshima which produced and marketed Abemaki cork was hit hard and facing imminent collapse after World War I, when importation of European cork was resumed. A group of Hiroshima investors and businessmen, headed by the chief of the principal bank involved, saw fit to save the failing venture, and transformed it into a publicly owned company. In January 1920, Toyo Cork Kogyo Company Limited was established. Toyo translates into Orient, and Kyogo means Industry.

Abortive try at passenger-car production: a 1940 prototype

Jujiro Matsuda was one of the founding members and became a director of the new company. Fifteen months later, President Kaizuka submitted his resignation for health reasons, and Jujiro Matsuda succeeded him.
Matsuda had never thought cork was a stable product and saw a definite limit to how far the company could grow with it, if it could grow at all. The engineer-entrepreneur in him saw the future of the company in producing more sophisticated industrial goods. In September 1927, the name of the company was changed to Toyo Kogyo Kaisha (Company), Limited.
The machinery division of Toyo Kogyo sought the patronage of the most powerful industrial complex in the western Japanese region, Imperial Japan's armed forces, who had a number of shipbuilding and armory installations. As a subcontractor of Nihon Seikosho (steel manufacturing works), Toyo Kogyo did machining work and supplied gauge tools to the military.
The military procurement was not very stable either, influenced as it was by budgetary expansion and contraction, political climates and international relations. Ups and downs were repeated with bewildering and unpredictable frequency. Again Jujiro Matsuda began searching for products that would support the company's planned growth. He found it in the automobile—to be precise, the small three-wheeler truck, Japan's motorized workhorse in the pre-WWII and immediate postwar periods.
There was a minor detour. Jujiro Matsuda could have turned his company into a potent competitor to Messrs. Honda and Suzuki, had his test production of motorcycles proved more lucrative. The company built and sold a batch of 30 machines under the brand name of Toyo Kogyo. One sample scored Mazda's first competition win in a Memorial Day race sponsored by the Fifth Army Division in 1930, defeating a British Ariel model.
Now, Toyo Kogyo's new motor vehicle must have one more wheel, and in the following year TKK began producing the Type DA tricycle. It was named **Mazda**, after **Ahura**

Mazda, the wise lord, supreme diety and creator of the world, the god of light in Zoroastrianism. The name of course rhymed very nicely with that of the incumbent President. D, by the way, stood for the differential with which the vehicle was fitted, and A for Number 1 in the series.

Toyo Kogyo attempted a premature entry into the passenger-car field with a prototype minicar in 1940, which had to be aborted.

The company was miraculously spared the devastation that descended onto Hiroshima on the fateful day of August 6, 1945 except for the shattered windows in its factories and offices, and was able to resume production after Japan's surrender.

Mazda's three-wheelers followed the familiar development route: ever bigger, more powerful and comfortable. The company showed its one-upmanship in the highly successful Type CT, introduced in 1950. The new model was powered by a brand-new air-cooled V-twin engine, displacing 1157 cc and producing a respectable 32 bhp; it was designed by the young Kenichi Yamamoto. Mazda's entry vehicle in the four-wheel field was based on CT mechanicals: the Type CA open-sided minitruck, whose styling reflected strong influence by the familiar four-wheel-drive vehicle used by the American Occupation Forces. The series was not a commercial success; only 100-odd vehicles were built in its four-year life span.

In December 1951, Jujiro Matsuda assumed the position of Chairman, and his son Tsuneji became the third President of Toyo Kogyo. Jujiro Matsuda passed away in March 1952 at the age of 77. The company was at the crest of its fortune then, and under the dynamic leadership of Tsuneji Matsuda it prospered further, moving up the product ladder—first to four-wheel trucks, and in May 1960 the first passenger car, the R360 two-seat coupe.

Rotarization

IN DECEMBER 1959, a West German manufacturer better known for its motorcycles shook the automotive world. NSU Werke Aktiengesellschaft of Neckarsulm, in cooperation with the Technical Development Laboratory (TES) of Felix Wankel at Lindau, had designed and developed a viable rotary engine. The official release mentioned that the well-known aircraft engine manufacturer Curtiss-Wright of Woodbridge, New Jersey, had already entered into a licensing agreement a year earlier, and was actively researching and developing the NSU-Wankel rotary engine, which certainly lent credence to the news.

President Tsuneji Matsuda (third from left), departs for Germany to conclude a tentative agreement with NSU Werke on development and production of the Wankel rotary engine, September 1960

As Executive Vice President, Kohei Matsuda led the first engineering delegation to Neckarsulm. Takashi Kuroda, who was to head the rotary-engine design group and is now in charge of Mazda's engineering, is seen in the group

Mazda delegation to Germany headed by Yamamoto (fourth from left) included engine designer Kuroda (extreme left, now head of Mazda's R&D)

Mazda was one of several Japanese manufacturers of automobiles, motorcycles, industrial powerplants and marine engines that were immediately attracted to this invention. The competition to join the NSU-Wankel licensee family was indeed fierce. Mazda was fortunate in having a compassionate visitor to its factory in Dr. Wilhelm Haas, the Federal Republic's Ambassador to Japan. The kindly ambassador expressed his gratitude for Mazda's hospitality and offered to reciprocate it. President Matsuda brought up the subject of Mazda's struggle among over 100 competitors (of which 34 were Japanese) for the coveted Wankel license. Two months later, in July 1960, Dr. Haas delivered good news from Neckarsulm: NSU was prepared to discuss an agreement. Matsuda promptly embarked on his first trip abroad. He concluded a tentative agreement with NSU and Wankel during his stay in Germany.

The agreement with NSU was subject to the Japanese Government's approval, which was granted in July 1961, upon which Mazda dispatched an engineering delegation headed by newly appointed Executive Vice President Kohei Matsuda (eldest son of President Matsuda) to Neckarsulm. Immediately upon the team's return, a Rotary Engine Development Committee was formed, drawing talents and resources from the Design, Material Research, Production Engineering, Manufacturing and Test Divisions. Executive Vice President Tokinosuke Murao, in charge of the company's engineering, directed the committee's activities and Yoshio Kohno, head of the Design Division, chaired it. An experimental single-rotor engine based on the design of NSU's KKM400 was built by the inter-departmental consortium, and tested on the bench as well as in a Mazda minivan.

In late 1962, deputy chief of the Design Division Kenichi Yamamoto was summoned to the office of President Matsuda to form an independent division for research and development of the Wankel rotary engine. Yamamoto had just returned from his visit to Neckarsulm in August, and knew numerous difficulties that had to be

Kohei Matsuda, son of the late Tsuneji Matsuda and fourth President. It was under his direction that the Project X605 RX-7 commenced. He was not able to launch the car

overcome before the rotary could become a practical automobile power unit. Little had he suspected that the task would be assigned to him.

In April 1963, the Rotary Engine Research Division was established, with 47 men forming four departments. The number, by the way, has a special connotation in the Japanese mind: the famous story of the 47 Samurais in feudal Japan who revenged their dishonored lord after years of hardship. Mazda's 47 Samurais were now fighting for their engineering honor.

The inner sanctum of the early Rotary Engine Research Division, with divisional chief Kenichi Yamamoto surrounded by senior engineers. From left, Masayuki Kirihara, Design; Shozo Karasuda, Research; Tadashi Kuroda, Design; Yamamoto and Kazuo Takada

The four departments in the division were:

Research, headed by Shozo Karasuda (a retired board member) with assistance from Ryuichi Nakao, now head of the Patent Division. They represented the new division as planners, negotiators and "diplomats."

Design, whose chief was Takashi Kuroda, who succeeded Yamamoto as the Divisional Manager in August 1973 and is now Managing Director in charge of Mazda's Research and Development. His staff engineers included Masayuki Kirihara, who was later dispatched to Neckarsulm as Mazda's resident liaison engineer. Later Kirihara established Mazda's West German marketing organization, the most successful among Japanese auto makers in Europe thereby earning the reputation of *gefährlicher Geschäftsmann*—"dangerous businessman" among his German colleagues. He now heads the Education and Training Division. Other members were Yasuo Tatsutomi, now in charge of the Engine Design Division and overseeing all engine-design activities; Tetsuo Fujiyama, today responsible for Mazda's racing activities; and "48th man" Hiroshi Ohzeki, now manager of the Fifth Engine Design Department. Ohzeki's deputy is Tomoh Tadokoro, one of a small "50th man" group.

Testing, was headed by Shoji Takada, now head of the Service Division. Under him were Dr. Takumi Muroki, theoretician and practitioner of rotary wizardry and now Senior Researcher at the newly established Technical Center; Masaru Mitsuyama, now serving as the head of the Engine Test Division; Yohji Tohyama, until recently Executive Vice President of MANA, Mazda's north American operations, director of early RX-7 competition activities and now in charge of export product planning; Kunio Matsuura, responsible for the racing rotary development; and Takaharu "Kobby" Kobayakawa, engineer-turned-technical-PR-man-par-excellence, who has since returned to his old domain as Senior Development Engineer.

Material Research, whose chief was Kei Matsui. There had been a division already dealing with materials and metallurgy, but Yamamoto insisted that his new division have an independent department that would fill its special and specific material requirements.

There were more engineers and technicians in the new division, too numerous to list here; today many of them occupy key engineering and other diversified positions at Mazda.

Yamamoto's new division literally worked day and night, first to solve the rotary's early problems (notably chatter marks and oil consumption), then to put the engine into series production, first on a limited scale for the small-volume Cosmo Sport.

President Tsuneji Matsuda had a grander plan for the new engine. His new program, "Rotarization," was pursued vigorously. He had a People's Rotary in mind, which was the reasonably priced and very fast (in a straight line, anyway) R100 coupe and its sedan variant, based on the company's piston-engine small-car chassis and body shell. There was a minor detour in the front-wheel-drive R130 coupe, another small volume specialty model, but then the movement gathered momentum, turning more Mazda products into rotary-powered. It culminated in two oddities, the American-market-only Rotary Pickup and the Japanese exclusive Rotary Parkway small bus.

Toyo Kogyo celebrated its 50th Anniversary in January 1970. A year later, it lost its leader in the sudden death of Tsuneji Matsuda of lung inflammation at the age of 74. Executive Vice President Kohei Matsuda, heir to the Matsuda clan, succeeded him as President.

President Kohei Matsuda followed in his late father's footsteps, continuing on the Rotarization route. His time was, however, a difficult one. It could be said that the fortune of the rotary is one of the most fascinating chapters in automotive history. The Mazda rotary emerged as a champion in the early stages of the clean-air battle, only to plummet in the aftermath of the Great Oil Crisis. "The Wankel rotary engine was evaluated, devaluated, and is now being re-evaluated, in an extraordinarily short span of time," observes rotary wizard Yamamoto. When NSU's early Ro80 developed durability problems, the Wankel's quality was questioned. When Mazda's interim detoxed engines used a little more fuel, the rotary was condemned as a gas guzzler. "If one type of reciprocating piston engine developed a cylinder wear problem, would you condemn the whole Otto-cycle family?" But then, Yamamoto reflects, had the Mazda rotary been installed in a car with a better chassis with more attractive, distinctive styling, it might have weathered the energy crisis.

It should be noted that it was President Kohei Matsuda who approved the Project X605, which became the RX-7. But even Mazda's successful re-entry vehicle for the rotary could not turn the tide in his favor; in December 1977 he stepped down from the presidency of the company his grandfather had founded. Director Yoshiki Yamasaki, soft-spoken but strong-willed production engineer-manager in his own right, succeeded Matsuda.

In November 1984, Chairman Masaji Iwasawa, formerly with the Sumitomo Bank, and President Yamasaki declared that Mazda Motor Corporation had now been fully restored to its health, and with that they handed the helm of the corporation to Moriyuki Watanabe and Kenichi Yamamoto.

First Cosmo Sport mockup. Moriyuki Watanabe of the Vehicle Design Division (Chairman of the Board since November 1984) stands behind the model

Tsuneji Matsuda returns from his triumphant trip to the Tokyo Motor Show with two prototype Cosmos. The welcoming group includes Moriyuki Watanabe and Kenichi Yamamoto

Former President Yoshiki Yamasaki, production-engineer-turned-chief-executive, launched the original RX-7 in spring 1978

Three pillars of engine wisdom

PRESIDENT YAMAMOTO ADVOCATES the corporate philosophy of the "three pillars of engines": the Otto-cycle reciprocating piston engine, Rudolf Diesel's compression-ignition engine and Felix Wankel's rotary, perfected by his company. Each is consigned to specific vehicle types and models. There aren't many "duals" or "triple" models, carrying two or all of these engines, left at Mazda. The big Cosmo and Luce 929 are the only models powered by all three, and they are not exported to America.

Mazda's current engine design and development organization reflects the management's balanced approach toward power-unit choices and development. New-generation rotary engines are designed by the Fifth Engine Design Department, headed by Hiroshi Ohzeki with the assistance by Tomoh Tadokoro and Noriyuki Kurio. The Fifth is one of departments comprising the Engine Design Division. Development and testing are carried out by the Fifth and Eighth Testing Departments, the former responsible for performance assurance and the latter reliability and durability.

Father of the Mazda Rotary, Kenichi Yamamoto, with the X605

Dr.-Ing. E. H. Felix Wankel, creator of the Wankel rotary engine, was born in August 1902 in Lahr/Schwarzwald (Black Forest). After a clerical apprenticeship in a scientific publishing house, he established a small workshop in 1924. Called WVW, the shop received the support of the German Air Ministry in 1936. In 1951 he established TES, where he formulated the Wankel rotary-engine principle

Rapport and mutual respect between two great designers are seen in this display of Mazda's Type 13B DEI engine at the Deutsches Museum in Munich. The engine was donated by President Kenichi Yamamoto; its special showcase was designed by no less a genius than Dr. Felix Wankel. A constructional masterpiece in itself, the case has a very thin frame, giving an impression that it is entirely made of glass panes, and is completely dust-proof

Noriyuki Kurio explains rotor housing construction to departmental chief Hiroshi Ohzeki and his staff engineers. Assistant Manager Tomoh Tadokoro is on the left

5

THE ROTARY ON THE TRACK

Early challenge

Cosmo 110S at the 'Ring

THE LATE Tsuneji Matsuda did not hide his dislike of those "noisy" race cars at the Japanese press introduction of the tiny Carol car. He would rather listen to the song of joy emitted by the smallest passenger-car four-cylinder engine in the world then, a liquid-cooled aluminum ohv four displacing all of 358 cc. Just the same, President Matsuda nevertheless did not stop his engineers from developing the noisiest racing cars of their time.

After putting the L10A Cosmo Sport on the Japanese market in May 1967, the Rotary Engine Research Division immediately began working on its racing conversion; the target was the 1968 Marathon de la Route, a gruelling 84-hour event run at the Nürburgring which was something of a cross between a circuit race and a tarmac rally.

Mazda's newly formed racing group did not have a clue as to what the competition would be—Kunio Matsuura, an engineer from RE Research, had barely "heard" of Porsches—and for that matter, what his group was getting into. They reasoned that an 84-hour run covering 10,000-kilometers (6250 miles) must be equal to a 100,000-km durability test on the road. That would indeed be a tough challenge, as few rotary cars had covered that much distance.

They prepared two cars to go through simulated 84-hour runs, at their own Miyoshi Proving Ground as well as at the Suzuka Racing Circuit. The results were far from encouraging. One car cooked its engine on the first day of the trial. A replacement unit seized, too.

Nevertheless, a team of two Cosmo Sports was sent to the 'Ring. In the event that started on August 21, 1968, one car crashed on the 81st hour after losing a rear wheel (broken axle), narrowly missing a tree and, according to Matsuura's vivid memory, aging its fearless and then young driver Yoshimi Katayama by a good ten years. The other Cosmo, piloted by European drivers, finished fourth overall.

The 'Ring Cosmo was powered by a modified production 10A twin-rotor engine with single chamber volume of 491 cc —a rather special engine as it had combination intake ports, i.e. a combination of peripheral and side ports. A batch of

Cosmo 110S at the Marathon de la Route, 1968. One car finished fourth overall

these engines had been built with production in mind, to be offered as a performance option in the Cosmo. They did not quite meet the expectation of Mazda designers, the Marathon engine producing only a fraction more than the L10B's 128 bhp gross. Officially it was rated at 130 bhp at 7000 rpm, despite its freed intake and exhaust. Breathing was through Nikki's Weber-clone twin-choke sidedraft carburetor (Mazda wanted to develop its own carburetors and commissioned Nikki to produce samples).

One of the major problem areas was lubrication. The Cosmo engine had a very shallow oil sump, about 1.2 inches deep, to lower the engine in the low car. Maintaining adequate oil pressure was critical under racing conditions, which imposed higher lateral acceleration; elaborate baffles had to be built into the sump. Another odd phenomenon particular to the rotary was that its oil level built up during the race. Oil was mixed into the fuel for gas sealing and lubrication; the mixture descended and accumulated in the sump, eventually blowing it out of the engine. A metering pump used in the lubrication system was employed to scavenge a part of the oil in the sump into a catch tank in front of the passenger seat. Each pit stop required a

change of cans, an operation Matsuura would rather have hidden from probing observers.

Aluminum-housing, combination-port 10A engine fitted with Nikki twin-barrel sidedraft carburetor. Note shallow oil sump of this engine type

Two Marathon contenders being shipped to Europe

R100 in European Touring Car Championship events

FOR THE 1969 and 1970 seasons, Mazda switched its racing wares from the Cosmo 110S to the new R100 coupe, which the company would like to promote in the world market. It also qualified as a touring car, and was thus eligible for the European Touring Car Championship.

By the end of 1968, the Hiroshima racing shop was able to coax 204 bhp from the 10A engine, specifically developed under the engine code 3883. It was based on the Cosmo's all-aluminum housing unit, not the production R100's M10A aluminum trochoid and iron side housing. Mazda engineers were worried that the engine with peripheral intake ports and aluminum housings might invoke official scrutineers' condemnation; to their great relief, that didn't happen (the rotary was such an unknown quality).

Mazda chose an Asian Event, the April 1969 Singapore Grand Prix, as a feeler; the R100 scored an outright win. In Singapore tune the engine produced 195 bhp at 9000 rpm, its maximum safe rev limit. A megaphone exhaust was tried on the R100, but proved to be vulnerable to the engine's fierce resonating cry

and split itself to shreds. Later a pair of straight pipes, of heat-resistant SUS steel, were used on the car.

Two cars were then entered in the Spa-Francorchamps 24-hour Grand Prix for touring cars in July 1969. The engine's output was deliberately held down to 187 bhp at a safe 8500 rpm for this long-distance event. The cars again developed lubrication problems, this time from copper piping to the air-cooled oil cooler, which split during the race. The oil cooler had to be bypassed and higher-viscosity oil got them through the arduous event. The two Mazda coupes finished fifth and sixth overall. As the top positions were occupied by the dominating Porsche 911S with token rear seating, the Mazda R100 could have been unofficially classified as a moral and truer touring-car winner.

The Mazda team was less fortunate in the 1969 Marathon de la Route, where three R100s were entered. One car retired with a hole in its fuel tank. Another spun in the rain and went over a cliff. The surviving car had its muffler bracket broken off by thermal shock in the wet. The muffler was a huge and heavy affair, to reduce exhaust back pressure which was the rotary's perpetual enemy; it weighed some 50 kg (110 lb). The car was

Mazda racing team campaigning in Europe

seen with a dangling silencer and flagged in by the official signaler. It had to be secured with baling wire, and the car set off again. Each prolonged pit stop counted against the competitor, so the driver was given a supply of baling wire and a wrench and instructed to stop at a designated service area to shore up the muffler—the do-it-yourself work did not count as a pit stop.

Then one of the two rotor chambers developed an exhaust-manifold crack, which added to the rotary's already raucous exhaust sounds. Flagged in again, the driver was given a blind main jet, which killed the offending chamber long enough to escape the officials' ears; then he would revert to the twin-rotor operation. The hard-working drivers repeated the tactics and finished fifth overall. The Marathon engine was in its mildest tune of the season, rated at 178 bhp at 8000 rpm.

The last race of the 1969 season was in the home country, the Suzuka Automobile Race meeting of November 1969, where Mazda expected to challenge the Japanese king of the touring class, Nissan's Skyline GT-R with its twincam 24-valve 2-liter inline six. The confrontation did not materialize, as the internationally contoured Mazda R100 with wide fender flares

was classified as a "racing car." The car ran with a high-strung peripheral 10A putting out 214 bhp, and scored an easy win in its assigned class.

In 1970 Mazda entered a factory team of R100s in three European touring-car races, the RAC Tourist Trophy (eighth, tenth and twelfth) in June, the West German Touring Car GP in July (fourth, fifth and sixth), and the July Spa 24-hour meeting (fifth overall).

Another notable event was the Le Mans 24-hour endurance race in June 1970, in which a Chevron B16 two-seater entered by the Belgian team of M. Bernève and Yves Deprès raced with the factory-supplied 10A engine converted to dry-sump lubrication. Factory engineer Kunio Matsuura attended to the venture. The engine developed 200 bhp, but the car's top speed in practice and qualification did not prove it: it looked more like 150 bhp. Matsuura attributed this to poor aerodynamics, which prevented the engine's breathing sufficient air. A brave endeavor, the lone Chevron retired in the fourth hour with a burst water hose.

In April 1971 Mazda's Competition Committee decided the following:

Winning R100 coupe at the 1969 Singapore Grand Prix for touring cars was a Mazda feeler toward serious racing ventures. A high power rating, 195 bhp at 9000 rpm, was coaxed from the engine for the sprint event

Type 10A, engine code 3883, developed in September 1968 for the Singapore event. Nikki-Weber carburetor is now mounted vertically

Engine code 3883 was based on the aluminum-housing Cosmo engine, not the volume-production M10A of the R100. Peripheral intake ports were used

1969 Spa-Francorchamps 24-hour race of the European Touring Car Championship series. One factory R100 finished fifth overall. The engine was "detuned" to 187 bhp at 8500 rpm

R100 coupes at the start of the 1969 Marathon de la Route

1) With the imminent implementation of safety and emission-control laws and regulations, the company's engineering resources must be concentrated in those directions. Therefore, all factory-scale international competition activities would henceforth cease.
2) The factory would continue to provide technical assistance and support to private teams and groups through Mazda-affiliated shops in Japan, specifically supplying engines to privateers.
3) Mazda would continue developing conversion kits for competition purposes.

Director Kenichi Yamamoto volunteered at the meeting, "International competition activities have been significant and useful in pursuing the new rotary engine's ultimate performance potential. The priority is, however, on technology that will ensure our survival as a manufacturer. One day, I earnestly hope, we shall return to the track."

1970 RAC Tourist Trophy race, where an R100 finished eighth overall. The peripheral 10A put out 210 bhp at 8500 rpm

1970 Spa-Francorchamps 24-hour endurance race, where an R100 finished fifth overall with the TT's 210-bhp engine

1970 Spa-Francorchamps 24-hour race

Belgian-entered Chevron B16 powered by a Type 10A engine provided by the factory, in the 1970 Le Mans 24-hour Endurance Race. The car did not finish

Slay the dragons—the Japanese scenes

RX-2 and RX-3 campaigns

TWO FORMER aircraft manufacturers joined their forces in November 1952. Tama Jidosha (Automobile), the remains of the former Tachikawa Aircraft, had been producing electric cars since 1947, but their days were obviously numbered. Tama approached Fuji Seimitsu Kogyo (Precision Industry), which had sprung from the former Nakajima Aircraft, about developing and providing a suitable gasoline engine. They renewed their old relationship (Nakajima used to supply engines to Tachikawa's fuselages) and the two comapnies eventually merged under the auspices of Bridgestone Rubber Company to become Fuji Seimitsu Kogyo in 1954.

Fuji, which later changed its corporate title to Prince Motor Industry, had a group of ambitious engineers, very much performance-minded. They launched the Skyline GT sedan, a stretched small family sedan powered by an overhead-camshaft 2-liter inline six borrowed from its senior sister model and given three sets of Weber two-barrel sidedraft carburetors.

The Skyline GT and its mid-engined pukka racing sister, the R380, began methodically pouncing their respective rivals on Japanese tracks.

In the industrial reorganization of the early seventies, with the imminent liberalization of foreign capital investment and imports, the smaller Prince sought shelter under the giant Nissan Motor Company's corporate arm, and in August 1966 it was absorbed into Nissan. Nissan allowed the Prince division to continue its competition activities; the second-generation racing Skyline GT-R was more potent than ever, with an R380 twincam 24-valve triple-carburetor 2-liter inline six and fully independent suspension. It became the undisputed King of Japanese touring-car racing.

The Hiroshima company was now set to challenge Skyline supremacy. Mazda's R100 ran in one Japanese event in 1970, in which the 10A engine was producing as much as 224 bhp and being taken up to 10,000 rpm. The R100 was fast on Fuji's grandstand straight, time and again passing the Skyline GT-R, only to be overtaken on the notorious banked section, where it was disconcertingly twitchy. One car finished third overall

Nissan's Skyline GT-R, King of Japanese Touring Car racing, was soon to be toppled from its throne by the rotary pretender

First close encounter of King Skyline and a pretender: R100 coupe at the 1970 JAF Grand Prix at Fuji

behind two factory Nissans. Toward the end of 1970, Mazda offered a sports conversion kit that tweaked the production cast-iron side housing 10A to 170 bhp. The R100's popularity among entry-level racers benefited greatly from this inexpensive conversion.

In June 1971 the Japan Automobile Federation, the sanctioning body of all competition activities in the country, decreed the ban of the peripheral-intake-port rotary. The new 12A two-rotor engine, with a widened trochoid housing bringing single chamber volume to 573 cc, had to conform to the new rule. Mounted in the RX-2, it produced 225 bhp at 8500 rpm in racing tune, now breathing from a real 48-mm twin-throat Weber (Mazda had by then given up on the Japanized carburetor, which could not match the Italian instrument's performance and quality). By the end of the 1971 season, the 12A's output was raised to 233 bhp, but the RX-2 was not still competitive. A smaller-engined Savanna (10A-powered RX-3) scored one win in December, after works Skylines had fallen by the wayside.

But it was in May 1972 Japanese Grand Prix that a trio of 12A-propelled RX-3s pounded the opposition. One of them took the pole position and the three Mazdas finished 1-2-3. The victory was resounding, and the Skyline GT-R's days appeared to be numbered.

The Japanese GP-specification 12A produced 240 bhp at 9000 rpm and maximum torque in excess of 160 lb-ft (22 kg-m) at 7500 rpm, using a 48-mm choke twin-choke Weber. The racing side-intake rotary had employed auxiliary "bridge ports," additional slits above the intake ports. In the 1972 engine this bridge port extended into the trochoid housing. The design invited controversy at JAF's post-race analytical meeting, but the organization did not pass any conclusion as to its legality. It did, nevertheless, lead to a conditional liberalization of the peripheral intake system: it would be allowed if "a minimum of 50 'peri'-engines are offered over the counter."

A factory RX-3 won the Super Touring Car championship in the Fuji Grand Champion Series in 1973, 1975 and 1976. The November 1973 Fuji GC event was to be the last confrontation of the RX-3 and Nissan's GT-R, where the former, now allowed to use a maximum rev limit of 9500 rpm, quickly established the class's course record and occupied the pole. A serious accident in the preceding event for pure racing cars canceled

RX-2 between a Nissan 240Z and a Porsche 910 in the 1971 Fuji 1000, where the Mazda finished third overall

Winning RX-3 at the Fuji TT 500-mile race, 1971

RX-3 winning the Touring Car Class in the 1972 Japanese Grand Prix

Auxiliary bridge port extending into the trochoid housing invited controversy in 1972, which eventually led to conditional liberalization of the peripheral-intake-port engine for racing in Japan

the meeting and prevented the last clash of the arch-rivals from taking place.

One unique feature of the factory RX-3 was its rear suspension: the live axle was laterally located by a Watt linkage in front of the axle. The arrangement, in a more space-efficient off-set location, was to be used later in Project X605, which became the original RX-7.

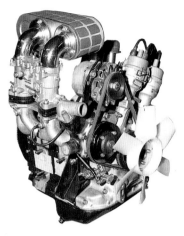

A Type 12A racing engine powered the RX-3

Japanese racing cars

IN OCTOBER 1973 the Arab sheiks and politicians shut their oil valves, putting the world into turmoil. A side effect in the far eastern isles was Mazda's withdrawal from factory-sponsored touring-car racing, where the RX-3 was now the invincible ruler. Mazda did not completely withdraw from the Japanese competition scene, but changed direction and concentrated in a more specialized arena, the Fuji Grand Champion series for two-seat racing cars, by supplying engines and supporting private rotary users.

The class was then dominated by another fire-breathing dragon, a Bavarian one: BMW's potent twincam 16-valve racing four.

Up to that time, what few rotary users there were in the Grand Championship Series had to rely on the basic touring-car Type 12A engine—with dismal results. A specialized engine would be required for mounting low and rigidly in a midship chassis that would also call for a shorter exhaust system with different power characteristics. By then the production 12A had progressed to Stage B, with a single distributor (Mazda's racing

100th win for Mazda: the 1976 Japanese Grand Prix at Fuji

group calls it "12B"). In racing tune it produced 250-plus bhp at 9500 rpm. The best it could achieve was an occasional fifth overall, so it was hardly a threat to the BMW power.

In 1976 the bigger-displacement 13B engine was introduced. Retaining side intake ports and wet-sump lubrication, the tuned 13B produced 280 bhp at 9200 rpm. The racing rotary continued to use one-piece carbon compound apex seals, which had an excellent self-lubricating capacity, but their thickness, 6 mm, was a serious deterrent to higher power output because it meant high friction. Even the father of the Mazda rotary was taken aback when engineer Matsuura suggested halving their width to 3 mm. But Yamamoto was naturally pleased with the subsequent report that the engine was running with no apparent trouble and squeezing out additional 10 bhp. The racing 13B was now producing at least equal if not superior power to the BMW, but the seasons's best placing was eighth overall.

The factory modified a racing 13B to peripheral-intake-port specification, installed it in a newly acquired March 75S two-seat racing chassis and commenced development work in 1976. The car displayed one quirk. Paul Frère, prominent European journalist and former racing driver, tried the March freshly out of the racing shop at its first sorting session at the Suzuka track, and found the car to oversteer to the left and understeer to the right. Mazda's own drivers continued to experience this curious trait, which was initially attributed to the chassis through the early development stage. The phenomenon ocurred even when the car was moving slowly in the paddock, and it suddenly hit engineer Matsuura that it was due to the gyro effect of the high mounted rotary. Rotating components were subsequently lightened and the engine converted to dry-sump lubrication, thereby lowering the installation height. These measures minimized the effect to an acceptable level. Now producing 290 bhp at 9000 rpm, the modified 13B propelled the March 75S to its first victory in the May 1977 Fuji 1000-kilometer race. By September of the year, the 13B was putting out 300 bhp; another March chassis, the 76S, powered by it won the Fuji International 200-mile event the same year. The condition attached to the approval of the 13B peri-engine in the Grand Championship Series was that its over-the-counter version would be made available in a sufficient quantity to private entrants. Its development consumed most of the 1977

Factory-sponsored March 75S powered by a 13B racing engine, circa 1976

Type 12A "Sports kit" engine

Racing apex seals. At top is a single-piece carbon-compound seal of 3-mm thickness, at bottom a two-piece metal seal

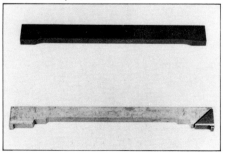

Pure peripheral-port trochoid (on left) with the production side-port housing

"Bridge" port above the normal intake port

season, and it was put on sale, carrying a price tag of 3 million yen—some 35 to 40 percent lower than the ongoing BMW quotation. The "Sports Kit" 13B included such features as a Weber DDW48IDA carburetor, dry-sump lubrication, aluminum flywheel and the ability to accommodate a racing-type twin-plate clutch. Private teams welcomed the rotary, whose numbers rapidly increased from a 3-rotary-to-14-BMW ratio in the first Grand Championship event of 1978 to 9-to-9 in the last event.

The 1979 season saw the first fuel-injected 13B: Lucas mechanical injection raised power to 311 bhp at 10,000 rpm. "Not as much as we had anticipated, and it was a devil of a system to tune," recalls Matsuura. But it proved powerful enough to secure the driver's championship of the season. In one race a fuel-injected 13B-powered car climbed from the tail end of the field to the top, which it held to the finish. This demonstration of superior power moved the race organizer to ban fuel injection on the 13B and add a 50-kg handicap weight to the rotary-powered car. The sheer number of the rotary brigade, now numbering 17 cars of the 22-car field in 1980, was not enough to overcome the handicap and lost the

Championship to BMW.

As the number of rotary-engine users increased, noise became a major problem. A few rotaries mixed into a larger company of reciprocating engines would not have been so offensive, but with more than a dozen banshees screaming at the same time, it was a different story. Engineer Matsuura thought it wiser to voluntarily reduce the racing rotary's noise level than be forced to accept mandatory and more stringent rules that the organizer might impose. A new silencing system called IR-4A was developed; it effectively reduced the engine's high exhaust noise from 125 dBA to 115, about the same level as the BMW's, as measured in front of the Fuji track's long straight. The system was offered to rotary users in 1981, who naturally showed their disdain for this power-robbing device, however small (about 3 percent or 10 bhp) Mazda claimed the loss would be. Matsuura remained adamant that the rotary should be fitted with the muffler system, and IR-4A has been serving the racing rotary ever since.

With the "Sports Kit" 13B project successfully launched in 1978 and the Grand Championship series in hand in the following season, Mazda's racing-engine group considered their GC

Type 13B racing engine with twin-throat Weber carburetor feeding peripheral intake ports

All-conquering rotary in the Fuji Grand Championship series of races, 1978

program successful and wrapped up official activities while continuing the support of private rotary users. Now they turned their full attention and efforts to another important ongoing project, factory participation in the American IMSA racing series with the newly launched X605 RX-7.

Fuji GC series now allows single-seat racing cars. The rotary faces formidable competition

Shades of an old Lancia-D50, the latest Mazda-powered contender is based on a March 842 F2 chassis with twin pontoon tanks

Bosch K-Jetronic fuel-injected 13B engine as used in the latest GC car

Mazda Racing Engines 1977

12A Sports Kit engine

	12A Sports Kit	Prod. 12A USA	Remarks
Displacement, cc	573 × 2	573 × 2	35CID × 2
Compression ratio	9.4	9.4	
Port type, intake	peri opens 86° BTDC closes 75° ABDC	side opens 32° ATDC closes 40° ABDC	
exhaust	peri opens 73° BBDC closes 65° ATDC	peri opens 75° BBDC closes 38° ATDC	
Carburation	Weber 48IDA twin-choke	4-barrel compound	
bore size, mm	48	primary 28 mm × 2 secondary 34 mm × 2	
venturi size, mm	43	primary 20/13/6.5 × 2 secondary 28/10 × 2	
Ignition	breaker point type*	breaker point	*factory CDI
Max. power, bhp/rpm	250 plus @ 9000	95 hp SAE net @ 6000	
Engine weight, dry	110 kg/242 lb**	146 kg/321 lb	**factory 224/102

13B Racing Engine (winning unit 1977 Fuji 1000 km race)

	13B Racing	Prod. 13B USA	Remarks
Displacement, cc	654 × 2	654 × 2	40CID × 2
Compression ratio	9.4	9.2	
Port type, intake	peri opens 86° BTDC closes 75° ABDC	side opens 32° ATDC closes 40° ABDC	
exhaust	peri opens 73° BBDC closes 65° ATDC	peri opens 75° BBDC closes 38° ATDC	
Carburation	Weber 48IDA twin-choke	4-barrel compound	
bore size, mm	48	primary 28 mm × 2 secondary 34 mm × 2	
venturi size, mm	43	primary 20/13/6.5 × 2 secondary 28/10 × 2	
Ignition	CDI pointless	breaker point type	
Max. power, bhp/rpm	290 plus @ 9000	110 hp SAE net @ 6000	
Engine weight, kg/lb	106/233	154/330	

Racing the RX-7

HIROSHIMA DISPATCHED A sortie in the form of two factory RX-3s to the Daytona 24-hour Endurance Race in 1978, in preparation for its foray into the IMSA GTU category with the racing RX-7 which was being developed in parallel to the roadgoing model. A skimpy air cleaner fitted on the engine gulped in a trochoid-full of Daytona's fine sand particles, which played havoc with the rotor sealing, and a sudden shower encountered during the race also delivered severe thermal shocks that split the exhaust system. The two cars forthwith departed the Florida track. "It was a total defeat, but certainly a lesson worth every yen we had spent on the jaunt," affirms engineer Matsuura.

Because the racing-car development progressed with that of the production X605 RX-7, as had that of the RX-2 and RX-3, when the RX-7 was presented to the visiting American enthusiast press in spring 1978 a GTU prototype was already there. As as soon as the veil of secrecy over the new car was lifted in Japan, a series of shake-down and development test sessions took place on the local tracks.

Two factory-prepared cars were entered in the 1979 Daytona 24-hour endurance race.

These cars incorporated modifications and improvements to preclude problems and troubles encountered in the 1978 event: with a dust-proof air cleaner, a reinforced exhaust system and coolant-level warning system. The racing 12A's development had been suspended; Japanese Grand Championship cars were now using the bigger 13B, in its last tune the 12A had put out 250 bhp. In the meantime, the production unit had received a number of internal improvements and was now known as "12B" in certain inner circles. Among other things the updated racing 12B had 3-mm-thick carbon apex seals and single side seals to reduce friction, which brought power up to 265 bhp at 8500 rpm. The single side-seal design had been tried on previous racing engines and was now standard on the production unit.

One of the two entries scored the GTU win at Daytona and finished fifth overall, closely followed by the second factory RX-7—an impressive debut for the brand-new sports car. Hiroshima's immediate aim was to topple the Nissan (then

Two factory-prepared RX-3s in the 1978 Daytona sortie, where they literally ate dust and retired

Mazda already had a GTU prototype ready when it introduced the production RX-7 to the American enthusiast press in spring of 1978

RX-7 had its first taste of victory in the GTU class of the 1979 Daytona 24-hour race

Class-winning RX-7 in the Mazda pit, 1979 Daytona

245

Datsun) Z's supremacy in the IMSA GTU category. Two more events on the west coast, at Sears Point and Portland (shorter-distance races), were tackled by the factory team with a sprint-tuned engine putting out 275 bhp at 9500 rpm. They finished third and second respectively, satisfactory results for the first year.

An interesting private excursion was undertaken at very high speeds by a Southern California firm specializing in the manufacture of high-performance parts for Mazda rotary-engine cars. The Racing Beat-prepared RX-7 powered by a tuned 13B engine and driven by Don Sherman, *Car and Driver* magazine's intrepid editor, ran in the 30th annual Bonneville National Speed Trials on September 28, 1978, and established a world speed record of 183.904 miles per hour for Class E grand touring cars.

Mazda decided to stay behind the scenes from 1980 onward, on all fronts: no more factory-prepared cars as such, but they would provide race engines and technical assistance to affiliated and private teams. In America, Mazda of North America (MANA), based in California, initiated "Customer Service" activities, directed by Executive Vice President Yohji

Tohyama—one of the original 47-man Rotary Engine Research Division. The RX-7 has since become one of the most successful production GT-based racing cars ever, winning the IMSA GTU championship for five years in row, from 1980 through 1984.

In 1980, Mazdaspeed, a Tokyo-based distributor-owned specialist (since then 80 percent of its stocks have been acquired by the Hiroshima company), fielded a joint onslaught on Europe's premier touring-car endurance event, the Spa-Francorchamps 24-hour race with Tom Walkingshaw Racing of Britain. It turned out to be an abortive try. The factory, nonchalant about the 1980 endeavor, decided to provide support to the Mazdaspeed-TWR combine for the 1981 race, and prepared an endurance-specification side-intake 12B engine producing 235 to 240 bhp. Three cars were entered, and the car driven by Walkinshaw and Pierre Dieudonnè scored the outright win. Tetsuo Fujiyama, responsible for coordinating Mazda's world competition activities, emphasizes the significance of the Spa victory: "A true highlight in our racing endeavors. Remember our first year in Europe, in 1969, when the R100 coupe threatened the leading BMW, only to retire at

1978 Bonneville Speed Trials RX-7, prepared and entered by Racing Beat of California

1980 IMSA GTU champion car

1981 IMSA GTU champion car

the 11th—or 23rd? —hour with mechanical failure. Now, the scene was reversed. It was the turn of our rivals to fall by the wayside."

Back in America, the RX-7 was sweeping up the GTU field. Not content resting on its laurels, Mazda decided to challenge the GTO category for displacement sizes over 2.8 liters (3 liters from the 1985 season). A 13B-powered GTO RX-7 won the class and finished fourth overall in the 1982 Daytona 24-hour endurance race. In the following year's event, Mazda scored the highest overall placing at Daytona, third overall with another GTO class-winning car. For the 1982 race Mazda used a Lucas fuel-injected 13B for qualification, which was rated at 330 bhp. Matsuura was not confident that the highly tuned injection engine would last the distance, so he reverted to a 310 bhp carburetted engine for the race.

1982 IMSA GTU champion car

1983 IMSA GTU champion car

1984 IMSA GTU champion car

13B-powered GTO RX-7 in a 1981 shakedown session

GTO RX-7 in the 1982 Daytona 24-hour race

1984 GTO champion RX-7

1981 Spa-Francorchamps 24-hour Touring Car race, where the TWR-Mazdaspeed RX-7 won outright

Camel Light cars

OF INTEREST and significance is the emergence of the Camel Light class in the American International Motorsports Association (IMSA) regulations. The rule specifies two-seat racing cars whose dimentional and displacement classifications are similar to those applied to the pure racing GTP category. The GTP Type 1 specifies a minimum weight of 700 kg (1540 lb) for two-valves-per-cylinder volume production engines, four-valves-per-cylinder racing engines under 2 liters and the rotary.

Two cars powered by Mazda rotary engines meeting the Camel Light rules ran the 1985 Dayton 24-hour race, both with British Argo JM16 chassis. One car driven by J. Marsh, R. Pawley and D. Marsh finished 10th overall and winning the class. The other Argo-Mazda finished 13th overall and second in the category. Mazda predicts that this segment will have more rotary-powered competitors and may even turn out to be an almost single engine-source class.

Camel Light Argo-13B in the 1985 Daytona 24-hour race

New GTO racer was developed in parallel to the road-going P747. It was shaped by Mazda's own design staff; body construction was commissioned to Mooncraft (not space-program related), chassis engineering by Mazdaspeed. A new racing three-rotor engine is a strong possibility

One-fifth model in Mazda's Miyoshi wind tunnel

RX-7 in international rallying

IN 1981 AN RX-7 driven by New Zealander Rod Millen was entered in the RAC Rally of the World Rally Championship Series, and finished 11th overall. Mazda then made a feasibility study of an RX-7 conforming to the International Group B rule. Mazda got serious about rallying, and in May 1983 established the Mazda Rally Team of Europe, based in the same compound as the company's European operation MOE (Mazda Motor Representative Office, Europe) in Brussels, Belgium. Put in charge of the team was Achim Warmbold, veteran German rallyist, with technical assistance provided by factory engineer Katsumi Sekita.

The team began campaigning in international and European events, starting from the 1983 Acropolis Rally in Greece using Group II RX-7 car powered by a "Spa tune" (referring to the 1981 24-hour touring car race) 12A. For the 1984 season, the team scaled up its efforts rallying more potent Group B RX-7s powered by bigger displacement 13B. One of the team cars finished ninth overall in the Acropolis Rally.

In the same event in 1985, the team's Group B rear-wheel-drive RX-7 driven by I. Carlsson scored third overall, and another car piloted by boss Warmbold finished sixth overall. Carlsson followed two four-wheel-drive cars (Peugeo 205 T16 and Audi Sport Quattro).

The MRT-E's Group B car is powered by a peripheral-intake-port 13B engine, breathing from a Weber 51IDA two-barrel carburetor and converted to dry-sump lubrication, putting out 300 bhp at 8500 rpm and 196 1b-ft (27 kg-m) of torque at 7000 rpm. It has a five-speed gearbox whose internal ratios are (first) 2.564, (second) 1.851, (third) 1.417, (fourth) 1.140 and a direct fifth of 1.000:1, combined to either of three final ratios (5.1, 5.3 and 5.8). Steering has been changed to a rack-and-pinion-system with a quick 13:1 ratio, and brakes are four-wheel ventilated discs. Wheel sizes are 6-to 9-inch width × 15 inch diameter for the front and 7- to 10-inch width × 15 for the rear, depending on events. Mazda's specifications list these vital dimensions:

Length, mm/in.	4250/167.3
Width	1770/69.7
Height	1265/49.8

TWR RX-7 in the 1982 RAC Rally

Mazda European rally team's RX-7 entry in the 1983 Acropolis Rally

Group B RX-7 entered by the Mazda Rally Team of Europe finshied third overall in the 1985 Acropolis Rally

Sixth-place RX-7 driven by the boss, Achim Warmbold, in the 1985 Acropolis

I. Carlsson, driver in the third-place RX-7 in the 1985 Acropolis event

Dirt-covered Type 13B rally engine is remarkably "clean" of the sundry ancillary equipment found on the production detoxed engine

Night scene in the '85 Acropolis

Wheelbase	2420/95.3
Tracks, front/rear	1548/60.9/1496/58.9
Weight, kg/lb	980/2156

A noteworthy private endeavor is Rod Millen's four-wheel-drive RX-7, modified by the Los Angeles-based team-owner-driver, to be campaigned in the Sports Car Club of America's Pro-Rally series.

The Millen RX-7, completed in 1983, employed part-time 4WD, without center differential or torque split. The car was powered by a 13B engine with Weber 51IDA carburetor, rated at 300 bhp at 8500 rpm. Vital statistics of the 1983 version included: overall length 4321 mm/170 in. on 2421 mm/95.3 in. wheelbase, overall width 1669 mm/65.7 in. on 1461 mm/57.5 in. front and 1430 mm/55.9 in. rear tracks, and overall height 1311 mm/51.6 in.. It gained about 110 lb over a rally 2WD RX-7, scaling 1036 kg (2290 lb).

Rod Millen's four-wheel-drive RX-7 campaigned in the SCCA Pro-Rally series

Front final drive unit and rack-and-pinion steering of Rod Millen's 4WD RX-7

Short lever on the left of the tunnel engages part-time 4WD in the Millen car

The Los Angeles-based Millen shop, where 4WD RX-7s are prepared

Le Mans and endurance racing

APART FROM THE Belgian endeavor in 1970, there had been two other private attempts of significance with Mazda's rotary engines at the famous Les 24-Heures du Mans. They were staged by a Tokyo-based racing-car constructor, Sigma Automotive and Racing. Sigma was run by Shin Kato, formerly of the Seventh Engineering Division of Toyota Motor Company, the racing division of the country's biggest automobile manufacturer. (This numerical slot in the corporate engineering structure has been left vacant since Toyota withdrew from factory racing.)

Sigma raced its slab-sided MC73 at the 1973 Le Mans race, using a tuned 12A engine putting out 250 bhp at 8000 rpm; it qualified 14th but retired in the 11th hour with a burst clutch. A more aerodynamically shaped car, the Sigma MC74, was also powered by a peripheral-port 12A, and finished 24th in the 1974 event. These were joint efforts by Sigma and Mazdaspeed, the latter then owned by Mazda's Tokyo distributor.

Mazdaspeed embarked on a five-year project to participate in the world's premier endurance race, beginning with an unsightly RX-3-based prototype called 251 which it raced in a number of Japanese events. The team took it on itself to run a highly modified "silhouette" RX-7, designated 252, in the 1979 Le Mans race. Its aerodynamically shaped body was designed by Takuya Yura, an outstanding Japanese racing-car designer who has since designed "25X"-series RX-7s and "7X7" Group C2 cars. The engine was a fuel-injected 13B with peripheral intake ports, Kugelfischer fuel injection and dry-sump lubrication, rated at 285 bhp at 9000 rpm. Mazda itself was not involved in the brave attempt, and all modifications to the engine were carried out by Mazdaspeed's shop.

The 252 lacked speed to qualify for the Le Mans start; Mazdaspeed was absent from the Sarthe circuit in 1980 but returned there the following year with two Type 253 cars, again silhouette RX-7s. It was a more serious endeavor this time, drawing technical expertise and support from Britain's TWR and Mazda-France. On this occasion the Hiroshima factory provided endurance-prepared 13Bs with Weber carburetors: a 300-bhp unit for qualification and one slightly detuned to 290 bhp @ 8500 rpm for the race. The team cars retired with

Takashi Ono's fancy of a Group 5 car on the original RX-7 theme. Ono designed the new P747 RX-7 and its GTO racing version.

Silhouette RX-7 "252" in an early shakedown test session. The car lacked speed and failed to qualify for the starting line of the 1979 French classic

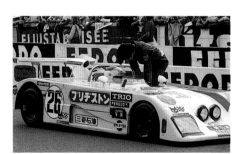

Sigma MC73, powered by 12A engine, in the 1973 Le Mans 24-hour endurance race. The car retired in the 11th hour

Streamlined MC74 in the 1974 Le Mans, also powered by 12A

Type 253 silhouette RX-7 in the 1981 Le Mans.
The two team cars retired with drivetrain
troubles

Factory-prepared racing 13B in the Le Mans
253 produced 300 bhp for qualification and
290 for the endurance race

Businesslike office equipment of the 253

Type 253 silhouette RX-7

Japanese driver team's 253 being pushed out
in the 1981 Le Mans race

Type 254, designed by Takuya Yura, being
constructed by Mooncraft of Shizuoka

Type 254 silhouette RX-7

Type 254 silhouette RX-7 in the Japan
Automobile Research Institute's Yatabe wind
tunnel

Night and day of the Type 254 at Le Mans,
1982. It finished 14th overall

Type 717C Group C-Junior car of 1983

717C in the Le Mans pit

717C in the 1983 Le Mans. The car won the
new C-Junior class

drivetrain problems.

In 1982 the 253 progressed to 254. The aerodynamics were further refined, reducing the drag coefficient to $C_D = 0.35$ in a wind-tunnel test. Taking other factors into account as well, Yura calculated a top speed of 277 km/h (173 mph) for the 1000-kg (220-lb) car. Mazda's racing engineer Matsuura again employed a familiar GTO tactic, using a Lucas-fuel injected 13B engine for qualification and a proven carburetted version with slightly less power for the race. This met with opposition from the organizer, who insisted that the same engine be used for qualifying and the race. Matsuura had to send for fuel-injection units from Japan, and just when they arrived, the organizer relented on the use of the detuned carburetor engine! Running in the IMSA GTX category and driven by Y. Terada, T. Yorino and Australian Alan Moffat, the Mazda 254 finished 14th overall in the 50th Le Mans endurance race.

In 1983 Mazdaspeed turned its attention to the new Group C-Junior category of two-seat racing cars, and built the Type 717C pukka racing two-seat coupe. The factory-tuned 13B engine was now fitted with Bosch K-Jetronic fuel injection and, because regulation limited fuel consumption, the 717C was equipped with a digital fuel-consumption readout. It won the Group C-Junior category and finished 12th overall in the 1983 Le Mans race.

The 1984 version was Type 727C, two of which raced in the Silverstone 1000 and at Le Mans—a familiar pattern taken by Mazdaspeed in its European campaign. They did not fare as well as the previous year's cars, one finishing 15th overall and the other 20th in the 24-hour race. More active and successful was the American tire maker B. F. Goodrich's team, which raced the Lola T616 Group C2 (C-Junior was renamed C2 in 1984) chassis powered by factory-prepared 13B engine rated at 330 bhp for sprint events and 310 bhp for endurance ones. It was the Lola that got the Group C2 honor at Le Mans, one T616-Mazda coming in 10th overall and another 12th.

Eighty percent of Mazdaspeed's stocks were now owned by Mazda Motor Corporation. It continued its endurance-race efforts, building a three-car fleet for the 1985 season. The "7X7" series now progressed to 737; meanwhile, the factory was readying the launch of Project 747, the new RX-7. The 737C is basically a refined 727C on a stretched wheelbase of 2530 mm (99.6 in.). Its chassis is typically racing car in that it has

Fuel-injection racing 13B with Bosch K-Jetronic

Three-dimensional fuel-injection metering cam of the racing 13B

Evolutionary 727C in a Japanese shakedown session

Engine bay of the mid-engine 727C

Type 727C in the 1984 Le Mans. One car finished 15th, the other 20th

B.F. Goodrich's more successful Lola T616-Mazda won Group C2 honors at the 1984 Le Mans, finishing a creditable 10th overall. Another B.F. Goodrich Lola-Mazda was close behind in 12th place

twin-tube aluminum monocoque construction. The suspension is contemporary racing design, with front unequal-length fabricated upper and lower arms, and a rear arrangement of upper I-arms and lower A-arms. Koni shock absorbers are used all around, and brakes are ventilated discs. Curiously, the 13B peripheral-port engine for Le Mans reverted to a Weber twin-throat carburetor for more consistent fuel economy. The endurance-tune 13B is officially rated at 300 bhp at 9000 rpm, mated to a Hewland FGA400 transaxle and installed in a car that is 4298 mm long, 1910 mm wide and 1065 mm tall (169.2 × 75.2 × 41.9 in.). The 730-kg (1609-lb) 737C finished third in the C2 class of the 1985 Le Mans race after having gearbox trouble.

The Hiroshima factory had been developing turbocharged rotaries since 1981. Early tests revealed that a single turbocharger installation would increase exhaust pressure, which cost performance; so Mazda engine designers adopted twin turbos, one per each rotor chamber. The turbocharger was Hitachi's very special HT20, with extensive use of exotic heat-resistant alloy components. Another enemy of rotary performance and reliability is detonation, which can occur

when the hotter charge in the combustion chamber is diluted with exhaust gas because of the large port timing overlap of the peripheral-port engine. For this reason, the turbo 13B employed a side intake "bridge" port arrangement with a slit-like auxiliary port above each main intake port, separated by a bridge. Rotor apex seals in the turbo 13B are a one-piece cast-iron design, sliding against the MCP trochoid. By comparison, the naturally asirated racing rotary still uses carbon apex seals and a solid plated trochoid.

Each rotor is fed by its own turbocharger, and elaborate boost control is employed; a usual wastegate shared between the two turbochargers plus a blow-off valve protecting the intake system, an intake-pressure relief valve for venting boost on deceleration, and a modulating valve that actuates the wastegate according to the engine's rpm to improve throttle response.

The intake charge is cooled by a dual intercooler system using air and water, the latter having its own cooling circuit. Fuel is injected by Bosch's K-Jetronic system, each rotor chamber having two injectors as in the latest RX-7 engine. The compression ratio is lowered to 7.5:1 from the production 13B's

Stretched 737C in the 1985 Le Mans. The car's best Group C2 positioning after 24 hours was third, a disappointment after years of hard work

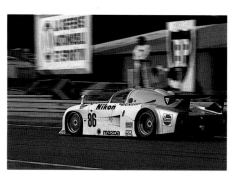

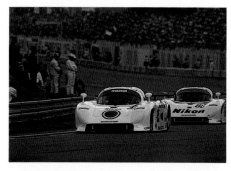

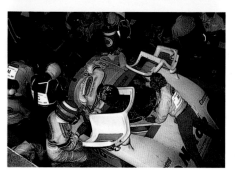

Curiously, Mazdaspeed reverted to carbureted 13Bs in the 1985 Le Mans

9.4:1. Thus set up, the racing 13B Turbo is rated at 500 bhp at 8000 rpm and produces a maximum torque of 442 Nm (326 lb-ft) at 7500 rpm.

The 727C had been designed to be powered by a 300-bhp naturally aspirated engine and nearly 70 percent more power was a bit handful for this compact car. So Mazdaspeed ordered a March 84G 2-seat racing chassis specifically for the turbo application. The March 84G-13B Turbo raced in the Fuji 1000-km race, which counted toward the World's Endurance Championship, in September 1984. It covered 153 of the 226 laps on the Fuji International Speedway before retiring with a crack in the plenum chamber.

March 84G two-seat racing car powered by turbocharged 13B engine, in an early test session

March 84G Turbo Rotary, whose boosted air is cooled by dual intercoolers (one air and the other water)

Twin-turbo fuel injected 13B engine is claimed to put out 500-plus bhp

March 84G Turbo Rotary in the 1984 Fuji WEC 1000 km: the single entry did not finish. Note large air intake on roof to introduce air to intercooler

Twin-turbo installation on 13B

Well equipped cockpit of the March 84G Rotary Turbo

A P P E N D I X

Mazda Rotary Engines

Keys:

e .... eccentricity. The amount of offset between the eccentric shaft centerline and the rotor centerline.

R .... radius or generating radius. The distance between the rotor centerline and the rotor's apex (in the Wankel rotary engine, there are three apices).

b .... width of the trochoid chamber.

$\mathbf{V_H}$ .... working chamber volume or single chamber capacity. It is obtained by the formula $\mathbf{V_H} = 3 \cdot \sqrt{3} \cdot \mathbf{Reb}$

type .... engine family designation

engine code ... specific engine designation

( ) .... Development/ Production year and month

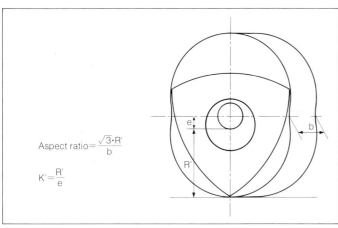

Aspect ratio $= \dfrac{\sqrt{3} \cdot R'}{b}$

$K' = \dfrac{R'}{e}$

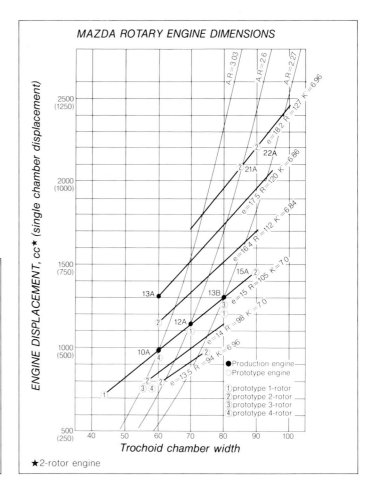

MAZDA ROTARY ENGINE DIMENSIONS

ENGINE DISPLACEMENT, cc★ (single chamber displacement)

Trochoid chamber width

● Production engine
○ Prototype engine

① prototype 1-rotor
② prototype 2-rotor
③ prototype 3-rotor
④ prototype 4-rotor

★2-rotor engine

I. EARLY EXPERIMENTAL ENGINES

Type 40A, engine code 0350 (April 1961)

THE FIRST Mazda-built rotary engine was based on the design of NSU's KKM400 unit, which the German firm had supplied. Development began in April 1961, two months after concluding the licensing agreement with NSU-Wankel, and was completed in November of the same year. It was tested on the bench as well as in a Mazda light vehicle in 1962. The 40A 0350 engine was a single-rotor unit with a working chamber volume of 386 cc (**e** = 14 mm, **R** = 90 mm, **b** = 59). The 0350 immediately ran into two major trouble areas that slowed early rotary development. Most serious were "chatter markes," or ripple-like uneven wear on the trochoid surface, which caused a sudden drop of power output after about 200 hours of operation on the bench; hardly less serious was atrocious oil consumption.

Chatter marks, a trouble similar to piston-ring flutter, were caused by frictional vibrations of the cast-iron apex seals against the chrome-plated rubbing surface of the trochoid chamber. The phenomenon was also affected by inadequate lubrication of the trochoid, the natural frequency of the seal elements and the coefficients of static and kinetic friction.

Heavy oil consumption and smoke emission were caused by inadequate oil sealing.

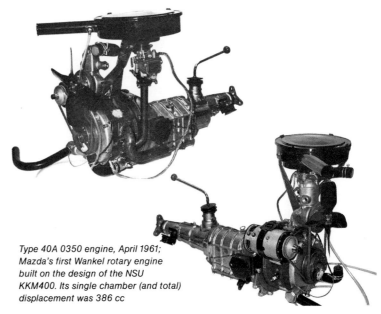

Type 40A 0350 engine, April 1961; Mazda's first Wankel rotary engine built on the design of the NSU KKM400. Its single chamber (and total) displacement was 386 cc

Type L8A, engine code 0353 (December 1962)

MAZDA'S FIRST twin-rotor engine was conceived and developed for installation in a vehicle. It had single chamber displacement of 399 cc from its internal dimensions of $e = 14$, $R = 98$ and $b = 56$. As in the 40A single-rotor engine, it had peripheral intake and exhaust ports. A batch of L8A engines was installed in various vehicle types for on-road test and evaluation.

The first breakthrough in solving the chatter marks came when cast-iron "cross hollow" seals were used. This apex seal had two longitudinal and several crossing perpendicular holes that helped reduce high-frequency vibrations, thus extending the trochoid's wear life considerably.

One of the L8A units was installed in a prototype L402A sports car in 1963, which was to evolve into the Type L10A Cosmo Sport.

The L8A two-rotor engine and its single-rotor version were displayed at the 1963 Tokyo Motor Show.

Like its derivative three and four-rotor engines, the L8A had dry-sump lubrication.

Type L8A twin-rotor engine. Note single spark plug per chamber and no oil sump under the housing (it had dry sump lubrication)

Type L8A 0353 twin-rotor engine, December 1962: the first two-rotor engine for installation in a vehicle, with a single chamber displacement of 399 cc. One of the L8A engines was installed in a prototype L402A sport car

Early Multis—engine codes 3804 and 3805 (December 1963)

THESE TWO multis were derived from the L8A 0353 two-rotor design, and shared the same trochoid dimensions, retaining a single chamber of 399 cc. The three-rotor unit is the 3804, the four-rotor version 3805.

Because of the rotary's structural needs, either the eccentric shaft or the main journal of the output shaft must be of the split-and-built-up design. The 3804 and 3805 employed the former, joined by Hirth-type radial serrations. Both the three and four-rotor units had a dry-sump lubrication systems and downdraft carburetors.

One of the four-rotor engine, fitted with an abbreviated four-stack exhaust system, powered the prototype open two-seater R16A.

No performance data was recorded of these early multis.

The R16A car was built in 1965 as the running test bed for the 3805 four-rotor engine

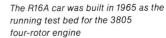

Engine code 3805, December 1963: a four-rotor version with built-up eccentric shaft employing serrated joints, 399 cc × 4. One such engine powered the R16A open two-seat prototype car

Engine code 3804, a three-rotor derivative of the L8A 0353 two-rotor engine; December 1963. Common to this entire engine group is dry-sump lubrication

II.PRODUCTON ENGINS

Type 10A family

●Engine code 3820 (prototype, October 1964)

THE TYPE L8A engine's internal dimensions were increased to obtain a single chamber displacement of 491 cc in October 1964. Vital dimensions of the enlarged 3820 two-rotor engine were: e = 15 mm, R = 105 mm and b = 60 mm, of which the former two served in the subsequent and further enlarged 12A and 13B series of production engines.

The 3820 engine had one of its twin distributors mounted vertically on the front cover and the other sticking from its side, supplying high-tension electricity to two sparkplugs per rotor-one of the production Mazda rotary's hallmarks.

The cross-hollow metal seal on the left, the first break-through in solving the chatter mark phenomenon. In the center is the single piece carbon seal adopted in the production 10A engine. On the right is the later two-piece metal seal

Type 10A, engine code 3820 (October 1964): an enlarged version of the two-rotor L8A, it has single chamber displacement of 491 cc and was forerunner of the 10A family of engines that powered early production cars

●Type L10A, engine code 0810 (May 1965)

THE 3820 design was further refined to become the 0810 that powered the pilot production Cosmo Sport (of which a batch of 60 cars was consigned to Mazda distributors and dealers in Japan from February through December 1966 for real-life evaluation) and from May 1967 the production version. The engine designation L10A was synonymous with that of the vehicle, but later the engine was referred to simply as 10A.

The L10A engine was a two-rotor unit sharing the same trochoid dimensions as the prototype 3820 (single chamber displacement 491 cc).

There was some head-scratching among the Japanese legislators as to how to classify and assess the Wankel rotary's displacement. They reached a temporary arrangement in taxing the 982-cc Cosmo; the commodity tax (like purchase tax, but included in the ex-factory price) would be equivalent to the percentage applied to cars under 2-liter capacity, and the annual automobile tax would be equal to the amount levied on cars in the 1-1.5-liter category. This formula of combined chamber displacement times 1.5 applies to the latest 13B-powered P747, which is still an under-2-liter car in Japan for taxation purposes. The material chosen for the trochoid housing of the production 0810 10A engine was, from the beginning, cast aluminum whose rubbing surface was hard-chrome-plated. It had aluminum-impregnated carbon apex seals, jointly developed by Mazda and Nihon Carbon and using Nihon's Pyro-Graphite carbon compound of high strength. The

Type 10A, engine code 0810 (October 1965): the first series-production Mazda rotary, inheriting the trochoid dimensions of the 3820 and its single chamber displacement of 491 cc. Producing 110 bhp at 7000 rpm, it powered the L10A Cosmo Sport

carbon-compound apex seal was to some extent self-lubricating, which helped relieve the critical trochoid-surface lubrication problem and give excellent wear rates of 0.8 to 1 mm in 100,000 km (62,000 mi.) of running. Housing wear was found to be even less (almost microscopic), and most important of all, chatter marks were completely eliminated by the new surface and seal material combination.

Unlike NSU which had adhered to peripheral inlet ports in its engines, Mazda engineers were strong advocates of the side-inlet arrangement for their production engines. A peripheral position offers better breathing than the somewhat restrictive side-port, and should bring in a considerable increase in brake mean effective pressure. Mazda designers, however, believed that it left something to be desired in low-speed torque, and that it was the cause of rough idling and engine rocking in their earlier prototypes. The side-port also gave better fuel economy, for at wider throttle openings the peripheral port would lose some

charge to the exhaust. Perhaps European and Japanese driving conditions had close bearings on NSU's and Mazda's respective choices of inlet port arrangements.

Each chamber had two side-intake ports. The inner port inhaled mixture from one of the four-barrel caburetor's 21-mm primary barrels. On wider throttle opening the outer port admitted a charge from a 28-mm secondary barrel. Each chamber had a single peripheral exhaust port. The side-housings were also of cast aluminum in the 0810 engine and its more powerful 0813 variation, and their rubbing surfaces were hot-sprayed with carbon steel layers for wear resistance.

The rotor was of ductile cast iron, and was provided with gas seal pieces and oil seal rings. There were more seal pieces in the earlier production Mazda rotaries than they currently have; double side seals and triple oil rings were used in the L10A and subsequent versions, for example. The rotor had an internally toothed gear on one side, affixed by spring loaded

pins which engaged with the side-housing-mounted stationary gear. These gears form the peritrochoidal phase gears that maintain the rotor in the correct relationship to the trochoid surface.

To accelerate the combustion process in the elongated combustion chamber, two spark plugs were used per chamber, firing in sequence. The leading plug fired at 2° ATDC and the trailing one at 7° ATDC. Force-feed lubrication was by a high-efficiency gear-type pump. Lubrication oil was also fed through the eccentric shaft into the rotor for rotor cooling, and an air cooled oil cooler was standard equipment. A very small amount of oil was injected by a metering pump into the carburetor for apex-seal lubrication, rather like modern two-stroke practice.

The L10A engine was water-cooled, the coolant flowing axially in the rotor housings. The complete engine weighed 102 kg (225 lb), considerably lighter than a conventional four-cylinder engine of similar output (which would weigh some

170 kg), and was much more compact at just 508 mm long, 594 mm wide and 544 mm high (20.0 × 23.4 × 21.4 in.). The production L10A 0810 developed 110 bhp at 7000 rpm and put out a maximum torque of 130 Nm (96 lb-ft) at 3500 rpm, both ratings being by the Japanese gross-power method used at the time.

Rotor of the 10A 0810 engine, with double side seals and triple-ring oil seals. The combustion recess on the rotor flank is symmetrical

1967 Cosmo Sport L10A, powered by the Type 10A 0810 engine

Pre-emission era rotary was relatively clean of accessories, and the engine proper is seen in the Cosmo L10A engine bay

● Type 10A, engine code 0813 (July 1968)

THE TYPE 10A 0813 was an uprated version of the 10A 0810 engine that powered the series L10B Cosmo Sport, launched in July 1968. Small-scale production of the model continued through September 1972.

The 0813 engine had its port timing and carburetion revised to produce 128 bhp at 7000 rpm and 140 Nm (103 lb-ft) of torque at 5000 rpm. It retained aluminum side housings as in the 0810, and there was no change in the engine's basic construction.

1968 Cosmo Sport L10B, powered by uprated Type 10A 0813 engine, producing 128 bhp at 7000 rpm

● Type 10A, engine code 0820 (production began 1968)

THE TYPE 10A 0820 engine was a detuned volume-production version of the 10A 0810/0813 that had powered the Cosmo Sport series.

The Cosmo venture, ambitious and honorable as it was, could hardly bring in adequate rewards for Mazda's enormous research investment. Then as now, the rule held that Japan was not a two-seater country. On the other hand, more practical sports sedans and 2 + 2 coupes were rapidly winning popularity among the Japanese.

Mazda was launching such a car, the Mazda R100 coupe, which had made its first public appearance as the RX85 prototype at the 1967 Tokyo Motor Show. The 0820 engine powered this volume production model.

The type 10A 0820 twin-rotor engine had identical dimensions and 491-cc single chamber displacement, but milder port timing and smaller carburetor bore sizes for an output of 100 bhp at 7000 rpm and a maximum torque of 98 lb-ft at 3500 rpm on the same 9.4:1 compression ratio. Comparison of the 0813 and 0820 is as follows:

	0813 (Cosmo)	0820 (R100)
Max power, gross, @ rpm	128 @ 7000	100 @ 7000
Max torque, gross lb-ft, @ rpm	103 @ 5000	98 @ 3500
Port timing:		
Intake opens, ° ATDC	25	32
Intake closes, ° ABDC	45	40
Exhaust opens, ° BBDC	75	75
Exhaust closes, ° ATDC	48	38
Port area, intake, cm^2	29	28
Port area, exhaust, cm^2	12	8
Engine dimensions:		
length × width × height, mm	655×575×610	625×575×630
in.	25.8×22.6×24.0	24.6×25.8×24.8
Engine weight, kg/lb	102/224	122/268

The rotor-housings were of aluminum alloy, now permanent molding casting instead of the Cosmo's sand casting, with hard-chrome-plated epitrochoidal bores and the carbon-compound apex seals were used. For cost and production reasons the 0820 had cast-iron side housings, as did the NSU's KKM612 engine that powered the Ro80 sedan, but differed in that the portions of the housings rubbed by the cast-iron side seals were induction-hardened whereas NSU sprayed metal coating onto them.

Another cost reduction was achieved by the choice of eccentric shaft material, which was now chrome steel instead of the Cosmo engine's chrome-molybdenum steel. As before, two side intake ports per rotor were employed, fed by a four-barrel compound carburetor. A single peripheral exhaust port let out burned gas, but the exhaust was no longer routed through the cooler side of the chamber as in the Cosmo engine; Mazda engineers had found that the coolant circulation was sufficient for balancing the asymmetrical heating of the housings.

The trochoid housings were water-cooled, with a sealed aluminum crossflow radiator and an overflow tank. Coolant flowed axially in the housings, as compared with NSU's circumferential flow.

Force-feed lubrication was by a high-output rotary pump, and oil was used to cool the rotors. An air-cooled oil cooler complemented the lubrication system.

● Type 10A, engine code 3877 DEVELOPED IN mid-1968 with emission control system by thermal reactor, was for the American-specification R100 coupe, launched in April 1969 and continued until early 1972.

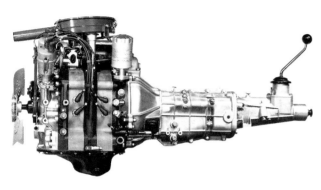

Type 0820 engine with cast-iron side-housings, rated at 100 bhp gross at 7000 rpm

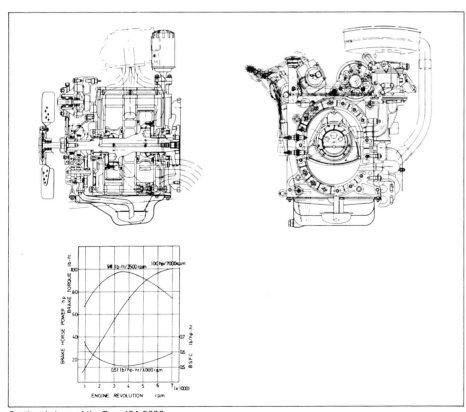

Sectional views of the Type 10A 0820 engine and a graph of its performance characteristics

The Mazda R100 coupe, powered by the Type 10A 3877 twin-rotor engine, was sold in the American market between 1968 and 1972. The same car continued through 1973 as the Familia Presto Rotary coupe in Japan

Familia Rotary SS, a four-door sedan version of the R100 coupe, was announced in Japan in April 1970

● Type 10A, engine code 0866 (production began 1971)
THE LAST of the 10A series, engine code 0866, powered Japanese versions of the RX-3 sedan, coupe and station wagon (called Savanna). It inherited the internal dimensions of earlier 10As but had its exhaust-port opening changed slightly to 80° BBDC.
Power output was now 105 bhp at 7000 rpm, maximum torque 135 Nm (99.5 lb-ft) at 3500 rpm. The engine's dimensions were (length) 635 mm × (width) 570 mm × (height) 664 mm (25.0 × 22.4 × 26.1 in.) and it scaled 128 kg (282 lb).
The exhaust system now included a cast-iron chamber

immediately aft of the exhaust ports to retain exhaust heat and partially promote oxidization, thus reducing some hydrocarbon contents. The exhaust-emission era was fast approaching Japan. The die-cast aluminum trochoid housing was now treated by a new surface-coating technique called TCP (Transplant Coating Process), developed by Doehler-Jarvis Division of National Lead Company. The trochoid bore was sprayed with 80C steel, onto which a thinner layer of chrome plating could be applied. The process improved productivity in manufacturing the rotor housings, as well as uniformity of the rubbing surface's finish.

Savanna series, announced in 1972, was the Japanese-market version of the RX-3. It was powered by a smaller Type 10A 0866 engine of 982 cc instead of the American model's 1146 cc Type 12A engine.
A 12A-powered coupe joined the Japanese series as the Savanna GT in 1975

An odd specimen of the Savanna series, this sedate-looking sedan with a less menacing front-end was a one-off model built by Mazda to the author's special order. Chairman Moriyuki Watanabe, then deputy chief of R&D, went to massive trouble to get this car built on the running assembly line

Type 13A, engine code 3847/0823 (March 1967)

IN THE reciprocating engine's parlance, this is a small-bore, long-stroke engine. The Type 13A two-rotor engine is an odd member of Mazda's production rotary-engine family. It was specifically designed and developed for a front-wheel-drive car, first shown at the 1967 Tokyo Motor Show as the RX87 and announced in October 1969 as the R130 Luce Rotary coupe

(internally known as the M13P). The R130 was produced for two seasons only.
Shorter length was a prerequisite to fitting longitudinally ahead of the front axle; thus its new internal dimensions of $e = 17.5$ mm, $R = 120$ mm and $b = 60$ mm, for a single chamber displacement of 655 cc.
It produced 126 bhp at 6000 rpm and 172 Nm (127 lb-ft) torque at 3500 rpm on a slightly lower (9.1:1) compression ratio. The

engine's outer dimensions were: 565 × 595 × 555 mm (22.2 × 23.4 × 21.9 in.) and its weight 137 kg (301 lb).
The 13A differed from the smaller 10A in that it had an integrated water-cooled oil cooler, its oil pump was driven by a chain and a portion of oil was metered into the carburetor float chamber for apex-seal lubrication.
No further development of this trochoid-size was pursued.

R130 Luce Rotary coupe (1970–72): Introduced as the RX87 prototype at the 1967 Tokyo Motor Show, as the production R130 Luce Rotary coupe in October 1969. Although it shares the Luce name with the older Mazda 1500/1800 sedan, and its styling showing a kinship to that Bertone-designed (chief stylist Giugiaro) model, it has an entirely new front-wheel-drive chassis. Its front suspension was by unequal length upper and lower arms, the rear suspension by independent semi-trailing arms. Brakes were a front disc/rear drum combination, steering by rack and pinion with power assistance in the top Super Deluxe model. Performance claims included a top speed of 190 km/h (119 mph) and a standing-start 1/4 mile time of 16.9 sec

Type 13A 3847/0823 twin-rotor engine, with 655-cc single chamber displacement for 1310 cc. Its development began in March 1967 for the 1970–72 R130 Luce Rotary coupe

R130 engine compartment with type 13A engine

Type 12A family

DEVELOPMENT OF this "bored" version of the 10A (**b** from 60 mm to 70 mm, for a single chamber displacement of 573 cc) began in March 1968 under engine code number 3872.

Earlier in April 1966, another combination of trochoidal dimensions was tried under the engine development code of 3830 (**e** = 16.4 mm, **R** = 112 mm and the same chamber width of 60 mm as the 10A) to obtain the 573-cc displacement but it was subsequently abandoned. The widened-bore 3872 was a more expeditious way to increase capacity. It became the first of the 12A family of engines, appearing in the RX-2 Capella car in May 1970. The RX-2 with emission-controlled 12A (engine code 3905) was launched in America in March 1971; the smaller RX-3 powered by the same engine followed a year later. And of course this was the power unit of the previous RX-7 series, from the original 1978 X605 through to the last P132 of 1985.

In Japan the 12A has powered various Mazda models, from the RX-2 through the intermediate 929 series (Cosmo and Luce cars) in naturally aspirated and turbocharged tunes.

Together with the bigger 13B engine, it has come through the two critical periods, first the emission-control movement in America and Japan, and later Oil Crises I and II. By the time the original RX7 was launched in 1978, more than 930,000 rotary engines had been produced by

The type 12A twin-rotor engine with single chamber displacement of 573 cc (1146 cc total) first used in the RX-2 series introduced in the American market in 1971. Development began in 1968 under engine code number 3872

An early Japanese 12A with cast-iron expansion exhaust manifold. Exhaust ports of three-hole honeycomb design, similar in the principle to the latest 13B's multi-chamber port insert, reduce radiating exhaust noise

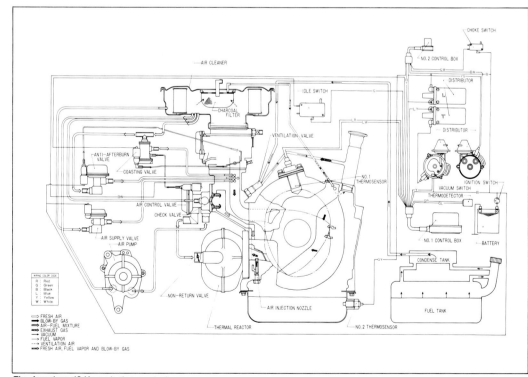

The American 12A's emission-control system by thermal reactor, secondary air injection and electronic ignition control

An early 12A rotor, with carbon apex seals and double side seals. Oil seals are now two rings. This is a Japanese-version engine with symmetrical combustion recess

An early U.S. 12A engine with tapering-recess-in-shallow-recess rotors. Carbon apex seals are still used

Mazda; during that turbulent decade, Mazda had made numerous improvements and refinements to the rotary, mainly on the 12A and its bigger sister 13B, to improve their fuel efficiency, driveability and reliability.

Mazda RX-2 coupe, powered by the 12A engine and introduced in America in 1971

The smaller RX-3 series of 1972, shared the 12A engine

1977 RX-3 SP in war paint and "snow plow" airdam

● Type 12A engine for the X605 and P642 RX-7 (produced 1978–1980)

THE BASIC trochoid dimensions remained the same in the twin-rotor 12A for the X605 RX-7: $e = 15$ mm, $R = 105$ mm and $b = 70$ mm for a single chamber displacement of 573 cc. In U.S. specifications, it produced 100 bhp SAE net at 6000 rpm (a much more realistic 100 bhp than that of the old R100, for instance) and 105 lb-ft of torque at 4000 rpm on a 9.4:1 compression ratio and a

four-barrel, two-stage compound carburetor. Exhaust cleansing was by a thermal reactor and secondary air injection.

Since the 1974 American model year, a new process called SIP (Sheet-metal Insert Process) had increased the strength of the trochoidal surface and improved productivity. In this process the aluminum-alloy trochoid housing is diecast around a sheet-metal insert which has a jagged surface for secure bonding. Hard chrome plating of the pinpoint-porous-chrome variety

that retains lubricant in minuscule pores is applied to the sheet metal. SIP improves the adhesion of chrome plating and eliminates spraying the trochoid surface with molten metal, which had been one of the most hazardous and least pleasant steps in the production process. Treatment of the sidehousing's rubbing surface had been changed, too. Originally it was hot-sprayed with 80C carbon steel, again a problematical process in the work environment. The Japanese version then

adopted induction hardening of the side-housing, first for its entire surface and then on just the rubbing portion. The latest treatment is gas soft-nitriding, by which a layer of Fe–C–N is depoisted onto the surface to improve side gas-and oil-seal wear and prevents corrosion. Mazda insiders call this process REST; used in conjunction with the double cast-iron seals with tapering lips and chrome-plated contact edges and enclosing in their grooves heat-resistant fluorized rubber O-rings, the

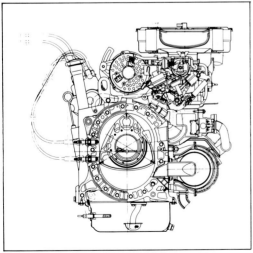

Thermal-reactor 12A for the X605 RX-7, March 1978

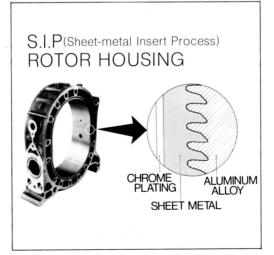

S.I.P (Sheet-metal Insert Process)
ROTOR HOUSING

CHROME PLATING   ALUMINUM ALLOY
SHEET METAL

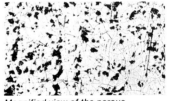

Magnified view of the porous chrome-plated surface

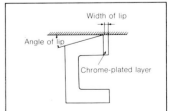

Width of lip
Angle of lip
Chrome-plated layer

Double cast-iron oil rings with tapering and chrome-plated lips helped solve long tormenting oil consumption

X605 RX-7 of 1978, powered by the 12A engine

process finally licked the long tormenting oil-consumption syndrome. Mazda's engine designers could now happily REST as far as the oil-consumption rate was concerned.

In the mid-1970s Mazda quietly changed the apex-seal material from the faithful carbon compound to cast iron, similar to ordinary piston-ring material. This was made possible by the new pinpoint-porous chrome-plating technique, which markedly improved trochoid and apex-seal lubrication. The metal seal had also gone through geometrical changes; the one used in the 12A for the X605 RX-7 had greatly

reduced leakage area. Another feature of the main seal body was that it was "crowned," so that it comformed to the trochoid surface's slight deformation under load. The rubbing tip of the apex seal was now crystallized in the form of carbides, a process called chill-hardening by an electron beam. The treatment gives the seal tip an almost ceramic-like composition, improving sealing and thermal efficiency. Furthermore the corner seal piece that kept the apex seal in place was of a new flexible design that kept the clearance to the rotor groove to a minimum for a tighter sealing. The rotor's combustion recess

was modified as well, to a LDR (leading deep recess) type with the leading spark plug position moved ahead by 5 mm. The new combustion chamber helped speed up flame propagation by virtue of increased squish effect. In this engine, ignition alternated between single-and two-plug operation: when the leading plug alone was used under part-load conditions, it resulted in better fuel economy as well as being advantagenous for emission control (hotter thermal reactor running).

The thermal-reactor system now incorporated a head exchanger that preheated secondary air injected into the intake port,

aiding reaction on a leaner air-fuel ratio; this contributed to the improvement in fuel economy too.

And the two-electrode sparkplugs had been replaced by a three-electrode type to obtain more stable ignition. The 12A engine for the X605 RX-7 measured 793 × 690 × 649 mm (31.2 × 27.2 × 25.6 in.), and weighed 158 kg (348 lb) with coolant and lubricant in the engine but excluding the radiator and oil cooler.

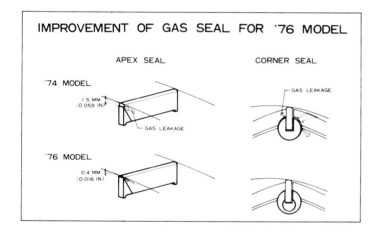

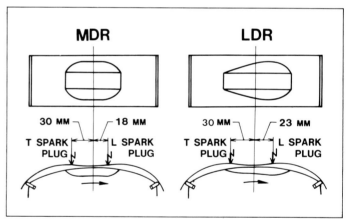

EXHAUST PORT INSERT

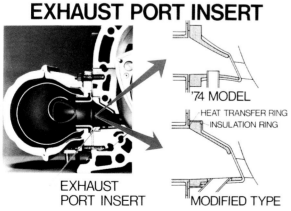

Heat transfer ring retains heat in exhaust gas while the insulating ring keeps heat from the rotor-housing. Heated secondary air is injected via angled passage

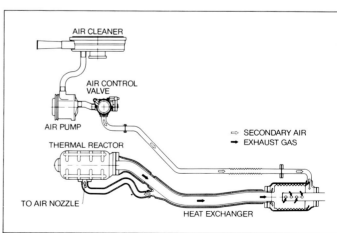

Heat exchanger in the RX-7 exhaust system preheats secondary air, aiding the thermal reactor's oxidization

●Lean-burn 12A (American P815, 130 and 132 RX-7s, produced 1981-85)
MAZDA'S STANDARD operating procedure is to try and prove anything new in the Japanese market first before exporting it. The policy is quite sound, in that the factory is within easy reach of the service network in the home country and can readily provide any advice, guidance and assistance that might be required on the new product.

The lean-burn 12A engine with catalytic-converter emission system was thus introduced in the Japanese P642 RX-7 in late 1979, while the American P642 retained the thermal reactor. America's RX-7 had to wait until late 1980, when the lean-burn 12A was put into the evolutionary P815 model.

In a major change from the previous thermal reactor, the lean-burn engine's new emission control system consisted of a high-energy ignition system, a downstream converter housing two beds of catalysts, and split-air secondary air injection by an engine-driven pump. At low speeds and on deceleration, the converter worked as an oxidizing catalyst; secondary air was injected into the intake port, burning a portion of the unburned hydrocarbons and carbon monoxides in the reactive exhaust manifold.

At medium speeds the port air injection was cut off; the front catalyst bed then principally treated oxides of nitrogen and some HC and CO as a three-way catalyst. The rear catalyst bed, supplied with additional air by the pump, took care of most of the residual HC and CO as an oxidizing catalyst.

Now running on the stoichiometric air-fuel ratio of 14.8:1 with three-way catalyst action, the 12A was consuming less fuel: a claimed improvement of 20 percent over the thermal-reactor Japanese RX-7. The American P815 RX-7 also got the improved-gas seal design, which included spring corner seals filled with heat-resistant elastic material to further reduce leakage area. For 1985 the 12A-powered P132 model also got a new monolith catalytic converter with improved efficiency.

With the catalytic converter system, twin sparkplugs per rotor now fired throughout the engine's operating revolution range, in contrast to the thermal-reactor version's alternation between two-plug and single-plug firing.

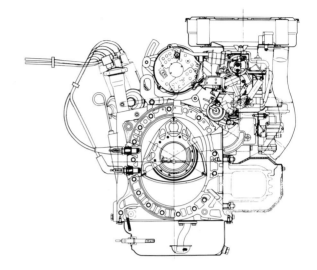

Lean-burn 12A engine was introduced in October 1979 with reactive exhaust manifold in place of thermal reactor. The main two-bed catalytic converter is downstream in the exhaust system

●Type 12A 6PI (Japanese models, produced 1982–85)
ORIGINALLY DEVELOPED under the VIPS designation (Variable Induction Port System), it was renamed, rather dryly, 6PI (six-port induction) and first introduced in the Luce sedan and Cosmo coupe series in 1981. In the side-port engine, port area and shape are worked for an optimum compromise of low-end torque and top-end power within the framework of the engine's maximum flow volume and its

given operating environments. The emphasis for cars sold in Japan, where driving is severely speed-limited, is on reasonable fuel economy and meeting the country's stringent emission standards.

The intake ports of the lean-burn 12A that powered the Japanese RX-7 opened at 32° ATDC and closed at 40° ABDC. It displayed good driveability and returned an acceptable 9.4 km/liter (22.1 mpg) in Japan's urban test cycle. There was,

however, a trade-off; with this timing top-end performance might not have been as good as needed in the few countries where high-end performance is a big priority. For this reason the 1981 European RX-7 had its intake-port closing delayed to 50° ABDC, at some sacrifice in low-speed torque and fuel economy.

The 6PI, with its rotating cylindrical valve controlling an extra intake port, could combine the better features of

the two engine configurations. Mazda engineers, however, put the 6PI's extended breathing ability to further improve economy, rather than power, and obtained a magic two-digit figure, 10 km/liter (23.5 mpg).

In the 6PI engine the valve-controlled auxiliary port is above the secondary main port, and is actuated by exhaust pressure. At low-rpm and load-conditions, the four-barrel carburetor's primary feeds the single-intake port on the inner housing. At medium speeds and loads, the secondary side feeds mixtures to the secondary main port. And at yet higher speeds and loads, increase in exhaust pressure turns the cylindrical valve opening the intake passage to the auxiliary power port. With the top-end adequately covered, the main ports may be sized, shaped and located so that port overlap is nearly eliminated, thus preventing charge dilution and blow-through; this stabilized idling and cuts fuel consumption.

In effect the 6PI engine has two torque curves.

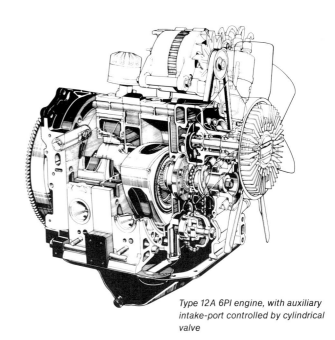

Type 12A 6PI engine, with auxiliary intake-port controlled by cylindrical valve

● Turbocharged and fuel-injected 12A (Japanese models, produced 1983–1985)
THE TURBOCHARGED and fuel-injected 12A has been confined to the Japanese market, powering first the Cosmo and Luce cars starting in late 1982 and (in its uprated version) the P132 RX-7 from September 1983 through the end of its model life. The 12A Turbo was the first production turbocharged and electronically fuel-injected rotary engine.
In its Turbo guise the 12A reverted to four side intake ports. Each bank has one injector, located in the intake port in near the port opening in the trochoid chamber. Because of this location, which is a cross between manifold and direct-injection methods, Mazda engineers call the fuel injection "semi-direct injection." The injector is actuated by electrical current and satisfactorily meets the rotary's widely varying fuel demands, from a 600-rpm idle to a full 7000-rpm operation. Air and fuel mixing is promoted at lower speeds by an air bleed to the injector nozzle receptacle, at higher rpm by a mixing-plate socket, an open-sided plastic tube with twin perforated plates. The plates splash and squeeze injected fuel, aiding mixture atomization.

The fuel-injection control unit is an analog type made by Nippon Denso; it works in conjunction with a Mitsubishi Electric digital emission-control computer. Fuel is injected once per intake stroke, simultaneously in both chambers. As there is a 180-degree difference in the two rotors' working phases, one chamber is injected at the beginning of the intake stroke (more precisely "travel" in the rotary), whereas the one in the

other chamber receives fuel when almost two-thirds of that rotor's intake travel are covered. As the rotary has an "internal" intake ports (each chamber takes in fuel and air on one side of the trochoid-housing and travels to the other side, where combustion occurs) chamber filling and mixture strength become uniform between the two banks, despite the staggered injection timing. Primary intake-port timing is unchanged from the carbureted

6PI engine: opening at 58° ATDC and closes at 40° ABDC. Opening of the secondary intake port is advanced to 32° ATDC; closing remains at 40° ABDC. The single peripheral exhaust port opens at 75° BBDC and closes at 48° ATDC.
Of interest in the air-only secondary intake port and manifold are dual throttle valves. A second butterfly valve is located upstream in the manifold; it opens slightly later than the

Original turbine blade and Impact design (right)

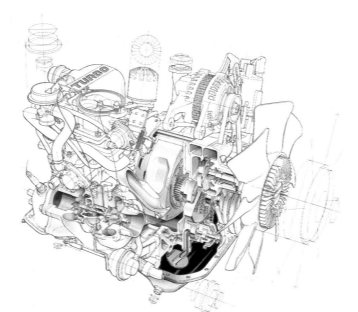

Turbocharged, fuel-injected 12A engine for the Japanese P132 RX-7 Turbo

lower one. The dual-valve arrangement prevents sudden air-pressure shocks and, together with the semi-direct injection system, allows a smaller plenum chamber.

The 12A Turbo was originally boosted by a Hitachi HT18-BM turbocharger with a 62-mm-diameter, 11-blade turbine and a 63-mm, 12-blade compressor, supplying a relatively modest maximum boost of 320 mm Hg (6.2 psi); typical for Japanese turbocharged reciprocating piston engine is about 400 mm Hg. Conversely, the compression ratio does not have to be lowered as much as that of the reciprocating piston engine: only to 8.5:1 from the naturally aspirated 12A's 9.4:1. The 1982 12A Turbo produced 160 bhp JIS at 6000 rpm and a maximum torque of 224 Nm (165 lb-ft) at

4000 rpm; 15–20 percent should be deducted to get the approximate SAE net values. Later, the engine was given a new turbocharger, Hitachi's HT18S-BM, with a smaller 57-mm turbine and 56-mm compressor, it was dubbed an Impact Turbocharger by Mazda engineers because it fully exploited the rotary's forceful exhaust-gas impact with its new turbine-blade shape. The new turbo added 5 more horsepower to the engine's output, as well as improving low-end torque chracteristics and minimizing turbo lag.

The 12A Turbo also has a knock-prevention system. Mazda engineers found in developing this engine that knocking would occur only under certain operating conditions: in a 2500–3750-rpm zone when intake temperature exceeds 85°

Celsius. The system, comprising of ignition-pulse, intake-temperature and boost sensors, detects this knock-prone zone and feeds a signal to the emission-control and fuel-injection computers, which in turn call for ignition retard and more fuel (in the latest 13B Turbo, a more usual piezometric knock sensor is used). Ignition is basically unchanged from that of the 6PI engine, which now employs semi-surface discharge sparkplugs.

As the turbo rotary's performance and consequently the thermal loads have been considerably increased (for the latter some 30 percent), lubrication of the trochoid sliding surface and turbocharger has become more critical. A new trochoidal surface treatment, called MCP or micro-channel porous plating, is

employed in the turbo rotary. It is a development of the pinpoint-porous chrome plating of the normal 12A; the pinpoint holes are interconnected by minuscule channels. Also, in contrast to the carbureted 12A's oil mixing in the carburetor for seal lubrication, the turbo rotary has separate oil injection: per chamber, one nozzle into the primary manifold and another directly into the trochoidal chamber, both fed by a metering pump. The turbocharger is also amply lubricated, thanks to the rotary's already adequate lubricating capacity (the rotors are oil-cooled too).

The 12A Turbo engine is 786 mm long, 548 mm wide and 638 mm tall (30.9 × 21.6 × 25.1 in.) and weighs 162 kg (356 lb).

Type 13B engine (produced 1973–1981)

THE 13B engine is the widest-bore production two-rotor engine, obtaining its single chamber displacement of 654 cc from $b = 80$ mm. Its trochoidal dimensions of $e = 15$ mm and $R = 105$ mm are common with the 10A and 12A.

It was introduced in the American market in the RX-4 series of sedan, coupe and station wagon in 1974. The same engine was shared by the unique Rotary Pickup launched in the same year. Later the American Cosmo (RX-5) got the 13B as well.

The carbureted 13B followed the same evolutionary path of improvement and refinement as the smaller 12A for better reliability and fuel economy. 1978 was the last year for the RX-4 and RX-5 models in the U.S., and the engine, too, bowed out temporarily from the American scene.

In Japan the 13B continued to

power Mazda's bigger passenger-car models and even a small bus, until 1981, when it was suspended from production.

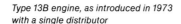

Type 13B engine, as introduced in 1973 with a single distributor

Thermal-reactor side of the 1974 Japanese 13B

Emission-control system of the 13B,
with the thermal reactor and heat
exchanger

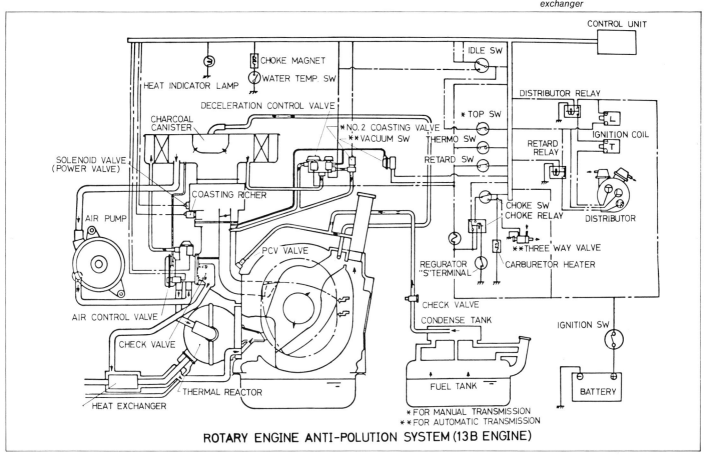

ROTARY ENGINE ANTI-POLUTION SYSTEM (13B ENGINE)

* FOR MANUAL TRANSMISSION
** FOR AUTOMATIC TRANSMISSION

Mazada RX-4 was the first model to be powered by the 13B. The car fell victim to the spiraling fuel price after Oil Crisis I

This very American-looking RX-4 successor, the Luce sedan of 1977, was also powered by the 13B. The Luce series, revamped since then, continues to this day

Roadpacer sedan, based on the Australian GM-Holden's Statesman body and running gear, was powered by the 13B and aimed at the Japanese executive class (1975–1978)

In the same year the RX-4 appeared, Mazda introduced the 13B-powered Rotary Pickup in America

Rotary Parkway mini-bus powered by the 13B twin-rotor engine, the largest rotary powered vehicle

13B DEI fuel-injected engine,
November 1983

●13B DEI (produced 1983–)
MAZDA REVIVED the big 13B two-rotor engine series in late 1983 in the Japanese intermediate Cosmo/Luce series and the American RX-7 GSL-SE. The engine had been updated to provide more power and better fuel economy through a combination of charge dynamics unique to the rotary, called DEI (Dynamic Effect Intake), and an electronically controlled fuel injection.

The new 13B also employed 6PI, which had appeared earlier in the Japanese carbureted 12A engine. Fuel was now injected by Bosch L-jetronic electronic fuel injection with one injector placed in the intake port of each chamber, as in the 12A Turbo. The DEI engine has long individual intake tubes growing from a box-like plenum chamber or "surge tank", as Mazda engineers prefer to call it. The plenum box is two-storied, its lower floor feeding into the two secondary intake tracts and the "mezzanine" into the two primary tubes. This plenum chamber is directly attached to the three-valve throttle chamber. A normal pendulum-type airflow meter and air cleaner are upstream of the throttle chamber-plenum box assembly.

Mazda engineers discovered that there was useful interaction of air between the two rotor chambers of the two-rotor engine: Because of the abrupt change in intake-port area as the ports are opened and closed by rotor motion, strong compression waves are generated. Waves are also generated just after intake opening, when part of the high-pressure exhaust in the expanding chamber is likely to rush backward into the intake manifold. The rotary's volumetric efficiency increase at high speeds was found to be due to the "tournament" effects of these two kinds of compression waves between the two rotors; Mazda's plenum box, with its lower floor for the secondary ports and mezzanine for the primary ports, utilizes this air interaction for positive charging of air into the working chamber. As measured immediately before intake-closing, intake air pressure is increased on the order of 100 mm Hg, so the system's effect could qualify as "pulse-positive charging."

The 13B DEI engine, as installed in the RX-7 GSL-SE, was rated at 135 bhp SAE net at 6000 rpm and produced a maximum torque of 180 Nm (133 lb-ft) at 2750 rpm.

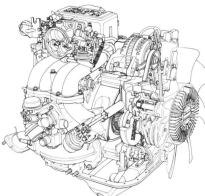

13B DEI engine with 6PI (auxiliary
power ports controlled by rotating
cylindrical valves)

Japanese specification Luce 929
4-door powered by the 13B DEI engine

●New 13B DEI (1986)
THIS IS the base engine for the P747 RX-7. See Chapter 1 for a full description.

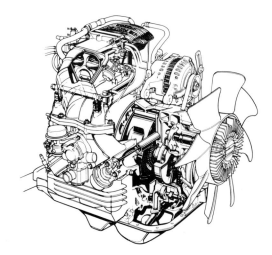

● 13B DEI Turbo (1986)
THE NEW turbocharged 13B DEI
is offered in the P747 RX-7. See
Chapter 1 for a detailed
description.

III.PROTOTYPE AND EXPERIMENTAL ENGINES

"New 400", engine code 3867 (September 1967)

THE PURSUIT of ultimate
efficiency has always been in the
minds of Mazda's rotary engine
designers and developers.
Having launched the
volume-production two-rotor 10A,
they sought a balance of equal
power and better fuel efficiency
in a smaller displacement version
with single chamber
displacement of 395 cc, which
was the "New 400" engine code
3867. Trochoidal dimensions
were divorced from those of the
10A, at $e = 13.5$ mm and
$R = 94$ mm, while the chamber
width remained the same at
$b = 60$ mm.
A further bored-out version
($b = 75$ mm) of this trochoidal
series was also built under
engine code 3893 in May 1969;
its single chamber displacement
was 495 cc.

*The new 400 engine is Mazda's
attempt to optimize performance and
economy in a smaller capacity engine
than type 10A*

Single-rotor engines, engine codes 3912 (January 1970), X002 (June 1970) and 3915 (March 1970)

MAZDA HAD been one of the original members of Japan's extraordinary "K-car" movement. The word **kei** translates "light", and these were passenger cars and commercial variants conforming to a set of regulated dimensions and engine displacement . The earlier K-car had to have a total displacement smaller than 360 cc; this was later raised to 550 cc. Mazda's passenger-car production began in 1960 with the diminutive R360 coupe, powered by an aluminum air-cooled V-twin engine. A more sophisticated four-seat sedan followed: the Carol 360 was propelled by a water-cooled OHV inline four-cylinder engine displacing the allowed 360 cc, transversely mounted in the rear overhang. The R360 was built until 1965, the Carol 360 from

Single-rotor engines: Narrow-bore X002 has chamber displacement of 360 cc, which Mazda hoped would fit in Japan's light car category

Larger single-rotor engines, 6A and 7A, intended for mini cars

1963 through 1970. With Honda's entry into the K movement, the segment saw a fierce horse power race (if you can imagine that) in the late Sixties. Mazda's suave inline four could not produce enough power to keep up with the hotter competitors.

But Mazda had the rotary. A bored-down (from 60 mm to 43.5 mm) half of the 10A with 356-cc chamber displacement was built under engine code 3912 in January 1970. It put out

35 bhp, far exceeding the 360 cc class norm of the time. Engine code X002, which was really the prototype power unit for a more powerful Carol replacement, followed.

It was said that the rival camps in the K segment objected fiercely to Mazda's plan. They insisted that a single-rotor rotary with 356-cc chamber displacement should not be allowed as a 360; instead, the chamber displacement should be multiplied by 1.5 to arrive at a

displacement equivalent to that of the normal reciprocating piston engine.

The Hiroshima company had to abandon the Rotary Carol project in the face of this opposition. Mazda also built single-rotor versions of the 12A and 13B engines with chamber capacities of 573 cc and 654 cc, designated type 6A and 7A respectively, for minicar projects in the early Seventies.

Engine code 2002, four-rotor (September 1971)

THIS IMPRESSIVE four-rotor engine could have powered Mazda's answer to Toyota's and Nissan's flagship sedan models. The type 2002 was two 10A engines in one, with the eccentric shafts' serrated ends mated in the center by a Curvic coupling. It retained the 491-cc single chamber displacement and side-intake ports, and developed 180 bhp at 6000 rpm.

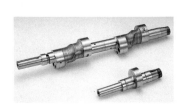

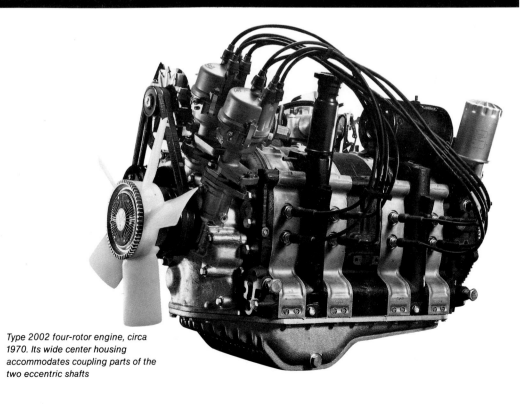

Type 2002 four-rotor engine, circa 1970. Its wide center housing accommodates coupling parts of the two eccentric shafts

Type R-II 21A (August 1972)

SPECIFICALLY DEVELOPED for the X020G sports car that was to compete against such high-performance GTs as the E-type Jaguar, Porsche 911 and Corvette, the twin-rotor 21A had the biggest single chamber displacement, 1046 cc, that ever saw the metal walls of the trochoid and side housings. Its internal dimensions were $e = 18.5$ mm, $R = 128$ mm and $b = 85$ mm. Power output was to be 180-bhp plus.

Oil Crisis I put an end to the 21A's development and the X020G project. A single specimen of this rotary behemoth and an unmachined rotor are kept at Mazda.

The type R-II 21A engine

Type 21A's trochoid housing and rotor without recess and seal grooves on the extreme right. On their left are the rotor housing and the rotor of the type 15A engine. The narrowest housing and rotor are those of Type X002 single-rotor engine

Super Rotary sports car: the 21A was developed for the X020G, intended to be a Corvette and Jag competitor

Type R-II 22A (August 1972)

PLANNED WITH the 21A was a yet bigger version, the 22A, with its trochoidal chamber width increased to 95 mm for an 1169-cc single chamber displacement. It did not progress beyond the planning stage.

Type 15A (March 1973)

THIS TWIN-ROTOR engine was an extension of the 10A-12A-13B line of engines, sharing their trochoidal dimensions of $e = 15$ mm and $R = 105$ mm. Its chamber width b had been increased by another 10 mm increment to 90 mm for 737 cc of single chamber displacement. The engine produced 135 hp gross at 5750 rpm and 196 Nm (145 lb-ft) of torque at 3500 rpm. A more practical proposition than the "monster" 21A, it too suffered in the aftermath of the Oil Embargo, and was shelved. A complete sample and

components are preserved in the Engine Testing Division's collection.

Mazda meant business with the 15A, which was fitted with a huge cast-iron thermal reactor to meet the emission standards of America and Japan

Type 15A engine developed in 1973: widest-bore version of the 10A-12A-13B trochoidal family

ROSCO advance engine

SHORT FOR ROtary Stratified COmbustion system, the ROSCO employs a reed valve in a primary peripheral intake port, an additional side-intake port and direct fuel injection. Under light load, air is supplied from the peripheral port only; fuel is injected into the swirl created by intake air. Injected fuel hits the swirl and is atomized. At the same time, it is carried to the leading side of the working chamber to form strata of rich mixture in the leading side and leaner mixture in the trailing side. The reed valve in the peripheral port prevents burned gas from blowing back into the intake manifold. Under high load the side port supplies a greater amount of air into the working chamber to produce higher power.

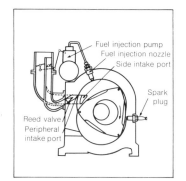

ROSCO

SCP System

STATIONARY COMBUSTION Process refers to a pre-combustion chamber developed by Mazda. The spherical pre-combustion chamber has a fuel-injection nozzle and a sparkplug on the side opposite to the trochoidal housing's intake and exhaust side. Under light load, fuel is supplied to the pre-chamber only, where it is ignited. Burning gas in the pre-chamber blows out and expands into the main working chamber, where any yet unburned portion is burned with fresh air introduced into the chamber. At higher loads, a separate carburetor supplies the air-fuel mixture into the normal side-port to augument the pre-chamber's fuel supply.

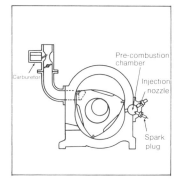

SCP

TISC System

TIMED INDUCTION with Super Charger is what TISC means; boost is provided by a high-efficiency air-pump. A rotary valve controls the air passage from the air-pump into an independent air-only side port above the normal intake port. It was TISC that gave birth to the 6PI system, which also has a positively controlled secondary power port above the normal intake port, but without supercharging.

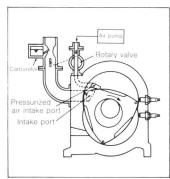

TISC

TISC engine with super air-pump boosting intake charge

Mazda P747 RX-7 with the key designers and engineers responsible for its creation.

① Kenichi Yamamoto	President	㉒ Jiro Maebayashi	Product Program
② Takashi Kuroda	General Manager R&D	㉓ Masaru Shiraishi	Power train
③ Michinori Yamanouchi	Deputy General Manager R&D	㉔ Hiroto Yamagata	Engine Testing
④ Akio Uchiyama	Program Manager P747	㉕ Makoto Ogasawara	Brake Research
⑤ Yasuo Aoyagi	Interior Design	㉖ Hiroshi Nakayama	Interior/Exterior Research
⑥ Sadao Umeda	Product Program	㉗ Hiroshi Kinoshita	Engine Design
⑦ Hideo Fujii	Manager, Electronics	㉘ Shunji Tanaka	Assistant Manager, Design
⑧ Tadashi Iwamoto	Electronics	㉙ Yuzo Ueoku	Engine Design
⑨ Hiroshi Yamamoto	Testing & Development	㉚ Hiroshi Ohzeki	Manager, Engine Design
⑩ Yasuo Tatsutomi	Div. Manager, Engine Design	㉛ Satoshi Yatomi	Assistant Manager, Engine Planning
⑪ Hirotaka Tachibana	Project Manager Testing & Development	㉜ Ushio Sakurai	Chassis Design
⑫ Ryoji Ooe	Electronics	㉝ Takao Kijima	Chassis Design
⑬ Chiharu Mizutani	Development	㉞ Toshihiro Wakimoto	Airconditioning System
⑭ Tatsuo Fukuyama	Electronics	㉟ Masaya Hamamoto	Product Program
⑮ Yoshinori Kurisu	Testing & Development	㊱ Takeshi Yamamoto	Body Design
⑯ Masami Sakata	Reliability	㊲ Naomune Moriyama	Product Program
⑰ Yoshimitsu Tanaka	Manager, Body Design Dept.	㊳ Shigemi Okada	Engine Testing
⑱ Minoru Fujimoto	Structure Research	㊴ Yasuji Oda	Project Manager, P747 Design
⑲ Takashi Abe	Div. Manager, Body Design	㊵ Takashi Ono	Exterior Design
⑳ Susumu Suto	Project Manager, PR	㊶ Toshio Yagi	Design
㉑ Yoshiaki Nakano	Noise & Vibration Research	㊷ Takaaki Itoh	Chassis Design
		㊸ Fumio Kageyama	Chassis Design

Index

PUBLICATION STAFF

Publication Director:	Masato Fujisawa
Assistand Publication Director:	Yasuo Umeda
Editorial Staff:	Masaaki Hori
	Hiroshi Kan
	Chikayo Tanaka
Layout Staff:	Kosaku Shibamura
	Katsura Takizawa
	Toshitsugu Utoh
Art Director:	Koichi Yazaki
Cover Design:	Etsushi Kiyohara
P747 RX-7 Photography:	Haru Tajima
Photographic sources:	Bob Hall
	Mazda Motor Corporation
	Mazdaspeed
	Motoring Press Service
	San'ei Shobo Corporation
	Hiroshi Seiki
	Yuji Shimizu
	World Rally Press
	Jack K. Yamaguchi
	Koichi Yazaki